CONDUCT DISORDER AND UNDERACHIEVEMENT

CONDUCT DISORDER AND UNDERACHIEVEMENT

RISK FACTORS, ASSESSMENT, TREATMENT, AND PREVENTION

HARVEY P. MANDEL

JOHN WILEY & SONS, INC.

New York • Chichester • Brisbane • Toronto • Singapore • Weinheim

Library of Congress Cataloging-in-Publication Data:

Mandel, Harvey P.
        Conduct disorder and underachievement : risk factors, assessment,
    treatment, and prevention / Harvey P. Mandel.
            p.   cm.
        Includes bibliographical references and index.
        ISBN 0-471-13147-4 (cloth : alk. paper)
        1. Behavior disorders in children.   2. Underachievement.
    I. Title.
        [DNLM: 1. Child Behavior Disorders.   2. Social Behavior Disorders—
    in adolescence.   3. Underachievement.   WS 350.6 M271c   1997]
    RJ506.B44M35   1997
    618.92′89—dc20
    DNLM/DLC
    for Library of Congress   96-23333

Printed in the United States of America

10   9   8   7   6   5   4   3   2   1

Preface

There is increasing interest in and mounting alarm about children and adolescents with behavior problems. For several reasons, the timing of this book on Conduct Disorder (CD) is not a coincidence:

1. The diagnosis of Conduct Disorder is becoming more prevalent (American Psychiatric Association, 1994), as are some of the more serious related behaviors, such as substance abuse (Loeber, 1990).
2. These individuals cause a disproportionate amount of difficulty for society.
3. A small proportion of conduct-disordered individuals are responsible for some of the most violent antisocial acts.
4. Recent changes of CD types in the *Diagnostic and Statistical Manual of Mental Disorders* (*DSM-IV*; American Psychiatric Association, 1994) have incorporated different pathways for childhood-onset and adolescent-onset types.
5. Enough data has been amassed about the risk factors associated with these different developmental trajectories to propose several multifactorial and interactional risk models.
6. Conduct Disorder can be one of the most difficult disorders to treat successfully. Antisocial behavior in some individuals will persist well into middle adulthood with negative consequences for most people who come in contact with these individuals.
7. Research findings from successful treatment approaches point to critical ingredients.
8. Results from successful prevention programs offer insight into factors that decrease the prevalence of this disorder.

Also, in light of the recent differentiation between childhood-onset and adolescent-onset CD, little attention has been paid to the possibility that academic underachievement plays a different role in the development of each trajectory. Further, there has been little differentiation between the most severe acting-out CDs and those who manage to stay in school and meet the less severe diagnostic criteria. The unstated assumption in the professional literature seems to be that once an individual qualifies for a CD diagnosis there is little further need to differentiate between those who meet the less severe or more severe criteria.

Because conduct problems fall on a continuum and many problematic behaviors don't lead to clinical referral, some researchers have identified subclinical levels of Conduct Disorder (Farrington, 1991b; Loeber, 1990). These researchers have found that these subclinical levels are strong predictors of future CD diagnosis.

Although some researchers implicate academic underachievement as a risk factor in the development of the disorder, other researchers conclude that underachievement is an associated consequence of this pattern. There is research evidence that (a) Conduct Disorder which develops in childhood is predictive of poor academic performance, and (b) lower academic performance in combination with lower intellectual functioning is associated with the development of CD. Thus, the relationships among CD, intellectual functioning, and academic attainment appear to be *bidirectional* (Bachman, Johnston, & O'Malley, 1978; Farrington, 1991a, 1991b; Ledingham & Schwartzman, 1984; Moffitt, 1993; Rutter & Giller, 1984; West, 1982). The position taken in this book is that underachievement can either lead to or can be a consequence of a CD pattern, and that it is much more fruitful to examine how each trajectory unfolds and what can be done to change the developmental pathways.

Chapter 1 contains a description of the disorder, encompassing diagnostic criteria, risk factors, motivation, and differential diagnosis. Included here is a discussion of the interactive nature of risk factors and formulation about developmental pathways. Chapter 2 presents a general review of assessment issues in dealing with CD underachievers and provides two case histories. The first is a case of a childhood-onset CD underachiever in which there were clear risk and perpetuating factors. The second is a case of adolescent-onset CD underachievement in which neither academic underachievement nor a disruptive behavior pattern emerged as a significant issue until early adolescence. In the second case, both family and school factors played a significant protective role during childhood. It was only with the changing demands of high school and interactions with a deviant adolescent peer subculture that both CD and underachievement emerged. Each case concludes with a discussion of the interaction between risk and protective factors.

Chapter 3 provides an overview of treatment approaches and outcome findings, while Chapter 4 is focused on prevention. Chapter 5 contains a review of research on the relationship between CD and underachievement, including issues of definition, risk factors, theoretical models, and types, as well as recommendations for future research. Chapter 6 provides an in-depth look at the stages of individual cognitively oriented therapy of CD underachievers. Therapy excerpts take the reader into the treatment sessions to capture the issues, struggles, and typical reactions of adolescent and therapist. Chapter 7 addresses frequently asked questions about CD underachievers. The Appendix lists instruments that have been used in research and assessment of the disorder, and the book concludes with an extensive list of References.

HARVEY P. MANDEL

Acknowledgments

Over the years many people have invested in me. I am grateful to my parents, Bernard Mandel and Ida Mandel, who provided me with strong and loving roots. In particular, observing how my father's pediatric practice played an important part in the lives of families from different cultural and racial backgrounds instilled in me a sense of wonder about children. It is a gift that has sustained me throughout my life. My parents also taught my sister, Rhoda, and me to draw on each other as an extension of our parents' care. Her own family and her professional work with Kids Help Foundation, which funds the Kids Help Line—a national toll-free 24-hour emergency phone line for troubled children—speaks to the models that my father and mother provided.

I want to thank my wife and professional colleague, Dorothy Mandel, the clinical director of the Institute on Achievement and Motivation, York University, Toronto, Canada. Dorothy's knowledge about families and younger children has enhanced the work of the Institute and allowed me to grow professionally. Much of the focus on families in this book reflects her wisdom. Our differences have always been our strength, both professionally and in our marriage, and for that and much more, I am most grateful.

The work of the Institute on Achievement and Motivation has been generously supported by the Counselling Foundation of Canada and by its President, Donald Lawson, and Executive Director, Elizabeth McTavish. In addition, some of the research has been supported by the Social Science and Humanities Research Council of the Canada Council. I appreciate the opportunity afforded me by a York University Faculty of Arts Leave Fellowship. This text is the result of the released time offered by the award.

In spite of their hectic schedules, Professors Debra Pepler and Jennifer Connolly of the Clinical-Developmental Program of the Psychology Department, York University, provided me with incisive feedback on earlier drafts of this manuscript.

I would like to thank Mary Wilensky, executive officer of the Institute, for preparation of interview transcripts, and Robin Mitchell, MA, and Adrienne Chin who sought out critical library information on which much of the literature review is based. In addition, I would like to acknowledge Gail Smith, the intake coordinator at the Institute. Her understanding about and ability to connect with adolescents paves the way during their earliest moments of professional contact with Institute staff.

I am also thankful for the continuing professional association with two colleagues in Chicago, Drs. Sander Marcus and Jotham Friedland. Together, we have developed a psychological test (Friedland, Marcus, & Mandel, 1996) that identifies different types of underachievers, including the Conduct Disorder type. In particular, I have valued the many years of productive collaboration with Sander Marcus, a coauthor on a recently published book for parents of underachievers (Mandel, Marcus, & Dean, 1995).

I am also deeply appreciative of the highest level of professionalism demonstrated daily by the staff at John Wiley & Sons, New York. In particular, I would like to thank Herb Reich, who showed early interest in this work as well as in my previous research and clinical activities, and more recently to Jo Ann Miller, Executive Editor, and her staff, who have brought this book to publication. I have been associated with John Wiley & Sons for almost ten years, and I continue to be impressed by their commitment to quality.

Finally, I owe a sincere thanks to all the teenagers and their parents with whom I have worked, and especially "Tony" and "Sam," the Conduct Disorder underachievers whose stories are told here. I hope our valuable shared experiences, which are documented through this book, will help others who suffer from these problems.

H.P.M.

Contents

Chapter 1

Conduct Disorder: Criteria, Course, Risk Factors, and Differential Diagnosis

GENERAL DESCRIPTION

Individuals diagnosed with Conduct Disorder (CD) exhibit a repetitive pattern of behavior in which they violate either the basic rights of others or important age-appropriate societal norms and rules. The behavior must entail more serious problems than the pranks and adolescent mischief that normally occur among teenagers. The prevalence of this disorder in children aged 4 to 18 years appears to have increased over the past 30 years and is presently estimated to range from 6% to 16% for boys and 2% to 9% for girls. These rates translate into approximately 1.3 million to 3.8 million cases in the United States (Kazdin, 1995).

In the *Diagnostic and Statistical Manual of Mental Disorders* (*DSM-IV;* American Psychiatric Association [APA], 1994), these problem behaviors are organized into four areas of functioning: (a) aggression toward people or animals, (b) destruction of property, (c) deceitfulness or theft, and (d) serious rule violations. In general, less severe misdeeds tend to emerge first, followed by escalation of problem behaviors. Boys tend to exhibit more confrontational actions (e.g., use of violence), whereas girls tend to use less confrontational patterns (e.g., lying, stealing).

The *DSM-IV* also distinguishes two types of CD based on whether the onset of the problem behavior occurred during childhood or adolescence. *Childhood-onset CD* is far more commonly diagnosed in boys than in girls and is often accompanied by more aggressive behavior. The male/female ratio for *adolescent-onset CD* is much more equal and has a better prognosis, probably because many children have been able to develop more normal peer relationships prior to the emergence of adolescent behavior

1

oblems (McGee, Feehan, Williams, & Anderson, 1992). Adolescent-onset CD teens tend to exhibit many of their behavior problems in the company of peers.

Diagnosed CD youth usually report difficulties at home and in the community, including school. They regularly blame others for these difficulties and maintain that they have been treated unfairly by those in authority. Often there is an external "tough" image accompanied by drinking, smoking, or other substance abuse. Such individuals have a low frustration tolerance, can be quite irritable, exhibit temper outbursts, and may often act recklessly and impulsively. Many are very active sexually.

Academic achievement does not appear to be a high priority for those with CD; issues of power and control are much more central. The manipulation of others to satisfy short-term needs is common, and the individual can be quite effective in choosing targets for manipulation. The defiance of authority has a gamelike quality in which the focus is on "winning." The young person appears to lack a sense of conscience or empathy for the plight of those who have suffered because of his or her problematic behavior. The overriding objective is immediate gratification. There is increasing evidence that CD children and adolescents may also suffer from other disorders (i.e., comorbidity), including learning disorders (LD), Attention Deficit/Hyperactivity Disorder (ADHD), and/or depression.

DSM-IV DIAGNOSTIC CRITERIA

The *DSM-IV* (APA, 1994, p. 90) lists a number of diagnostic criteria for CD. At least three of the following criteria must have occurred during the previous year, with at least one criterion being present during the past six months. In addition, there must be significant impairment in social, academic, and/or occupational functioning.

Aggression toward People and/or Animals
1. Often bullies, threatens, or intimidates others.
2. Often initiates physical fights.
3. Has used a weapon that can cause serious harm to others.
4. Has been physically cruel to people.
5. Has been physically cruel to animals.
6. Has stolen while confronting a victim.
7. Has forced someone into sexual activity.

Destruction of Property

8. Has deliberately engaged in fire setting with the intention of causing serious damage.
9. Has deliberately destroyed others' property (other than by fire setting).

Deceitfulness or Theft

10. Has broken into someone else's house, building, or car.
11. Often lies to obtain goods or favors or to avoid obligations (i.e., cons others).
12. Has stolen items of nontrivial value without confronting a victim.

Serious Rules Violations

13. Often stays out at night despite parental prohibitions, beginning before the age of 13 years.
14. Has run away from home overnight at least twice while living in parental or parental surrogate home (or once without returning for a lengthy period).
15. Is often truant from school, beginning before the age of 13 years.

BEHAVIORAL COURSE OF CONDUCT DISORDER

Many researchers report that once the pattern develops (and if conditions sustain or enhance its existence), altering it becomes difficult and requires mobilization of many resources (Loeber, 1982; Olweus, 1979, 1981; Olweus, Block, & Radke-Yarrow, 1986; Robins & Ratcliffe, 1979). The stability coefficients of CD for boys appear to be only slightly higher than for girls (Olweus, 1981). In addition, "The further an individual has progressed to more serious antisocial acts, the less likely he/she will reverse to a nondeviant lifestyle" (Loeber, 1990, p. 24). Fergusson, Horwood, and Lynsky (1995) have reported that stability coefficients can vary depending on the method of calculating stability and change, and cautioned measurement error tending to inflate the rate of change.

Lewis et al. (1991), who followed the course of the disorder in male and female delinquents over a 12-year period, reported that girls had a higher mortality and suicide rate than boys, perhaps reflecting different gender-related social expressions of the disorder's symptoms. In a study on the course of CD in 54 short-term hospitalized female adolescents (aged 13–16 years), Zoccolillo and Rogers (1991) found that the condition worsened over time. Most of the subjects (84%) had never been hospitalized before, nor had they sought help for mental health reasons (73%). By follow-up (2 to 4 years later), "Six percent had died a violent death, the majority had dropped out of school, one-third were pregnant before the age of 17, half were arrested, and many suffered traumatic injuries" (p. 973). Comorbid diagnoses of depression or anxiety disorders did not improve outcome. In fact, in a longitudinal study, Zoccolillo, Pickles, Quinton, and Rutter (1992) found:

> A latent class model that used both the retrospective and contemporaneous indicators of conduct disorder confirmed the very high continuity with adult social difficulties. Conduct disorder appeared to be an almost necessary condition for multiple social disability in adults in these samples. (p. 971)

Research on adolescence has shown that petty and nonescalating antisocial behavior is the norm (DiLalla & Gottesman, 1989). The typical course of CD was examined by LeBlanc, Cote, and Loeber (1991), who compared a male control group of adolescents with a known group of delinquents. These researchers identified three stages of delinquency—occasional, transitory, and persistent: "In our data, the dominant, relatively low level of stability in the adolescent sample [i.e., control group] points to the existence of occasional delinquency. Our data leads us to expect that persistent delinquents have passed through occasional and transitory delinquency before consistently offending" (p. 41).

Many factors have been implicated in the development of CD. Researchers have clarified the differences in early-onset and later-onset factors (Lahey, Loeber, Quay, Frick, & Grimm, 1992; Loeber, 1989; Moffitt, 1993; Safer, 1984). For example, Safer (1984) isolated grade of onset of serious disruptive behaviors as the single most powerful discriminating factor in generating subgroups among CD adolescents: "Students whose misconduct began in the early elementary school were characterized by a prominent degree of developmental-educational limitations, whereas those with a later onset were—like the control group—remarkably free of early risk factors" (p. 603). White, Moffitt, Earls, Robins, and Silva (1990) reported that the single best predictor of antisocial disorders by age 11 was the existence of behavior problems in the preschool years. In a research review, Loeber and Dishion (1983) found that the major predictors of delinquency were "the parents' family management and techniques (supervision and discipline), the child's conduct problems, parental criminality, and the child's poor academic performance" (p. 68).

The *DSM-IV* (APA, 1994) has formally divided CD into childhood-onset and adolescent-onset types. More is known about the childhood-onset type which appears to begin in early childhood with the emergence of Oppositional Defiant Disorder (ODD). This noncompliant, angry, argumentative, and irritable behavior worsens with the emergence of more serious behaviors, including lying, fighting, and stealing. For a very small percentage (approximately 4%) even more serious behaviors evolve, including crimes against property and/or violence against others. Hinshaw, Lahey, and Hart (1993) postulate:

> Childhood-onset antisocial pathway begins formally with the emergence of ODD in early childhood . . . with some youths progressing to both aggressive and nonaggressive symptoms of CD in middle childhood, and even fewer progressing to the most serious symptoms of CD by late childhood or adolescence. (p. 45)

It is important to recognize, however, that many children diagnosed with ODD do *not* progress to the more serious childhood-onset CD. In fact, many of these children will no longer exhibit ODD by the time they enter adolescence (Hinshaw, Lahey, & Hart, 1993). It appears that powerful mediating variables other than ODD are predictive of the emergence and persistence of CD. These include biology, family environment, school factors, and peer influences. This issue will be described in the next section.

In contrast to most young children, many adolescents exhibit some infrequent and episodic antisocial behavior. Only a small percentage of these teenagers engage in persistent delinquent activity. Most teenagers with adolescent-onset CD exhibit less severe behavior and are not as aggressive as those with the childhood-onset type. They did not exhibit ODD in their childhood years, and the emergence of this pattern appears to be related to negative influences of a deviant peer group.

Patterson (1982) and Patterson, DeBaryshe, and Ramsey (1989) have proposed a pathway for CD. It begins with ineffective, coercive parenting, which leads to their child's disruptive behavior. This in turn leads both to academic failure and rejection by peers. School failure and peer rejection create conditions for the next step—depressed mood and gravitation to deviant but accepting peers, usually in late childhood or early adolescence.

Robinson (1985) proposed modifications of Patterson's coercive family model, "in which a conduct disorder is conceptualized as a deviation from normal maturation determined by the interaction of person, behavior, and environment" (p. 597). The dyadic parent-child relationship, the role of attachment, the role of synchrony (i.e., the ability of parents to align or calibrate their behavior to meet the needs of their child), the ability of parents to behave in a concerned manner toward others and provide their children with abstract reasons for doing so, and the ability and willingness of parents to impart social values directly through modeling, teaching, and sanctioning of these values, are all incorporated in the expanded model. In addition and concurrently, the child's intellectual development (e.g., from preoperational to operational thinking) and other mediating variables, such as parent pathology, adequacy of social support networks, and marital difficulties, are integral aspects of the modified model.

Lahey and colleagues (1995) reported on the course of CD over a 4-year period in 171 outpatient clinic boys (mean age 9.5 years): "For most boys with CD, the number of symptoms fluctuated above and below the diagnostic threshold from year to year but remained relatively high. Lower SES [socioeconomic status], parental antisocial personality disorder (APD), and attention deficit/hyperactivity disorder were significant correlates of CD in Year 1" (p. 83). The only group that improved over the 4-year study included those CD boys whose fathers were not diagnosed APD and who had above-average intelligence. In other words, higher intelligence and the absence of an APD father were protective factors. Similar results were reported from a 6-year longitudinal study (Loeber, Green, Keenan, & Lahey, 1995): "Low SES of the parent, ODD, and parental substance abuse best predicted the onset of CD. In addition, ADHD predicted an early onset" (p. 499).

Loeber (1990) postulated the following developmental sequence for the emergence of disruptive behaviors in childhood and adolescence: difficult temperament (postnatal); hyperactivity (noticed by parents more once walking begins); overt conduct problems such as aggression (after age 2); withdrawal and poor peer relationships (during preschool); academic problems (Grades 1 or 2); covert or concealing conduct problems such as truancy, stealing, substance use (later childhood and early adolescence); association with deviant peers, delinquency, and recidivism (all three during adolescence). Rubin, Chen, McDougall, Bowker, and McKinnon (1995) confirmed the relationship between childhood aggression and adolescent delinquency.

A recent study (Moffitt, Caspi, Dickson, Silva, & Stanton, 1996) has provided additional support for the differentiation between childhood-onset and adolescent-onset CD. These researchers studied the developmental histories of 457 males from ages 3 to 18 years, and found that "males whose antisocial behavior follows a life-course-persistent path differ from males who follow an adolescence-limited path" (p. 399).

The pathways for child-onset and adolescent-onset CDs appear to be different even though they may contain several common factors. The implications of these differences for treatment will be addressed in Chapter 3.

ISSUES OF DIFFERENTIAL DIAGNOSIS

Developmentally, it is typical for many adolescents to engage in *isolated antisocial acts,* either on their own or as part of a peer group. Some adolescents may even be susceptible to peer pressures to act out against authority in antisocial ways. Therefore, single acts of antisocial behavior should never lead to a diagnosis of CD. In reaching a diagnostic decision, the critical issue involves the frequency and duration of such acts. The antisocial behavior must be repetitive and must have been a frequent problem for at least 6 months (APA, 1994). A key is to check whether there has been a significant impact on social and/or academic functioning. Isolated illegal acts seldom produce permanent noticeable deterioration in these two areas.

Reactions against authority are not unique to conduct disorder. The *Oppositional Defiant Disorder (ODD) underachiever* also exhibits disobedient behavior (APA, 1994; Mandel & Marcus, 1988; Samuels & Sikorski, 1990). In a recent review of these disorders, Loeber, Lahey, and Thomas (1991) conclude that although there is overlap between these two conditions (e.g., mild aggression and lying), and although they are developmentally related, unique aspects emerge:

> Age of onset for ODD is earlier than for most CD symptoms. Nearly all youth with CD have a history of ODD, but not all ODD cases progress to CD. The disorders demonstrate the same forms of parental psychopathology and family adversity but to a greater degree for CD than for ODD. (p. 379)

In a later review, Lahey and colleagues (1992) also concluded that the adolescent-onset CD appears to develop without signs of ODD.

In my own clinical experience, ODD behavior generally does not violate the basic rights of others nor does it violate major adolescent behavioral norms. Further, the individual typically feels some remorse for disruptive behavior (although not at the time it occurs), whereas the individual with CD seldom does. And even when a person with CD shows signs of remorse, it may be motivated by the desire to avoid or lessen negative consequences rather than being heartfelt.

Some children and adolescents exhibit *fluctuating moods,* including heightened irritability and some antisocial behavior. In those cases, the behaviors tend to be short-lived and nonrepetitive.

There is increasing evidence that some children and adolescents with CD show signs of *comorbidity* for other disorders such as *Attention-Deficit/-Hyperactivity Disorder* (ADHD; APA, 1994). It has been difficult to evaluate the degree to which these are separate disorders or variations of the same behavior pattern: "Factor analyses typically yield distinct but correlated dimensions in the area of hyperactivity and conduct problems/aggression; separate factors of inattention are sometimes found. Recent studies provide support for the separation of aggressive, hyperactive, and aggressive-hyperactive subgroups of children" (Hinshaw, 1987, p. 443). Individuals with comorbid CD-ADHD tend to exhibit more aggressive behavior than those without ADHD and have a poorer prognosis (Hinshaw et al., 1993; Moffitt, 1990a; Walker, Lahey, Hynd, & Frame, 1987).

There is also controversy about the degree to which *academic underachievement (AU)* plays a role either in the development and/or maintenance of disruptive behavior disorders, such as CD and ADHD. Frick and colleagues (1991) used a statistical regression formula to identify underachievers and noted: "The apparent relation between CD and AU was found to be due to its comorbidity with ADHD" (p. 289).

The CD underachiever may also exhibit one or several *Learning Disorders,* such as a Mathematics Disorder, Reading Disorder, or Disorder of Written Expression (APA, 1994), or one or several *Communication Disorders,* such as an Expressive Language Disorder, or a Mixed Receptive-Expressive Language Disorder.

There is mounting evidence that many individuals with CD also experience more lasting *affective disorders,* especially *dysthymia* and *anxiety* (Berndt & Zinn, 1984; Biederman, Newcorn, & Sprich, 1991; Chiles, Miller, & Cox, 1980; Delameter & Lahey, 1983; Gray, 1987; Kashani et al., 1980; Kashani et al., 1987; Kovacs, Paulauskas, Gastonis, & Richards, 1988; Marriage, Fine, Moretti, & Haley, 1986; McBurnett et al., 1991;

Puig-Antich, 1982). The degree to which each individual is aware of the existence or extent of the dysthymia will vary greatly and may be related to prognosis in treatment.

Individuals with CD will also vary in the amount of available psychic energy. Some may exceed normal limits and be considered *hypomanic.*

An alternative to the diagnosis of CD underachiever is *Child* or *Adolescent Antisocial Behavior* (APA, 1994). This diagnosis should be considered where the student is underachieving but the conduct problems are isolated and not part of a repetitive pattern that meets the diagnostic requirements for CD. Often these conduct problems appear in conjunction with major psychosocial stress.

WHAT MOTIVATES INDIVIDUALS WITH CONDUCT DISORDER?

Individuals with CD resist authority and have difficulty with self-control and delay of gratification. But what things consistently motivate them? And are the answers distinct for the childhood-onset and adolescent-onset types?

Three theories have been used to explain delinquent motivations: (a) *rational-choice,* (b) *strain,* and (c) *subcultural deviance.* Empirical and clinical support has been found for each (Cimler & Beach, 1981; Cusson, 1983; Mandel & Marcus, 1988; Mandel, Marcus, & Dean, 1995; Wilson & Herrnstein, 1985) as well as for an integration of these theories (Farrington, 1993).

Using self-report, Cusson (1983) summarized reasons that delinquents gave for their behavior. These included personal material gain, arousal (e.g., thrill seeking by using drugs or playing chicken), approval of peers (gaining of social respect and status), a way of proving toughness to oneself or to others, a safety valve to relieve internal pressure, retaliation to "square" accounts, escape from unpleasant situations (e.g., school truancy), and/or satisfaction of sexual needs. These self-stated reasons can be subsumed under economic, arousal, and self-esteem needs.

Researchers have also speculated about several other motivations. These include anger as a response to being hurt (Berkowitz, 1989), anger triggered by cognitive processes in which the child attributes malicious intent in others (strike before you are struck), and/or antisocial activity based on a rational decision (Wilson & Herrnstein, 1985). Farrington (1993) distinguished between short-and long-term energizing factors as well as unfolding motivational stages, integrating many of the previously discussed variables in a model of delinquent behavior.

Agnew (1990) found that motivations to commit antisocial acts vary depending on the severity of the act: "Violent crimes are committed primarily for retaliation/revenge. Drug offenses are committed primarily because of social pressure, with self-gratification/pleasure also an important reason" (p. 267).

RISK FACTORS FOR CONDUCT DISORDER

Research over the past 20 years has identified a number of contributors to conduct problems in children and adolescents. At present, there is controversy about whether some of these factors are the cause, simply related to other causes, or the result of the antisocial behavior. Also, many descriptive and diagnostic labels have been used for children and adolescents with behavioral problems (e.g., juvenile delinquency, disruptive behaviors, aggressive behaviors, attentional problems, oppositional behavior, psychopathic and/or sociopathic behavior). In the following subsections, I will summarize the variables that have been implicated as risk factors for CD.

Male and Female Conduct Disorder

Are the developmental pathways identical for boys and girls diagnosed with CD? For every three studies on male CDs there is only one focused on their female counterparts (Zoccolillo, 1993). Research subject pools have come primarily from youngsters apprehended because of criminal acts (predominantly boys). The diagnostic criteria for CD were originally derived from these predominantly male samples, thereby excluding criteria that could have resulted in a higher CD prevalence in girls.

Some researchers recommend considering *sex-specific CD criteria* for females (Zoccolillo, 1993). For example, Lewis and colleagues (1991) found that CD females are arrested less often and for less serious offenses than CD males. Therefore, any criterion based on frequency of arrests could be interpreted differently for males and females. Other researchers recommend against the use of sex-specific criteria and suggest expanding the diagnostic criteria by including other serious externalizing problems (Zahn-Waxler, 1993).

Shanok and Lewis (1981) compared the histories of incarcerated and nonincarcerated delinquent females: "Accidents and injuries, head and face injuries, perinatal difficulties, neurologic abnormalities, and child abuse were found more frequently in the histories of incarcerated girls" (p. 211). Are the more serious medical problems of incarcerated female delinquents the product of a different etiologic pathway from that of non-incarcerated female delinquents?

If CD *prevalence rates* are examined by dividing youngsters into child and adolescent groups, the childhood-onset type is far more commonly diagnosed in males than in females, ranging from 3 : 1 to 4 : 1 (Anderson, Williams, McGee, & Silva, 1987; Esser, Schmidt, & Woerner, 1990; Offord et al., 1987). In contrast, the *male/female ratio for adolescents* is approximately 1 : 1 (Esser et al., 1990; Kashani et al., 1987; McGee et al., 1990).

Caspi, Lynam, Moffitt, and Silva (1993) explored the interaction of biological and environmental factors in the etiology of adolescent female delinquency. More specifically, they examined the impact of *early menarche* on delinquent behavior in mixed versus same-sex school settings. Their findings are intriguing because they point to a developmental interaction. For example, compared with subjects from an all-girls school, early-maturing girls from a coeducational school were much more involved in antisocial activities by age 13. Girls in a coed school who matured "on time" did not engage in more antisocial activity by age 13 than did their all-girls school counterparts. By age 15, however, these coed-based female teens had begun to show a slight increase in their antisocial behavior compared with their same-sex school counterparts. In contrast, girls from a coed school who matured late engaged in the same small amount of antisocial activity as did their same-sex school counterparts. The authors hypothesize that early biological development interacts with exposure to male delinquent culture in the coed setting. They also found that girls who reported childhood-onset behavior problems (i.e., occurrence long before menarche) had already been involved with delinquent peers whether they matured early, on time, or late. These researchers speculate that individual differences may combine with what they term *transition events*: "A transition event that is characterized by ambiguity, novelty, and uncertainty (the early onset of menarche) is likely to accentuate the effects of preexisting attributes (behavior problems) or behavior (delinquency)" (Caspi et al., 1993, p. 28).

Pepler (1995) concludes:

There is evidence to suggest that somewhat different mechanisms influence the development of aggression in girls and boys. As knowledge of these mechanisms increases, we will be able to articulate different components for intervention, depending not only on the age, but also on the gender of the children at risk. (pp. 28–29)

Biological Factors

A number of studies point to *heredity* as an important contributor to antisocial behavior (Cadoret, 1978; Cadoret, Cain, & Crowe, 1983; Crowe, 1974; DiLalla & Gottesman, 1989; Faraone, Beiderman, Keenan, & Tsuang, 1991; Mednick, Gabrielli, & Hutchings, 1984). Reid, Dorr, Walker, and Bonner (1986) found that antisocial behavior was higher in monozygotic twins reared apart than in dizygotic twins reared apart. Reviews by Rutter and colleagues (1990) and Plomin, Nitz, and Rowe (1990) have highlighted the role heredity plays in aggression, criminality, and antisocial personality. Comings (1995) reported on the role genetics may play in the development of CD by reviewing studies of Tourette's syndrome and ADHD probands and their relatives. His findings support the role of genetic factors in both Oppositional Defiant Disorder and Conduct Disorder.

Using data from three twin studies, Cadoret et al. (1983) highlighted the interaction between heredity and environment in the development of adolescent antisocial behavior:

> Results indicate significant increases in antisocial behavior when an adoptee has both a genetic factor and an adverse environmental factor present. The increase in number of antisocial behaviors due to both genetic and environmental factors acting together is far greater than the predicted increase from either acting alone. (p. 301)

Mednick et al. (1984) concur:

> In a population of adoptions a relation was found between biological parent criminal convictions and criminal convictions in their adoptee children. This claim holds especially for chronic criminality. The findings imply that biological predispositions are involved in the development of at least some criminal behavior. (p. 893)

DiLalla and Gottesman (1989) reviewed studies that address the issue of heredity in the development of delinquency and criminality, and emphasized the interaction between these two contributors: "Twin and adoption studies show that criminality increases with the presence of criminality in biological relatives; the environmental effects of having a criminal parent also increase the risk of adoptee criminality" (p. 339). Dodge (1990) criticized efforts to pit nature against nurture in etiological research on childhood CD: "It is recommended that instead of focusing on the relative sizes of effects, researchers should focus on the questions of which mechanisms operate and how they *interact* during transactional development" (p. 698).

Werner and Smith (1982) found biological risk factors for conduct disorder included premature birth, low birth weight, minor injuries during birth, and impaired breathing at birth. Mrazek and Haggerty (1994) found that damage to the *central nervous system* (e.g., during birth) and chronic illness during childhood also increase the risk of developing conduct disorder.

Autonomic responsiveness has also been a target for research on CD (Delameter & Lahey, 1983). Raine, Venables, and Williams (1990) reported a significant difference in the skin conductances of criminal and control subjects. They concluded: "The genetic predisposition to criminal behavior may find its expression in part through smaller autonomic orienting" (p. 933).

Biochemical factors have also been implicated. In a 2-year prospective study, Kruesi and colleagues (1992) recently reported that a specific level of 5-hydroxyindoleacetic acid, a *serotonin* metabolite, was predictive of physical aggression in severely disruptive hospitalized children and adolescents. Some researchers have reported serotonergic dysfunction in sociopaths (Lewis, 1991), linking the inability of the psychopath to learn from experience (punishment or nonreward) to similar findings from animal learning research on low serotonin levels. McBurnett and colleagues (1991), in their study of comorbidity of CD and anxiety disorder found that *salivary cortisol* "may be a useful biological marker of arousal associated with behavioral inhibition system activity in children with CD" (p. 192).

It has long been known that antisocial and substance abusing (SA) adults show changes in dopaminergic regulation and levels of monoamine oxidase (MAO). But is there any relationship between antisocial, substance-abusing fathers and their sons' MAO levels? Gabel, Stadler, Bjorn, Shindledecker, and Bowden (1995) studied the relationship between substance abuse by antisocial fathers and levels of specific biological markers in their children. Two chemicals were studied: (a) homovanillic acid (HVA), a metabolite of dopamine (DA), and (b) MAO, an enzyme that facilitates the chemical conversion of DA to HVA. A total of 65 children and teens participated, ranging in age from 6 to 15 years:

> The findings indicated that MAO activity was significantly higher in boys of SA fathers with CD than (1) in boys of non-SA fathers with CD and, (2) in boys of SA fathers without CD. The findings support the concept of doaminergic dysregulation in sons of SA fathers, manifested by alterations in MAO activity levels in those youths with CD. (p. 135)

Lewis, Shanok, Pincus, and Glaser (1979) reported that the more violent juvenile delinquents in their sample exhibited major and minor *neurological abnormalities*. Since the childhood histories of the most violent juvenile offenders contained evidence that they had observed extreme physical abuse as children, one wonders whether they too had been the victims of abuse and may have experienced neurological damage. Did these neurological abnormalities cause the serious acting out or were they result of damage caused during their own or someone else's acting out?

Pointing to research on *perseverative responding* for reward, dysfunctions in *noradrenaline and serotonin* activity, and low levels of *electrodermal response* in severe CDs, Quay (1993) proposes a psychobiological model for the development of the undersocialized, aggressive type of CD, the most severe type described in the *DSM-III-R* (APA, 1987). This would probably equate to the childhood-onset severe type described in the current *DSM-IV* (APA, 1994). Quay (1993) also describes the interaction of these factors with the environment:

> The persistence of aggression over generations (Eron & Heusmann, 1990) suggests that those likely to have the predisposing biology will also be exposed to aggressive parental role models. It may also be possible for experience to have an effect on those neurotransmitters that are involved in the function of the two systems. (p. 176)

Neuropsychological and Cognitive Processes

In examining *neuropsychological factors* in CD, Hurwitz, Bibace, Wolff, and Rowbotham (1972) reported that juvenile delinquents performed poorly on a test of motor development and on sequencing skills when compared with normals. Brickman, McManus, Grapentine, and Alessi (1984) found that *expressive speech* and *memory scales* on the Luria-Nebraska Battery differentiated delinquent from nondelinquent adolescents.

Moffitt and Silva (1988c) reported significant differe
trol group, a non-attention-deficit disorder (ADD) de)
an ADD-delinquent group on neuropsychological m
delinquents with past ADD were more cognitively impan
ADD delinquents, both groups scored significantly below nondelinqu.
[i.e., the control group] on verbal, visuospatial, and visual-motor integration skills" (p. 553). Raine and Jones (1987) found similar differences between antisocial and hyperactive children, and adolescents (ages 7–15)
on neuropsychological measures. They concluded that test results point to
two distinct conditions, supporting earlier biochemical research (Rogeness, Hernandez, Macedo, & Mitchell, 1982).

In a review of neuropsychological studies, Moffitt (1993) reported that
two cognitive factors play important roles in the development of CD. Her
review implicates *lesions in the left frontal lobe* and that lobe's involvement with the *limbic system* as causal factors in the specific *verbal skill
deficits* (e.g., expression and comprehension) and *executive dysfunction*
(e.g., poor inhibitory control) seen in delinquents with ADHD. Her review has been criticized by Pennington and Bennetto (1993) who propose a more cautious approach to data interpretation and who recommend
further investigation. It is fair to say, however, that biological factors play
a role in the development of extreme antisocial behavior, although the
exact genetic, biochemical, and physiological mechanisms are not yet
fully understood.

Temperament has also long been thought to be predictive of behavior.
For example, infants with "good" temperaments were thought to be less
likely to develop disruptive behavior problems. But the results of several
studies reveal that the relationship between temperament and behavior
is neither simple nor direct (Kandel et al., 1988; Schonfeld, Shaffer,
O'Connor, & Portnoy, 1988; White, Moffitt, & Silva, 1989). They found
that infants with difficult temperaments, low IQs, and family difficulties
tended to develop disruptive behavior problems, whereas infants with difficult temperaments, high IQs, and family difficulties did not. It appears
that a *high IQ acts in a protective manner,* decreasing the probability of
disruptive behavior and possibly preventing subsequent underachievement.

Perceptions, attributions, and problem-solving skills constitute the
world of cognition and many children with disruptive behavior problems
exhibit cognitive difficulties (Crick & Dodge, 1994; Shirk, 1988). For example, Andrew (1977) postulated that a significant discrepancy between
verbal and performance scores on IQ tests (labeled *intellectual imbalance*)

ay increase the chances of delinquency in children and adolescents. Haynes and Bensch (1981) reported that the P > V discrepancy was predictive of greater recidivism in delinquents. Those delinquents who did not reoffend did not show this P − V discrepancy. Interestingly, the magnitude of the discrepancy was not related to the severity of the acting out.

One cognitive factor—IQ—appears to play a positive or *protective role* in the development of delinquency. Using subjects from Denmark, Moffitt, Gabrielli, Mednick, and Schulsinger (1981) found that, once they controlled socioeconomic status, there was a significant negative correlation between IQ and delinquent behavior. In a confirmatory study using juvenile delinquents from New Zealand, White, Moffitt, and Silva (1989) reported similar results. Subjects were rated at the age of 5 years according to delinquency risk factors and later tested for delinquency outcome: "By varying subject selection procedures, we also found that a very high IQ may help boys, even those at risk, to stay free of delinquency altogether" (p. 719). These findings are consistent with those cited in the section on the mediating role of IQ in combination with temperament and disruptive childhood behaviors (Kandel et al., 1988; Schonfeld, Shaffer, O'Connor, & Portnoy, 1988).

But how does a higher IQ mediate severe disruptive behavior? It is hypothesized that a higher IQ increases the possibility of at least some academic success. This would be especially true for individuals with a higher verbal IQ, as it is much more highly correlated with academic success than is performance IQ. Such success may mitigate against acting out because it results in a range of personal benefits for the student (e.g., praise, status, increased mastery, or control). In addition, a higher IQ may reflect a greater capacity for problem solving. In contrast, youngsters with lower IQ may have a more limited cognitive capacity to perceive alternatives to problems. This lower ability to generate options may lead to a more rapid increase in frustration and behavioral deterioration.

To my knowledge, very few studies have compared higher functioning and less severe CD underachievers with lower functioning and more severe CD underachievers. In my clinical experience, these higher functioning CD underachievers tend to have at least an average verbal IQ. Many have a discrepancy between verbal and performance IQs in favor of the verbal, and some have a high verbal IQ. In light of the preceding research findings (White, Moffitt, & Silva, 1989), these CD underachievers are more likely to have a positive prognosis, in spite of many risk factors, because of a verbal intellectual advantage.

Do social class and/or race change this P > V pattern in CD? Controlling for race and social class, Walsh, Petee, and Beyer (1987) reported that most delinquents still exhibited the P > V pattern. There is also growing evidence that certain *cognitive and linguistic problems* precede the emergence of disruptive behavior (White, Moffitt, & Silva, 1989). Schonfeld, Shaffer, O'Connor, and Portnoy (1988) found that three factors appear to carry equal weight in accounting for the diagnosis of CD in their sample of 17-year-olds: cognitive functioning, parent psychopathology, and evidence of childhood aggression. The researchers noted: "A closer look at the data tentatively suggested that a *broad deficiency in acculturational learning,* rather than narrowly focused social cognitive differences or native endowment, constitutes a key element in the link between cognitive functioning and conduct disorder" (p. 993). The two cases to be presented in Chapter 2 will highlight how intellectual functioning, language problems, and social acculturational factors interact to change the risk of CD.

The learning styles and academic histories of adolescent delinquents and nondelinquents appear to be quite different. Meltzer, Levine, Karniski, Palfrey, and Clarke (1984) found significant differences in the kind and frequency of errors both within and across the following educational skills areas: *reading style and errors, spelling style and errors, the mechanics, organization and formulation of writing,* and *math errors.* Further, as early as Grade 2, 45% of the delinquents exhibited *delays in reading* and 35% *delays in handwriting,* whereas only 14% of the control group showed these delays. In fact, the authors suggest that early learning difficulties may be a risk factor for delinquency.

Skoff and Libon (1987) found deficiencies in *executive functioning* in approximately two thirds of the juvenile delinquents in their sample. Specifically, these delinquents were moderately to severely impaired in at least one of the following executive functions: *mental planning, establishing and maintaining a mental set, shifting set,* and *mental control.*

Not all researchers have found cognitive differences. Tarter, Hegedus, Alterman, and Katz-Garris (1983) reported no relationship between cognitive status and severity of violent behavior in juvenile offenders. Slaby and Guerra (1988) found that aggressive antisocial adolescent offenders had a dysfunctional, predictable pattern of *problem solving,* which included hostile problem definition, choice of hostile goals, low frequency of seeking the facts, creation of few alternatives, and poor anticipation of the consequences of their choices. These teens also strongly believed aggression was a legitimate response that boosted self-esteem and did not cause undue suffering to others.

Negative attributions play an important role in triggering aggressive responses in juvenile offenders (Nasby, Hayden, & DePaulo, 1980; Steinberg & Dodge, 1983). Dodge, Price, Bachorowski, and Newman (1990) found that even when race, IQ, and socioeconomic status are controlled, those delinquents who held hostile attributional biases (e.g., "You got a problem, dude?") were much more likely to act out aggressively against others, often when the stimuli from others were benign. In fact, addressing these hostile attributions is one of the key elements in many treatment programs.

Dodge, Bates, and Pettit (1990) reviewed studies on the development of aggression in children and found most designs confounded by issues of socioeconomic (e.g., poverty) and biological factors (e.g., early medical problems and/or temperament). In their rigorously controlled study they reported: "Physical abuse is indeed a risk factor for later aggressive behavior even when the other ecological and biological factors are known. Abused children tended to acquire deviant patterns of processing social information, and these may mediate the development of aggressive behavior" (p. 1678).

In a more recent study, Dodge, Bates, Pettit, and Valente (1995) confirmed this finding. Through interviews with mothers, they explored the degree to which 584 kindergarten children had been exposed to physical abuse. Several years later, when the children had reached Grades 3 and 4, the research team examined the current reports of teacher-rated acting-out behaviors of these same children:

> Early abuse increased the risk of teacher-rated externalizing outcomes in Grades 3 and 4 by fourfold, and this effect cannot be accounted for by confounded ecological or child factors. Abuse was associated with later processing patterns (encoding errors, hostile attributional biases, accessing of aggressive responses, and positive evaluations of aggression), which in turn, predicted later externalizing outcomes. (p. 632)

Early physical abuse undoubtedly is a risk factor for externalizing behavior. What Dodge et al. (1995) have explored is the mediating role of social information-processing.

Are *expectations* about future interpersonal difficulties predictive of the development of behavioral problems? Allen, Leadbeater, and Aber

(1994) reported that at-risk teenagers (mean age 16.8 years) who did not expect positive outcome in future problematic social interactions were much more likely to engage in hard drug use within the following year than those whose expectations were more positive. They also found that the level of soft drug usage in at-risk adolescents was predictive of future delinquency and poorer problem-solving effectiveness. The authors concluded: "Negative expectations reduce competence by decreasing the effort placed into adaptive behavior and increasing the likelihood of choosing maladaptive strategies in problematic situations" (p. 338).

It has long been a clinical "truth" that individuals with CD do not learn from experience and make repeated errors in judgment and behavior (Shapiro, Quay, Hogan, & Schwartz, 1988). Newman (1987) experimentally explored this issue using "disinhibited" adult subjects, including a sample of psychopaths. When disinhibited subjects were placed in situations where money was the reward, they did not slow their response time following an incorrect reaction (i.e., they *perseverated*). Following failure, some psychopaths responded even more quickly on the next trial whereas most control subjects slowed their responses to consider alternative solutions. Speeding up after an incorrect response was highly correlated with failure to learn from the "punishment" and was characteristic of the disinhibited groups.

In a parallel study, Newman, Patterson, and Kosson (1987) reported that building in a delay during which psychopaths could not respond decreased perseverative behavior. They recommend that this principle of forced delay be incorporated in treatment programs. Scerbo and colleagues (1990) reported similar findings in adolescent psychopaths.

Another research area of cognitive functioning in CD is based on Kohlberg's stages of *moral development* (1978). Early research by Campagna and Harter (1975) showed that sociopathic adolescents had lower scores on measures of moral development than did normal adolescents. A similar finding was reported by Bear and Richards (1981) for children with conduct problems. However, an overview of these studies shows that delinquents as a group, as is true for normal adolescents, showed a wide range of stages of moral development, including more mature levels: "Thus, acquisition of conventional [moral] concepts in no way prevents delinquency" (Jurovic, 1980, p. 716). Having the cognitive capacity for higher moral levels does not automatically lead to implementation of these concepts in daily life.

Several behaviors seen in CD can be judged within the context of moral development. For example, Stouthamer-Loeber (1986) reported that early persistent lying is a strong predictor of later delinquency and poor adult adjustment. Another characteristic involves the externalization of blame. Nucci and Herman (1982) reported that children with behavioral problems were less likely to assume personal responsibility for their actions.

Affective Processes

As mentioned earlier, negative hostile attributions play a role in triggering conduct problem behavior. Aside from the cognitive issue, however, the role of affect in the development of conduct disorder has also been studied from a number of different perspectives. One research direction has focused on the ability of individuals to take the role of others and experience *affective empathy*. Ellis (1982) reported that delinquent adolescents were either "significantly delayed or arrested in the development of empathy" (p. 123). This was confirmed in a later study by Kaplan and Arbuthnot (1985), who reported that on unstructured empathy tasks, delinquents scored significantly lower than an adolescent control group. A more recent study reconfirmed these findings (Matthys, Walterbos, Van Engeland, & Koops, 1995): "CD boys perceived their peers more from an egocentric point of view. They paid less attention to the peers' inner, personal worlds, and instead attended more to the peers' external qualities" (p. 357).

McKeough, Yates, and Marini (1994) explored the thinking process in behaviorally disturbed and normal groups of 6-, 8-, and 10-year-old boys of equivalent intelligence. Four tasks were used: (a) creating a story that contained a problem and a solution; (b) understanding the role of mother through two pictures, one depicting a girl slipping from a roof and the other depicting a fire in a child's room; (c) testing empathy by showing videotapes of emotionally charged situations and asking the child to describe how the character felt and why; and (d) asking the child to explain the meaning of words that describe human emotions.

The behaviorally disturbed boys were significantly lower in their scores of intentionality compared with the control group. And although the disruptive boys increased the complexity of their cognitions with increasing age (as did the control group), they were consistently behind their same-age control peers at each age level. In other words, disruptive boys were less able to create reasonable solutions, understand the adult role, empathize, and explain the meaning of emotional terms. These boys with behavioral problems were unable to decode or misread the experiences of others.

The relationship between *mood shifts* and the emergence of disruptive behavior has also been examined. Weinberger and Gomes (1995) used a time series and path-analytic methods in their study of problem behavior in a day-treatment sample of 20 preadolescent boys: "The boys did engage in emotional acting out, in that their morning moods predicted their subsequent disruptive behavior. Boys' mood changes served as a mediator between the intensity of interpersonal conflicts and decrements in their self-restraint" (p. 1473). In addition, these researchers found that the boys who reported the lowest personal distress and were rated by their teachers as the greatest deniers of stress (i.e., defensive process) tended to show the strongest relationship between mood and acting-out behavior.

The role of depression and its relation to CD will be explored in the following section.

Comorbidity Issues

The simultaneous existence of more than one disorder in a child or adolescent has received much research attention over the past 10 years (Kashani et al., 1987; Offord, Boyle, & Racine, 1991). For example, in a study in Puerto Rico, Bird, Gould, and Staghezza (1993) reported high levels of comorbidity across four major diagnoses: ADD, CD/OD, depression, and anxiety.

In general, five comorbid conditions typically are associated with childhood-onset CD:

1. *Attention Deficit/Hyperactivity Disorder (ADHD),* including inattention and/or hyperactivity and/or impulsivity (Biederman, Munir, & Knee, 1987; Faraone, Biederman, Keenan, & Tsuang, 1991).
2. *Substance abuse* (Lynsky & Fergusson, 1995).
3. *Depression* (Biederman, Newcorn, & Sprich, 1991; Holmes & Robins, 1987; Taras, 1993) and *Bipolar Disorder* (Kovacs & Pollock, 1995).
4. *Anxiety* (Russo et al., 1991; Russo et al., 1993).
5. *Academic underachievement* (Mandel & Mandel, 1995; Mandel, Marcus, & Dean, 1995; Taras, 1993).

Attention Deficit/Hyperactivity Disorder

Schachar and Tannock (1995) studied cognitive and developmental risk patterns, and psychosocial factors among CD, ADHD, and comorbid CD + ADHD. The pure CD group had experienced a greater degree of stress in their environment and exhibited specific difficulties in math. The pure ADHD group had significantly greater difficulty on cognitive measures requiring inhibition and flexibility of response, and demonstrated developmental delays and reading problems:

> The ADHD + CD group was similar to the ADHD group on cognitive, developmental, and reading measures and similar to the CD group on psychosocial and arithmetic measures. These results support the distinctiveness of ADHD and CD and the hypothesis that the comorbid condition of ADHD + CD is a hybrid of pure ADHD and pure CD. (p. 639)

Dykman and Ackerman (1993) reported that children with ADHD are much more likely to exhibit oppositional or conduct disorder than those with ADD. In their study, McArdle, O'Brien, and Kolvin (1995) reported that for both younger and older children, hyperactivity was strongly linked to CD. There is mounting evidence (Loeber, 1988; Moffitt, in press; Robins, 1966) that these children are more likely to continue their antisocial pattern well into adulthood and that the antisocial acts will become more serious, often leading to physical and sexual abuse. Further, individuals with comorbid CD and ADHD are more likely to exhibit heightened aggression, a wider range and greater persistence of antisocial behavior, and significantly higher peer rejection rates than those with only one of these disorders (Farrington, Loeber, & Van Kammen, 1990; Magnusson, 1987; McGee, Williams, & Silva, 1984; Milich & Landau, 1989; Offord, Sullivan, Allen, & Abrams, 1979; Walker, Lahey, Hynd, & Frame, 1987). Therefore, the most reasonable assumption is that the effects of ADHD combine with other predisposing and/or precipitating factors to increase the chances of the development of CD (Hinshaw, Lahey, & Hart, 1993; Hinshaw & Mednick, 1995). A study by Fergusson and Horwood (1995) has shed some new light on the relationships among CD, ADD, IQ, academic achievement, and the probability of the development of Conduct Disorder or Oppositional Defiant Disorder. I will review it in some detail in Chapter 5.

In addition, the sex of the child also interacts with the comorbidity of CD and ADHD. Even though the prevalence of comorbid CD and ADHD for boys is far more common than it is for girls, Szatmari, Boyle, and Offord (1989) found that girls with a diagnosis of ADHD have a 40:1 greater risk for comorbid CD diagnosis.

Not all studies have found a relationship between impulsivity and CD. In their study of 111 impulsive outpatient preadolescents and young adolescents (82 boys; 29 girls), Halperin and colleagues (1995) found that children who initiated fights and who were diagnosed as CD or Oppositional Defiant Disorder were not impulsive. It is possible, however, for children with CD who do not initiate fights to be impulsive. This raises the issue of subgroups within the CD diagnosis.

Substance Abuse

Another CD comorbid condition is substance abuse. Lynsky and Fergusson (1995) reported that early-onset CD is a risk factor for later substance abuse, often not showing itself until early adolescence These researchers also found, however, that this risk was *not* true for a diagnosis of ADD without hyperactivity. Thus a child with ADD (*absence* of hyperactivity and CD) is at much less risk of later substance abuse than a child with a CD diagnosis.

Johnson, Arria, Borges, Ialongo, and Anthony (1995) examined the rates of growth of conduct problem behaviors of 408 students ranging in age from middle childhood to early adolescence:

> Early alcohol use without parental permission was associated with higher levels of conduct problem behaviors by the ages of 10–12 years and higher rates of growth in those behaviors during the transition from late childhood to early adolescence for both boys and girls, although the levels differed by sex. It may be that unsanctioned early alcohol use puts youths on an accelerated pathway of conduct problem behaviors and development of conduct disorder in adolescence. (p. 661)

The finding of a relationship between CD and Substance Use Disorder (SUD) in psychiatric adolescent inpatients was also reported recently in two separate studies (Grilo et al., 1995; Young et al., 1995).

Depression and Bipolar Disorder

Research findings point to the emergence of depression following the development of CD in adolescents (Biederman, Newcorn, & Sprich, 1991; Chiles, Miller, & Cox, 1980; Holmes & Robins, 1987). We now know that the prevalence of CD with depression is much higher than first suspected (Kovacs, Paulauskas, Gatsonis, & Richards, 1988; Offord, Boyle, & Racine, 1991). A recent study by Taras (1993) found that in a sample of high school CD underachievers, about half showed significant depression while half showed almost no sadness. This comorbidity pattern was quite different from other types of underachievers (e.g., Anxiety Disorder underachiever or Academic Problem underachiever).

The coexistence of CD and depression has implications for symptom expression, course, and treatment. For example, Pfeffer, Plutchik, and Mizruchi (1983) studied inpatient and outpatient children between the ages of 6 and 12 years who fit into one of four groups: nonassaultive/nonsuicidal, assaultive-suicidal, suicidal-only, assaultive-only. They reported that the pure assaultive group was characterized by the *absence* of depression, whereas depression occurred in both the suicidal-only and assaultive-suicidal groups.

Apter and colleagues (1995) extended the preceding findings on the relationship between aggression and depression in their recent study of 163 suicidal adolescent psychiatric inpatients. They found:

> There are hypothetically two types of suicidal behaviors during adolescence: a wish to die (depression) and a wish not to be here for a time (impulse control). The first type of suicidal behavior characterizes that seen in disorders with prominant depression such as major depressive disorder and anorexia nervosa, and the second characterizes disorders of impulse control such as conduct disorder. (p. 912)

In a longitudinal study, Harrington, Fudge, Rutter, Pickles, and Hill (1991) focused on depressives with and without CD, but did not study the outcome of CD with and without depression. They found 21% had diagnoses of both CD and depression, and long-term outcome measures did not differ for depressed children with and without CD.

Puig-Antich (1982) found that in children with CD and major affective disorder, successful treatment for depression also resulted in improvement in CD symptoms. My clinical experience and that of my colleagues also points to a better prognosis for those CD underachievers with comorbid depression. Our speculation is that depression makes these youngsters more vulnerable, thereby increasing opportunities for a therapeutic alliance. Perhaps CD underachievers with comorbid depression have experienced somewhat different developmental pathways than those with a single diagnosis of CD. I will address related treatment issues in Chapter 3.

In a longitudinal study, Kovacs and Pollock (1995) reported on the prevalence, age of onset, and course of comorbid CD in 23 bipolar disorder children and adolescents (average follow-up age, 8.1 years). The lifetime comorbidity rate was 69%. In approximately 48% of the cases, CD developed first, while in about 30% of the cases, CD developed after the emergence of the Bipolar Disorder: "Comorbid CD may exist in a large portion of young patients with BP disorder. Comorbid CD in bipolar youths appears to be associated with a somewhat worse clinical course. The overall indications are that comorbid CD may identify a subtype of very early onset BP disorder" (p. 716).

Anxiety Disorder

Walker and colleagues (1991) examined Anxiety Disorder as a coexisting condition with CD. They reported: "Boys with CD and comorbid anxiety disorder were markedly less impaired than boys with CD alone" (p. 187). In a review of studies on comorbidity in child and adult disorders, Zoccolillo (1992) concluded: "For both sexes, both depressive and anxiety disorders co-occurred with conduct disorder (and its adult outcomes) far more than expected by chance in childhood, adolescence, and adulthood" (p. 547).

More important, the developmental impact of CD with anxiety is not static. Russo and colleagues (1991) found that boys aged 7 to 12 years with comorbid anxiety disorder and CD (controlled for ADD) showed lower sensation-seeking scores than CD boys without anxiety. In a subsequent study, however, Russo et al. (1993) found that in preadolescents and adolescents, aged 9–14, there was no difference in sensation-seeking scores between comorbid CD/anxiety and CD only groups. It appears that the protective component of anxiety is operative only in children with comorbid CD/anxiety. By adolescence, its protective influence wanes.

Academic Underachievement

Does underachievement increase the probability of the development of CD, or does the presence of CD increase the probability of academic underachievement? The answer is complex. Each may be true, but under differing circumstances. I will address these questions in greater detail in Chapter 5.

A recent report highlights the relationship of comorbid or mixed diagnosis of CD to severity of symptoms (Noam, Paget, Valiant, Borst, & Bartok, 1994). They found: "The mixed disorder group is characterized by the most severe symptoms in each of the pure affective and conduct disordered groups" (p. 519). A related study adds credence to the negative impact of comorbidity. Marriage, Fine, Moretti, and Haley (1986) found that in CD with depression, the depressive symptoms were more severe than for the pure depressed group. In other words, comorbid diagnosis predicts increased severity of symptoms.

A study by Biederman, Faraone, Mick, and Lelon (1995) has shed some light on the pattern of development for comorbid conditions. They studied 424 clinic-referred adolescents who had histories of major depression and at least one other comorbid condition, including ADHD, CD, and anxiety disorders: "For the most part, comorbid disorders preceded the onset of major depression by several years" (p. 579). One could speculate that, at least for most of these adolescents, not being able to resolve the difficulties presented by one disorder eventually led to the development of a major depressive disorder.

What about the long-term prognosis for comorbid CD? Keller and colleagues (1992) followed children who had been diagnosed with Attention Deficit Disorder, Conduct Disorder, and/or Oppositional Defiant Disorder. Over 30% of the children had a comorbid diagnosis: "Rates of recurrence were high following recovery from each of these disorders" (p. 204). Thus, comorbidity may increase the probability of recurrence.

Family Variables

A number of predisposing family-based factors for CD are listed in the *DSM-IV* (APA, 1994): *parental rejection, inconsistent management with harsh discipline, early institutional living, frequent shifting of parent figures* (e.g., from parents, to stepparents, to grandparents, to friends, back to parents), *large family size, involvement with delinquent groups,* and *the presence of an alcoholic father.*

Parental substance abuse has been found to be a risk factor for both Oppositional Defiant Disorder and Conduct Disorder (Reich, Earls, Frankel, & Shayka, 1993). These researchers also found, interestingly, that the children of alcoholic parents did not have an increased risk for depression.

In a major epidemiological study, Offord, Boyle, and Racine (1991) found that three factors were independently highly predictive of CD: *family dysfunction, male sex,* and *large sibship.* Rogers, Forehand, and

Geist (1981) found that parents of CD children "issued more commands, emitted more negative behavior toward their children, and perceived their children and themselves as less well adjusted than the parents in the nonclinic group" (p. 139). In a study of differentially diagnosed under-achievers, Schwartzbein (1992) found that parents of adolescent CD un-derachievers had significantly poorer dyadic adjustment scores than parents of achievers. He also found that families of CD underachievers were more disengaged than families of achievers.

Research has also focused on the mother-child relationship in exam-ining risk factors in CD. For example, Anderson, Lytton, and Romney (1986) compared the responses of mothers of behavior problem 6- to 11-year-old sons with matched mothers of normals: "The findings suggest that the child's, and not the mother's, behavioral tendency is the major in-fluence in CD" (p. 604).

Lytton (1990) reviewed "studies of interactions between unrelated mothers and children, reaction to punishment, autonomic reactivity, bio-chemical factors, and drug treatment and longitudinal studies of delin-quency. Evidence from this research and from research on parental influences is interpreted as demonstrating the primacy of the child's own contributions to CD within a reciprocal parent-child interactive system" (p. 683).

The impact of an aggressive child on mother-child dyadic interactions was studied by Snyder, Edwards, McGraw, Kilgore, and Holton (1994). These researchers found greater frequency and intensity of *bidirectional* aversive exchanges in dyads with an aggressive child than in nonaggres-sive child dyads. Both child and mother contributed to the expression, maintenance, and escalation of aversive/coercive dyadic exchanges.

Studies have questioned the influence of maternal parenting for CD by examining the influence of *parental antisocial personality disorder (APD)* on the prediction of delinquency. Lahey and colleagues (1988) compared two samples of clinic-referred children. The first group was diagnosed as CD, while the second contained children with a range of diagnoses other than CD. They found that CD children were much more likely to have an APD parent than the children with other diagnoses.

In a related study, researchers (Lahey et al., 1988) also reported that both mothers and fathers of CD children were more likely to exhibit APD and abuse drugs. The mothers also tended to exhibit more depression or *Somatization Disorder.* Further, when CD coexisted with Attention Deficit Disorder (ADD), the fathers were much more likely to "have a history of aggression, arrest, and imprisonment" (p. 163). This was not true for the group with ADD only indicating that parent psychopathology is linked to CD and comorbid CD-ADD, but not to ADD alone. They also found that comorbid CD-ADD children's group exhibited much more serious and aggressive antisocial behavior, which was true for the fathers as well. These results confirmed work by West and Prinz (1987), who found increased probability of CD in the children of parents involved in criminal activity, exhibiting APD, or abusing alcohol.

Frick and colleagues (1992) compared a control group, clinic-referred Oppositional Defiant Disorder (ODD), and CD children (7–13 years of age) on degree of maternal supervision and discipline and on the existence of APD in the father: "When both paternal APD and deviant maternal parenting were entered into a 2 × 2 logit-model analyses predicting CD, only parental APD was significantly associated with CD, and no interactions between parental adjustment and maternal parenting were found" (p. 49). Apparently, the father's psychopathology (and not the behavior problem child's or the mother's psychological adjustment) was predictive of future delinquency.

Additional factors that emerge in the prediction of disruptive behaviors in young children include low socioeconomic status (Rutter, Tizard, & Whitmore, 1970), single parenthood (Webster-Stratton, 1990), maternal depression (Campbell, 1990; Williams, Anderson, McGee, & Silva, 1990), parental conflict and physical violence (Jouriles, Murphy, & O'Leary, 1989; Porter & O'Leary, 1980; Widom, 1989).

Lewis, Pincus, Lovely, Spitzer, and Moy (1987) found that *abuse* or *family violence* were the most significant factors differentiating incarcerated delinquents and nondelinquents: "This constellation also distinguished the more aggressive from the less aggressive subjects in each group" (p. 744). In a later study, Lewis, Lovely, Yeager, and Femina (1989) reported: "The interaction of intrinsic vulnerabilities (cognitive, psychiatric, and neurological) and a history of abuse and/or family violence was a better predictor of adult violent crime" (p. 431).

Further, a study by Eron, Huesmann, and Zelli (1991) points to the interaction of violence within the family. They reported that harsh punishment by parents of CD children, which can be a response to disruptive child behavior, often increases the acting out and violent reactions in the CD child. Kazdin stated: "The relation between child deviance and punishment is likely to be that each begets and promotes the other, and, in the process, they both become more extreme" (1995).

Yet the question still remains: Are these factors related more to the cause or the consequences of other risk factors? For example, Grinnell and Chambers (1979) found "little or no relationship between broken homes and middle-class delinquency" (p. 395). Hennessy, Richards, and Berk (1978) reported similar findings.

In a study of 12- to 17-year-old conduct-problem youth, Goldstein (1984) found:

> It was the youths from father-absent households with low supervision who had a greater likelihood of conduct problems. In households with a high degree of supervision, youths from father-absent families were no more likely than those from father-present families to demonstrate conduct problems. (p. 679)

Farnworth (1984) in a study of low-income minority families also found: "When both parents are employed and the father is present, delinquency is reduced. This suggests that a fruitful research focus in the future may be the economic dimensions of black families rather than their structure" (p. 362).

In a study on the impact of race and family structure on delinquency, Matsueda and Heimer (1987) found that in *both* white and black groups, single-parent families had less parental supervision, which permitted increased opportunities for delinquent affiliation and ultimately deviant behavior. They also found interesting differences between the two groups: "Blacks from broken homes who also live in troubled neighborhoods are more likely than those residing in trouble-free neighborhoods to associate with delinquents, and, consequently, violate the law. We were unable to locate such an interaction in the nonblack model" (p. 836).

Larzelere and Patterson (1990) found, however, that in young boys the "direct effect of SES on delinquency was not significant after controlling for parental management, which was modeled as a second-order factor consisting of parental monitoring and discipline" (p. 301). Webster-Stratton (1989) compared the mothers of conduct-problem children under three conditions: single, maritally supported, and maritally unsupported. She found significant positive correlations between marital dissatisfaction and mother stress, perceptions of greater seriousness of child behavior, and child noncompliance: "However, the single mothers reported significantly greater child behavior problems and perceived themselves as more stressed than the other two groups of mothers" (p. 417).

So what conclusions are reasonable to reach about the contribution of single-parent homes to the development of CD? In a review of this issue, McCord (1994) states:

> In studies that control for social class, evidence fails to support a view that paternal absence causes crime. Rather, correlates of single-parent homes such as paternal alcoholism and criminality or lack of supervision and poor socialization practices within the home seem responsible for elevated rates of CD found among subsets of single-parent families. (p. 322)

Loeber and Schmalling (1985) distinguished between *overt* and *covert* behaviors in CD. Overt behaviors included arguing, tantrums, and fighting, while covert behaviors included stealing, truancy, and fire setting. There is some evidence that those children who exhibit both covert and overt antisocial behaviors are at greatest risk for future problems.

Kazdin (1992) used this distinction to study the families of overt and covert CD children. He divided his subjects into four groups: high and low overt, and high and low covert CD. Those high in overt antisocial behavior came from families "with significantly greater conflict and less independence among family members" (p. 3). The families of the high overt children "showed significantly lower family cohesion and organization and less of an emphasis on moral-religious values" (p. 3). In this study, therefore, different family interaction patterns were related to differences in the kind of antisocial behavior these children exhibited.

Attachment problems in the parent-child relationship, especially during preschool and early school years have been implicated in the development of disruptive behaviors in children (Greenberg, Speltz, & DeKlyen, 1993; Henggeler, 1989; Waters, Posada, Crowell, & Lay, 1993). Sroufe, Egeland, and Kreutzer (1990) found that children raised in a high-risk environment with poor attachment showed significantly greater subsequent disruptive aggressive behavior, poor peer relationships, and affective problems than children raised in the same environment with early secure attachments.

The issue of attachment was also described clinically in four older CD adolescents in residential treatment (Penzerro & Lein, 1995). Acting-out behaviors tended to increase around impending discharge from residential treatment, and the ambivalences in the boys about their attachments to professional care staff were described. Previous unresolved attachments were also predictive of continued acting-out behavior in response to impending significant relationship loss.

Disruptive behavior problems appear to develop in response to both the direct influence of factors already reviewed and the indirect negative impact of other variables, such as child-rearing practices (Forgatch, Patterson, & Skinner, 1988; Snyder, 1991). Researchers have noted the importance of positive parenting and not just the absence of coercive child-rearing practices (Pettit & Bates, 1989).

Having a delinquent brother increases the likelihood of delinquent behavior in male siblings (Jones, Offord, & Abrams, 1980). Loeber, Weissman, and Reid (1983) found that adolescents who have been assaultive in the community came from families with a significantly greater frequency and severity of fighting with their siblings. Thus, these youth later express in the community what they have learned from a physically abusive sibling relationship. However, the negative impact of this relationship can be attenuated. Jones et al. (1980) found that the probability of delinquency in sibling males decreases as the number of sisters in the family increases: "These results are interpreted in terms of male potentiation and female suppression of antisocial behaviour in boys" (p. 139).

Greenberg et al. (1993) proposed an interactional risk model across four risk domains: (a) biological (e.g., difficult temperament), (b) family ecology (e.g., response to adversity), (c) parenting (e.g., coercive), and (d) quality of attachment (e.g., poor versus good):

> In the development of this model, we assumed that as the number of risk factors increases, the probability of problem behavior also increases. In addition, the relations among risk factors and disruptive behavior problems are expected to be transactional, and significant change may occur in risk status across time. Finally, different combinations of risk factors may lead to disorders whose forms or symptoms are different. (p. 205)

The implications of such bidirectional, interactive risk models for differential treatment are intriguing.

Peer Influences: Early Exclusion Followed by Later Inclusion?

While specific family problems have been implicated in the development of childhood-onset CD, peer group delinquency has been reported as a critical risk factor in adolescent-onset CD (APA, 1994; Jensen, 1972). In addition, the contribution of peers to the development and maintenance of aggression and impulsivity in much younger children has been documented. Olson (1992) found that as early as preschool, boys involved in aggressive and impulsive interactions with their peers early in the school year gradually became targets of *peer rejection* and retaliation later in the year. This early peer rejection isolates the aggressive child and may play a role in the maintenance of aggression in conduct-problem preschoolers (Hoza, Molina, Bukowski, & Sippola, 1995).

In a longitudinal study, Bierman and Wargo (1995) found that aggressive-rejected boys, when compared with aggressive-nonrejected or rejected-nonaggressive boys, exhibited more conduct problems at a 2-year follow-up. And although each group showed some conduct problems, poorer social skills, and higher levels of isolation from peers or peer dislike, these three factors did not impact in the same way for each group. It appears that aggressive-rejected boys are at greatest risk for the development of conduct problems.

Taylor (1990) confirmed peer rejection of aggressive, low-achieving students in Grades 2 through 5. Similar results had also been previously reported by Coie and Kupersmidt (1983) and Dodge, Coie, and Brakke (1982), and more recently for students in Grades 5 and 6 (Little & Garber, 1995). They found that aggressive elementary school students are rapidly rejected by nonaggressive peers. We also know that once peer rejection occurs, it is very hard to reverse (Bierman, 1990).

Peer rejection as a risk factor may impact boys somewhat differently than girls. In a longitudinal study, Coie, Terry, Lenox, Lochman, and Hyman (1995) followed 1,147 children from Grade 3 to Grade 10. They found that boys who had shown aggression and who also were rejected by peers in Grade 3 gradually developed more serious internalizing and externalizing problems. On the other hand, early reported aggression in girls was only predictive of later externalizing problems, as measured by self-report. In addition, for girls, peer rejection alone was predictive of psychological disorder, as measured by parent report. Some boys who exhibit aggression early and are not rejected by peers may not be at as great a risk as boys who both exhibit aggression and are rejected by peers.

Further, Price and Dodge (1989) distinguished two types of aggression in peer relationships. The first is *reactive aggression,* which they found was triggered in response to peer rejection. In contrast, *proactive aggression* was triggered in response to being the target of proactive aggression from peers. These responses suggest that motivation for aggression can have more than one source.

Craig and Pepler (1994) and Pepler and Craig (1994) used naturalistic videotape observations of elementary school students to document the extent and nature of bullying in the schoolyard. These researchers found that nonaggressive rejectors of bullies frequently provoke rejected aggressive youngsters, precipitating further difficulties for the at-risk child.

Attachment to *deviant peers* is predictive of later use of drugs for both males and females (Elliott, Huizinga, & Ageton, 1985). This predictive course has been confirmed by other researchers (Swaim, Oetting, Edwards, & Beauvais, 1989), who found that "the hypothesis that young people take drugs to alleviate emotional distress does not hold up well; emotional distress variables, with the exception of anger, produced only very small and indirect links to drug use" (p. 227). It appears that in teenagers, association with a peer drug culture is predictive of drug use, whereas emotional disturbance is not predictive.

Keenan, Loeber, Zhang, Stouthamer-Loeber, and Van Kammen (1995) found that individual deviant behavior in early adolescence increases dramatically within a deviant peer group. These researchers speculate that this influence may be specific to adolescent-onset CD only.

According to Patterson and Dishion (1985), the development of conduct problems in adolescence has its roots in ineffective parent monitoring and poor academic skills. Dishion, Patterson, Stoolmiller, and Skinner (1991) reported that academic failure and peer rejection at age 10 were highly predictive of early and continuing involvement with delinquent peers. Therefore, existence of a delinquent peer culture interacts with these two precursors (ineffective parenting and poor academic skills) to dramatically increase the likelihood of delinquent activity. These findings have been confirmed by Dishion, Capaldi, Spracklen, and Li (1995).

Kupersmidt, Burchinal, and Patterson (1995) examined how peer relationships in childhood predict behavior in early adolescence. They investigated 880 third- and fourth-grade students in a longitudinal 4-year project. They found that problems in both dyadic peer and group peer relationships were predictive of later externalizing problem behavior. They also found that risk factors had a cumulative action.

French, Conrad, and Turner (1995) studied how rejection impacts antisocial and non-antisocial adolescents. Their sample consisted of 501 students in Grade 8 (ages 13–14), who were reassessed again in Grade 10 (ages 15–16) and compared with 1,082 Grade 10 classmates. By Grade

10, the rejected-antisocial teens exhibited significantly greater affiliation with a deviant peer group, drug use, depression, truancy, more behavior problems in school, and low academic achievement. Because they did not find any differences at follow-up between respective rejected and accepted groups, the authors question the role of rejection in the later development of psychopathology.

What do delinquent adolescents derive from their peer relationships? Two theories have predominated, each with a significant bias:

> Major delinquency theories differ significantly in the ways in which they have portrayed friendship patterns of male and, more recently, female delinquents. *Psychological studies* and *control theory* depict delinquent peer relationships as inadequate or exploitive and cold, whereas *subcultural theories* generally emphasize the intimacy and solidarity of the delinquent gang. (Giordano, Cernkovich, & Pugh, 1986, p. 1170)

The reality is that delinquent peer relationships are much more complex.

Giordano et al. (1986) found that in some respects adolescent delinquent peer relationships are quite similar to nondelinquent peer relationships. The typical length and frequency of peer contacts were very similar and both groups believed that they could "be themselves" with their friends. Delinquent and nondelinquent adolescents reported similar patterns on intrinsic and extrinsic benefits they derived from their friendships.

But important differences did emerge between delinquent and nondelinquent peer relationships. Extent of self-disclosure to peers was slightly higher for delinquent adolescents. Adolescent delinquents reported significantly *higher levels of conflict* with peers. Delinquents reported that they both influence and are influenced by their delinquent friends to a greater extent than was the case for nondelinquent teens.

Yet not all delinquent peer relationships are riddled with friction. For example, female delinquent relationships were characterized by less overt peer pressure and conflict and greater intimacy than those of their male counterparts. In a related finding, Gaffney and McFall (1981) reported that female delinquents showed significantly greater social skills when dealing with adults than they did in dealing with peers. And to add to the complexity, differences were also found between peer relationships of black delinquents and those of their white counterparts. Black delinquents reported longer lasting but less intense relationships than delinquent whites.

How does academic underachievement affect peer relationships and are the consequences the same for male and female underachievers? Leonoff (1993) found that as male underachievers progressed through high school they reported decreased popularity with both male and female peers. Female underachievers reported decreased popularity only with opposite-sex peers.

Aggressive rejected male underachievers do not always end up as isolates. As their popularity decreases with the larger peer group, many develop and maintain friendships with other aggressive and rejected youngsters (Cairns & Cairns, 1992; Cairns, Cairns, & Neckerman, 1989; Cairns, Cairns, Neckerman, Gest, & Gariepy, 1988).

Although not directly related to the question of the development of CD, a qualitative study by Amber (1994a) focused on the effect of peer abuse on both children and their parents. The negative impact of peer abuse lasted beyond the school day and its ripples were played out at home in negative interactions with parents. Many victims of peer abuse continued to suffer years after the abuse had ceased. And many parents were ignorant of the extent of their children's suffering: "What we see is that, in addition to direct victims, peer abuse also has secondary victims, the parents in this case" (Amber, 1994a, p. 125). Her findings argue strongly for a multidimensional causality model.

Early peer group influences for CD likely involve *exclusion* through rejection, isolation, and provocation (hostile attributions by nonaggressive "normal" peers aimed at the aggressive, antisocial youngster). Peer group influences for CD in late latency and early adolescence, however, likely involve rejection by the antisocial teen of the normal group and *inclusion* in mutually satisfying delinquent activities. In addition, an article by Tremblay, Masse, Vitaro, and Dobkin (1995) pointed to the possibility that there may be subgroups of at-risk boys who are much more highly influenced by peers, and these subgroups may be at greater risk for affiliation with and control by a deviant peer culture.

Community and Societal Contributions

Do structures in the immediate community have any impact on the development of delinquency? This question has been addressed by a voluminous sociological literature; only several representative studies will be reviewed here.

Sociologists and social psychologists have studied the relationship between *attachment to traditional community institutions* (e.g., the family, school, religious groups) and deviancy. Social control theory predicts an inverse relationship—the greater the number and strength of these attachments, the lower the probability of delinquent behavior. A number of researchers have questioned the simplicity of this theoretical position (Liska & Reed, 1985), pointing out that the relationships are much more complex than previously thought. Attachment to conventional community institutions and deviant behavior are reciprocal variables, each impacting the other and each influenced by other variables (e.g., social status).

What role does the community play in the relationship between the delinquent's *perceived risk of punishment* and self-reported delinquency? Jensen, Erickson, and Gibbs (1978) found that there was a much greater inverse relationship between the individual's appraisal of the risk of getting caught in the specific contemplated antisocial act versus his or her assessment of the chances of any juvenile getting caught in that community. Thus although community standards are a contributing deterrent to antisocial behavior, they are not as important as the juvenile's assessment of the risk of arrest in a specific set of circumstances.

Is there a significant relationship between *unemployment rates* and delinquency rates? Farrington, Gallagher, Morley, St. Ledger, and West (1986) reported a significant positive relationship, especially for crimes against property designed for material gain, for 15- to 16-year-olds, for adolescents who were prone to delinquency, and for youths with entry level poor-paying jobs.

How do community contextual factors influence the development of CD? In the sociology literature, three major community variables have been theoretically linked to delinquency (Simcha-Fagan & Schwartz, 1986): (a) *Social disorganization:* the degree to which a community is unable to define its values and create structures to help individuals and groups solve problems; (b) *Subcultural deviance:* the degree of cohesion and support within a deviant subgroup (e.g., in the case of delinquency, creating and sustaining antisocial "career" opportunities); and (c) *Societal reaction:* the extent to which the larger culture uses class bias to assign special status to any subgroup (e.g., greater number of lower class individuals labeled as criminals).

Using an all-male stratified sample, Simcha-Fagan and Schwartz (1986) found that two specific community factors were strongly related to delinquency:

Two distinct community-level constructs, congruent with the mechanisms proposed by social disorganization and by the subcultural perspectives, are provided strong support . . . the community's ability to sustain organizational participation and the extent of disorder-criminal subculture. (p. 694)

The issue of community can be broadened to encompass violent and criminal models that children and adolescents are exposed to through television, movies, video games, and so on. Socializing "agents" include not only the family and immediate community, but also the global village. Some research findings point to the strong, cumulative, negative influence of excessive *media violence* on some individuals (Huesmann & Malamuth, 1986). Lefkowitz and colleagues (1977) have pointed to the increased risk for violent behavior in children who have been exposed regularly to TV violence and aggression, a tendency that continues in adolescence and adulthood. More recently, Strasburger (1995) found similar results for violent movies and video games.

But not all reviews produce the same result. Heath, Bresolin, and Rinaldi (1989) report that a "small but genuine association appears to exist between media violence and aggression" (p. 376). Developmental issues are important here as well because the extent of the negative influences will depend on, among other things, the age of the at-risk individual and protective or predisposing family factors.

Amber (1994b) also addressed the impact of global changes on parenting: "Western societies have seen a spiralling increase in juvenile delinquency, violence among children, gang wars, and unsupported adolescent pregnancy. As children's environments have become more complex, more dangerous, and less supportive, we can expect parenting to become more difficult" (p. 535). Our changing world society may be a contributing factor to CD in children and adolescents, and blaming parents, especially mothers, for adolescent-onset CD not only is an inaccurate reading of the process but may do harm.

A NOTE ABOUT PROTECTIVE FACTORS

Many of the protective factors appear to be the absence of risk factors and can be conceptualized as falling into three major categories (Garmezy, Speltz, & DeKlyen, 1993; Kazdin, 1995; Werner & Smith, 1992): (a) the

TABLE 1.1   Summary of Conduct Disorder Risk Factors

Main Factors	Research Focus
1. Hereditary	Twin studies
2. Biological	a. Autonomic responsiveness
	b. Serotonin
	c. Salivary cortisol
	d. Electrodermal response
	e. MAO

	f. Neurological abnormalities
	   frontal lobe lesions
	   expressive speech and memory

	g. Perseverative responding
	h. Premature birth, birth injury, low birth weight
	i. Temperament
3. Cognitive processes	a. IQ (protective factor)
	b. Intellectual imbalance (P > V)
	c. Reading, spelling, writing, math problems
	d. Problem solving deficits—(executive)
	e. Negative (hostile) attributions
	f. Expectations about outcome
	g. Moral development lag or arrest
4. Affective processes	a. Affective empathy deficit
	b. Moods and mood shifts
5. Age of onset	a. Childhood vs. Adolescent Onset Types

6. Sex	a. Prevalence rates for male and female CDs
	   childhood type: M:F :: 4:1
	   adolescent type: M:F :: 1:1

	b. Impact of menarche on female CD
7. Comorbidity	a. ADHD
	b. Depression
	c. Anxiety
	d. Academic underachievement
	e. Substance abuse
8. Family	a. Parent-child attachment

	b. Child-rearing practices
	   parental supervision
	   discipline

	c. Abuse and/or physical violence at home
	d. Sibling abuse and/or violence

TABLE 1.1 *(Continued)*

Main Factors	Research Focus
	e. Antisocial Personality Disorder in parents
	f. Substance abuse by parents
	g. Depression/Somatization Disorder in mother
	h. Overt vs. Covert behaviors and the family
9. Motivation	a. Rational-choice theory
	b. Strain theory
	c. Subcultural deviance theory
10. Peers	a. Early peer rejection
	b. Deviant adolescent peer group affiliation
	c. Control vs. Subcultural theories
	d. Popularity differential for males/females
11. Community	a. Perceived risk of community punishment
	b. Attachment to community institutions
	c. Unemployment rates
	d. Social disorganization
	e. Subcultural deviance
	f. Societal reaction
	g. Media violence
	h. Socioeconomic global change

child or adolescent attributes (e.g., good temperament, higher verbal IQ), (b) family attributes (e.g., sound child-rearing patterns), and (c) external supports (e.g., positive relationships with nondeviant peers, significant relationship with a teacher). As Kazdin (1995) pointed out, "These factors tend to be interdependent and reciprocal." He added, "It is useful to conceptualize many of these factors as part of transactions between the child and the environment" (p. 64).

The previous review provides affirmation that many variables have been implicated in the development of Conduct Disorder. Table 1.1 summarizes these and related factors.

HOW RISK FACTORS INTERACT

Even those researchers who focus on a limited number of risk factors for CD concede that whether an individual develops the disorder will depend on an interaction of risk and protective factors. *Multifactorial, developmental,* and *interactional,* or *bidirectional,* approaches have been proposed that incorporate the psychological, contextual (e.g., community), and psychobiological contributors to the development of CD (Loeber, 1990; Susman, 1993).

Research has clearly identified both risk and protective (resiliency) factors for CD. Rutter (1991) has noted a significant shift in this research focus: "It is apparent that the shift was not just from vulnerability to resilience, but also from risk *variables* to the process of *negotiating* risk situations" (p. 182). These mechanisms, by which the factors combine with individual differences to produce the observed outcome, are now targets of intense research.

A number of researchers (Kazdin, 1995; Rutter, 1991) have described important principles regarding mechanisms of risk and resilience. There are eight such principles:

1. The presence of a risk factor does not automatically mean that a child has been fully exposed to that factor. Even though a risk factor exists in a given situation, other protective factors may act to diminish its impact.
2. "Over time, several risk factors may become related" (Kazdin, 1995, p. 61). For example, poor academic performance in elementary school may result in early school dropout, which in turn may increase the probability of the development of CD.
3. The full impact of many risk factors is only seen in situations where multiple risks co-occur. Single risk factors rarely have the same long-term negative consequences as do multiple risk factors acting simultaneously (Rutter, 1979; Yoshikawa, 1994).
4. Resilience and risk factors are constantly changing attributes: "If circumstances change, the risk alters" (Rutter, 1991, p. 184). For example, the impact of marital discord will vary depending on the age, temperament, and sex of the at-risk child (Kazdin, 1995).
5. "Many vulnerability or protective processes concern key *turning points* in people's lives, rather than long-standing attributes or experiences as such" (Rutter, 1991, p. 187). These turning points can change a developmental path for better or for worse.
6. Risk mechanisms lead directly to disorder, whereas vulnerability/protective mechanisms act indirectly, interacting with the risk

factors. The nature and impact of protective mechanisms become evident in the interaction and in the outcome.

7. The presence of protective mechanisms in determining a positive outcome is not as critical for low-risk children as it is for high-risk children (Rutter & Quinton, 1984).
8. Even in situations with multiple risk factors, many children do not experience long-term negative consequences (Richters & Martinez, 1993).

Let us return now to a closer examination of those risk factors implicated in CD to examine their probable *processes*. For example, why is the CD prevalence rate so much higher for preadolescent males than for preadolescent females? Rutter (1991) cited studies showing that, as a result of family discord, boys were more likely to:

1. Develop behavioral rather than emotional problems, including disruptive oppositional behavior (Rutter, 1982; Rutter & Quinton, 1984).
2. Trigger more negative reactions from parents and peers because of their disruptive behavior (Fagot, Hagan, Leinbach, & Kronsberg, 1985; Patterson, 1982; Rutter, 1982).
3. Be exposed more directly and often to parental conflicts (Hetherington, Cox, & Cox, 1982).
4. Be more vulnerable to physical hazards, reflecting perhaps a greater neurodevelopmental susceptibility than is true for girls (Earls, 1987; Richman, Stevenson, & Graham, 1982).
5. Be institutionalized when the family breaks up and therefore be exposed to greater risk outside the family (Packman, 1986).

Rutter (1991) concludes:

It may be inferred that the protection afforded by being female is in part a result of lesser exposure to the risk factor, a reduced exposure that is a consequence of the immediate family context, the chain of interactions that follows, and the sequelae of family breakdown. (p. 191)

Once a clinically referred preadolescent or young adolescent female has developed a CD, however, she is at much greater risk for teenage pregnancy (Kovacs, Krol, & Voti, 1994); having Conduct Disorder is itself a risk factor for pregnancy. Therefore, Principle 2 may play itself out differently for at-risk boys than at-risk girls.

If we add to the preceding mix a child whose temperament is characterized by inflexibility, negative affect and mood, and general untidiness (what Rutter has labeled adverse temperament), we increase the likelihood of adverse parental reactions. And what if we add maternal depression and paternal substance abuse to those interactions?

And in the classroom, these disruptive behaviors may eventually trigger similar negative reactions in teachers and peers. Thus the damage from the interaction of factors within the family often is compounded outside the family. In addition, school problems will likely feed back into the already escalating family stress, through, for example, the demands directed at the parents by school personnel to address problem behavior and poor academic performance. These demands will add to negative chain reactions. In Chapter 5, I will address in detail how the risk and protective factors for the development of CD interact to increase or decrease the risk of academic underachievement.

The negative impact of family discord on a child's behavior can be diminished by the presence of just one sound parent-child relationship (Rutter, 1978). Further, even if experiences that enhance self-esteem and self-efficacy are not available within a family, they may be available outside the family through a caring and competent teacher or athletic coach. Tennant, Bebbington, and Hurry (1981) have labeled these counterbalancing factors "neutralizing" life events.

Finally, Loeber (1990) has distinguished between *risk factors* and *causal factors*. For example, if family risk factors are involved in the development of CD, researchers could assume:

- More than one child/family should be affected.
- Multiple family problems should increase the risk more than solitary family factors.
- More severe family problems should result in more serious antisocial child behavior *(a dose-response relationship)*.
- As family problems mount, non-antisocial children should begin to develop antisocial problems.

In addition, Loeber surmised that a valid causal factor should still show up in outcome measures, even when other factors are statistically partialed out. There are "many forms of evidence which can assist researchers in transforming a risk factor into a causal one" (p. 5). Farrington (1995) summarized many of the key findings from the Cambridge Study in Delinquent Development, which followed 411 males from age 8 to age 32. I have already summarized many of the risk factors uncovered in this study. Farrington reported, however, that several factors were associated with an eventual decrease in the frequency of offending behavior. These included getting married, obtaining employment, and moving away from the geographic area where subjects had spent their childhood and adolescent years. Thus, despite many risk factors (e.g., low intelligence, poor school performance, impulsivity, parental criminality, ineffective parenting, poverty), external protective factors can change the course of the disorder.

Chapter 2 will provide an overview of assessment issues and CD, as well as two case histories, one of a childhood-onset underachiever and the second of an adolescent-onset CD underachiever. The interaction between risk and protective factors in the developmental pathways of each case will be highlighted.

Chapter 2

Assessment

> Diagnosis and assessment are fundamental to research that is designed
> to understand the nature of antisocial behavior, its causes, correlates,
> and clinical course.
>
> KAZDIN (1995, P. 48)

Professionals confront a number of unique issues in the assessment of Conduct Disorder (CD) and underachievement. How these issues are expressed and dealt with will depend to some extent on the professional setting (e.g., hospital, outpatient clinic, private practice, school psychologist's office) as well as on the degree of dysfunction in both child and family. The focus in this chapter will be on psychological assessment, including testing, diagnostic interviewing, and collection of historical information and data from independent sources.

CHOOSING AN ASSESSMENT BATTERY

Some antisocial behavior is overt (e.g., threatening or attacking others) and relatively easy to document. Some is covert (e.g., stealing or fire setting) and often difficult to substantiate. In addition, individuals with CD typically do not exhibit their entire antisocial repertoire across all venues (e.g., home, school, community). These facts make assessment complex and distinctive.

Kaplan (1988) stressed the importance of an overview of the context within which disordered conduct occurs:

> Is it situation-specific? Does it fit into a developmental paradigm? What
> are the familial, genetic, intrapsychic, and reactive factors that con-
> tribute to the cause of the antisocial behavior? Is there a coexistent neu-
> ropsychiatric or medical disorder that causes or exacerbates the conduct

disorder? What role do sociocultural and peer factors play in the emergence of the antisocial behavior? (p. 576)

McMahon and Forehand (1988) identified a number of critical areas to assess in behavior problem children. These include the parents' perceptions of the child's problems, teacher perceptions, each parent's personal adjustment, marital interaction, nature and levels of parental stress, and the extent to which the mother is socially isolated from community resources. Andrews, Garrison, Jackson, Addy, and McKeown (1993) examined the differences between mother ratings of their adolescent's behavior from the adolescent's self-ratings, and concluded that because the two perspectives are different, each is critical in any assessment of conduct disorder.

Because CD is multidetermined with a high probability of comorbidity and coexisting family and peer problems, assessment materials and processes must reflect this heterogeneity. Academic skill deficits, learning disabilities, attention deficit problems, depression and anxiety, social skills deficits, substance abuse, family and parent psychopathology, peer rejection and/or deviant peer involvement, and other conditions may be present. Usually, a combination of tests, semistructured diagnostic interviews (child/adolescent, marital, and family), independent information from the school (teachers, vice-principal, etc.), other appropriate professionals (e.g., probation officer), along with results of previous assessments will provide a more complete perspective.

McMahon (1987) argues for an expansion of methods and data sources when assessing CD, including not only the cognitive characteristics of the child but those of the parents as well. In addition, he argues for assessment of the personal adjustment of each parent and the nature and quality of each parent's significant social relationships outside the family.

Many tests, instruments, and observational and interview procedures have been developed specifically for the study, assessment, or treatment of Conduct Disorder. Approximately 50 of these are listed in the appendix. Often it is not possible to obtain needed information from all sources because of economic limitations, time constraints, lack of information, or resistance. Assessment conclusions may have to be based on incomplete information. Professionals at the Oregon Social Learning Center have suggested a "multiple gating" approach to assessment of at-risk children. This includes an initial, less time-consuming screening with short interviews and questionnaires, followed by time-intensive interviews for those children identified at greatest risk or exhibiting the most serious acting-out behavior. McMahon (1987) proposed similar assessment structures and stages. These and other methods of rationing professional resources can maximize the effectiveness and target children most at risk for CD and its complications.

Kernberg and Chazan (1991) have developed a "readiness" for parent training assessment, in which parental attachment to the conduct-disordered child, parental motivation for professional instruction, and parental ability to form a working partnership with the therapist are all assessed in a series of observation and trial sessions.

Professionals at the Institute on Achievement and Motivation at York University in Toronto, Canada, have developed a standard procedure for the assessment and differential diagnosis of academic underachievement (Mandel, Friedland, & Marcus, 1996; Mandel & Mandel, 1995; Mandel & Marcus, 1988), which includes screening for cognitive strengths and liabilities, academic skill deficits, perceptual-motor abilities, obtaining teacher, parent, and student behavior ratings, reviewing developmental and academic history, work habits, conducting both individual and family semi-structured diagnostic interviews, using both objective and projective personality tests, and assessing career interests for adolescent underachievers.

ENHANCING ASSESSMENT ATTENDANCE

What type of disruptive child gets referred for professional assessment, and by what process? Griest, Forehand, McMahon, and Wells (1980) found that clinic-referred children were more seriously disturbed and less cooperative than nonreferred conduct-disordered children. They also found:

> When considering child behavior, parent behavior, parent perceptions of child adjustment, and parent reports of personal/marital adjustment, the parent perceptions of the child best differentiated the two groups. Therefore, the child's behavior alone is insufficient for him/her becoming the identified client. Instead, both the child's behavior and the parent's adjustment are important in the process. (p. 144)

It appears that the parents who do not refer their conduct problem child for a professional assessment have made their judgment not to seek help solely on the basis of their own perception of their child.

Requests for a professional assessment for disruptive and/or antisocial behavior almost always occur under crisis conditions. The severity and intensity of the crisis will vary greatly, but there will be pressure and tension, often from sources external to the family, such as the school or the courts. Most assessments, however, do not take place within hours of the original request. And the conditions that precipitated the request often change by the time of the assessment.

Canceled appointments or no-shows are typical. In child-onset CD, this may be a reflection either of parental and/or child pathology. For adolescent-onset CD, it may also reflect a planned or an impulsive decision by the teen to "disappear" hours before the scheduled appointment, making it impossible for a responsible parent to carry through with the assessment. Even initial attendance is not predictive of consistent future attendance.

So what to do? Most practitioners recommend the following actions to increase and/or maintain assessment attendance:

- Contact the family several days in advance of the assessment (e.g., by phone) to verify and remind. Any potential difficulties with attendance can be discussed along with potential solutions.

- Consider holding an initial assessment session in the family's home. Not only does this allow the assessor to observe the family in its natural environment, it also permits the professional to explain the assessment and its consequences and reach a verbal agreement with the participants. Capaldi and Patterson (1987) used these and other practical means (e.g., participation incentives) to enhance treatment attendance and compliance.

- The appointment times of additional assessment sessions should be clear to parents and the child or adolescent. Reminders should continue.

ASSESSMENT CONTRACTING

Most assessments serve a number of purposes. For CD, this is true not only about the assessment results but about their potential impact on the child's life at home, in school, and in the community. Therefore, the purpose should be clearly explained (e.g., uncovering deficits that may be contributing to problem behavior). This contracting phase should also include a statement about how results will be shared with the child and family, as well as who will have access to the results once the assessment is completed (e.g., school, family doctor, juvenile court).

Limits to confidentiality should also be stated and any questions answered. Absolute confidentiality should never be promised when dealing with conduct-disordered students. This is especially critical for adolescents, because the consequences of absolute confidentiality may be more serious. Further, refusing absolute confidentiality tends to increase the veracity of student information, particularly when the therapist has indicated that facts will also be gathered or verified with other appropriate sources.

Policies regarding cancellations and missed appointments must be stated and agreed to. This will avoid unnecessary misunderstandings.

PREDICTABLE STUDENT AND ASSESSOR REACTIONS

Students with Conduct Disorder have predictable reactions to both the assessor and the assessment process. These include a wariness about and need to test the limits of the assessment situation. Limit testing can take many forms—not showing up, trying to take over the testing situation by controlling the flow of questions and answers, refusing to complete a test, putting the tester on the defensive through intimidation, "seduction," selective and/or false reporting, and so on. These predictable reactions also occur in psychotherapy and will be elaborated in greater detail in Chapters 3 and 6.

Just as there are predictable client reactions to the assessment, there are predictable assessor reactions. These include excessive wariness and/or detachment (self-protection), fascination with the student's acting-out feats (perhaps reflecting the assessor's identification with the student), gullibility (accepting statements as facts based on the student's selective and/or slanted reporting), need to rescue (assuming an exaggerated advocacy role), anger at having been manipulated (e.g., having been taken in by unfulfilled promises), and a desire to reject the student because of his/her immoral antisocial behavior (repulsion). In short, a range of potential negative countertransference reactions may be triggered during both the assessment and treatment of these clients.

How does the therapist maintain a working relationship during the assessment and at the same time ensure that countertransference reactions do not interfere with the assessment? Self-awareness is one of the most important tools. Knowledge and understanding of the disorder help as well. It is important to realize that if the professional is experiencing these reactions, it is a sure sign that something is happening—a relationship with the student is developing. And the elements it has generated are similar to those triggered in other helpers, such as teachers, and probation officers. These predictable professional reactions are instructive and valuable.

RECOMMENDATIONS: A BRIDGE TO TREATMENT

At the conclusion of an assessment, the professional must generate recommendations, sometimes in the absence of critical information. For example, frequently one parent is cooperative while the other is either unavailable or resistive (passively or actively). Information gaps will exist. These need to be pursued and if unavailable should be documented in the report.

The nature of the disorder dictates that assessment findings will suggest multiple problems. The professional should be familiar with specific programs and/or specialists who can address the problems and who are willing to coordinate treatments.

The professional should be prepared for resistance to the recommendations. And just as there are ways to encourage assessment attendance, there are means of improving compliance with the recommendations. One way to combat this reluctance is to inform the family at the beginning of the feedback that a number of problems have been uncovered, each of which requires attention, but that not all members of the family need to be involved in all treatments. It is also important to describe the long-term prognosis and course of CD to decrease the chances of recommendation rejection. Each abandoned recommendation increases the probability of continued problems.

When resistance to implementing the recommendations is high, it is still important to describe the probable course, without seeming to "beg" the family into treatment. Inform the family that services are available when things get worse, and wish them well. If the problems improve on their own, which is a highly unlikely possibility, the family will reap the benefits as they prove you wrong. If the problems worsen as is likely, you have at least gained some credibility because of your earlier prediction.

CASE HISTORIES

This section contains two case histories of CD underachievers. Tony (Case 1), a 17-year-old male, presents a history of childhood-onset CD underachievement. Sam (Case 2), a 16-year-old male presents a history of adolescent-onset CD underachievement.

These cases were selected because each highlights both risk and protective factors. In particular, in the second case, one could speculate that a number of protective factors delayed the emergence of both the CD and the academic underachievement until adolescence. In addition, a verbatim transcript of Case 1 highlights the exchanges in the individual Semi-structured Diagnostic Interview for Underachievers (SSDIU) (Mandel & Mandel, 1995; Mandel & Marcus, 1988). Case 1 will be reintroduced in Chapter 6 to illustrate individual cognitive therapy. This approach will provide the reader with a detailed view of how assessment findings bridge to treatment and inform the treatment process.

Case 1: Childhood-Onset CD Underachievement

Reason for Referral and Developmental History

Tony, an 11th-grade student, was an attractive 17-year-old, male Caucasian of mixed cultural descent. His father was a carpenter and his mother worked as an executive assistant for an insurance company. He had one younger sister, aged 13, and a younger brother, aged 10, and described his family as lower middle class. Both parents had been employed in their present jobs for a considerable length of time and the family had lived in their home for many years.

Tony was referred to the Institute on Achievement and Motivation at York University by a mental health professional because of Tony's chronic academic underachievement. His mother made the initial contact and she and Tony came for the intake interview. Her husband was unwilling to come because he did not think that Tony needed much help and could be "straightened out" with firmer discipline.

In the intake interview, Mrs. B. reported that she had experienced no difficulties with either her pregnancy or delivery of her eldest son. All other developmental milestones had been normal. In a separate interview with the intake worker, Mrs. B. divulged that she had met her husband on a blind date and that she had gotten pregnant on their second date. She described him as being tall, handsome, and charming. She also admitted that their marriage had been stormy and that periodically he drank to excess. She had considered leaving him a number of times, but each time they had somehow reconciled. She said that she was not in love with him any more, but had decided to remain married for the sake of the children and because of her strong Catholic convictions.

Tony's teachers had first raised concerns about him when he was 8 years old. He was described as a distractible, oppositional, immature underachiever who had difficulty completing his work. He did not put much effort into most of his school subjects although his teachers rated him as having much greater potential. Teachers noted Tony's increasing punctuality problems, distractibility, and lack of self-discipline or acceptance of responsibility for school achievement.

At the beginning of Grade 5, Tony's mother requested a private educational assessment because of continuing concerns about her son's underachievement. Results from the Wide Range Achievement Test (WRAT) showed that Tony was at grade level in math, one grade level ahead in reading, and one grade level behind in spelling. Tony's ability to read isolated words was well developed but he gave quick answers and did not attempt items more than once. In math, neither addition nor multiplication facts were automatic, which often led to careless errors. Results from the Peabody Picture Vocabulary Test (PPVT) put Tony at the 99th percentile. The examiner commented that Tony communicated in a pseudo-mature fashion with excessive volume as if he were proclaiming his viewpoint rather than sharing it. In any discussion, he tended to react as if the conversation was an argument. Spontaneous comments were almost always non-task-related, and Tony showed little or no interest in his assessment performance.

The examiner recommended that the school provide special assistance to improve Tony's attention span and task completion. She also recommended that a behavioral management program be instituted in the classroom. In addition, individual and family assessments were recommended because of (a) Tony's comments about his relationship with his mother (issues of control and power struggles); (b) his parents' marital relationship (his parents had talked openly about the possibility of separation and had argued intensely in Tony's presence), and (c) Tony's role in that relationship (acting as a buffer and lightning rod for differences between his parents). The individual assessment was not done.

On his Grade 5 final report card, Tony's teacher commented: "Tony has continued to experience difficulty in most areas of the academic program. When he puts his mind to it and takes his work seriously, he can do well. More self-discipline is needed in settling down to work."

The family assessment led to a recommendation for family therapy. The family was seen for several sessions, but as Mr. B. refused to contribute or continue, therapy gradually evolved into alternating individual outpatient therapy for Mrs. B. and for Tony, which lasted intermittently over a 4-year period.

Mrs. B.'s sessions focused on parent management issues (how could she deal with Tony's behavior problems despite the disagreements between herself and her husband), on her marital difficulties (assessing the issues and options), and coping with her reactive depression episodes. Disagreements continued between Mr. and Mrs. B. about how to deal with Tony's acting-out behavior, and there was little consistency in either parental expectations or consequences for his misbehavior.

Individual therapy sessions with Tony focused on helping him develop better social skills in school and at home. Treatment issues included specific bullying incidents, role playing and rehearsal to increase self-control, discussion of prosocial behavior options, choice of peers, and school course requirements. During this 4-year period of nonregular attendance, there was some improvement in Tony's academic performance, although this was not sustained.

Because of changes in treatment staff, Tony first saw a male therapist intermittently for about 2 years, followed by a female therapist. When the female therapist announced her departure from the agency, Tony announced that he was terminating therapy.

During the 4-year treatment period, many of the problems that Tony experienced were not discovered or shared by all adult helpers until long after they had occurred. In addition, some incidents that occurred in the community were only discovered years later because Tony was willing to divulge them.

Although Tony continued to experience behavioral difficulties in school, he was always promoted because he was bright, articulate, and a good reader. His teachers tried many approaches including behavioral contracting, but these approaches were not effective over the long term. As each approach failed, teachers tended to withdraw from Tony, leaving him to complete assignments. This pattern of intense involvement followed by withdrawal was also typical of his mother's interactions with him at home.

At the beginning of Grade 8, his mother again requested an independent educational assessment because of her concerns about academic performance. On the WRAT, Tony scored one grade level above in reading, at grade level in math, and three grade levels below in spelling. The examiner commented that Tony showed much less confidence in his ability than his performance would indicate and exhibited very poor awareness of time constraints. Tony scored at the 94th percentile on the PPVT. The examiner commented that on this test of receptive vocabulary Tony performed in the rapid learner classification. He showed ease with the task, attended well, and displayed no impulsivity. He was able to generate a range of effective strategies. On the Raven's Standard Progressive Matrices, Tony scored at the 75th percentile.

On a Grades 8–9 academic skills test, Tony experienced no difficulty with oral reading, showed good comprehension, and was able to produce a competent and creative writing sample judged to be at grade level. However, his spelling was poor.

Throughout his school years, his academic performance had shown a clear and sustained deterioration from Grade 6, where his GPA was in the mid-60s, to Grade 11, where it was 40%. In Grade 6, his teacher noted that Tony had shown commendable progress, but needed to produce greater effort. By the first year of high school, however, his teacher commented that Tony had shown "a total lack of effort, satisfactory achievement in physical education but improper uniform, and inconsistent and poor work habits." By Grade 10, his teacher wrote: "Little effort shown, more effort required, wastes time needlessly, and neglects homework and study."

During his first year of high school, Tony was involved in a knife-wielding incident and was referred to a children's mental health agency for evaluation. He met with a social worker for six sessions. She then reported to the school that she doubted Tony would be involved in such incidents again. The aggressive and threatening behavior was labeled an aberration.

In the middle of Grade 11 on the recommendation of the school, Tony was transferred to an independent study program. He would continue to follow his academic program but not in a regular classroom. The program involved individual contracting between Tony and his independent studies teachers, with Tony deciding when and if to ask for help. Attendance was not required, except for tests, handing in projects, and final exams. Although Tony had some difficulty with this structure, he was able to maintain himself in the program. At the time of the current assessment, he stated that he predicted that he would be able to graduate from high school as a result of this program.

During this period, Tony's mother continued individual therapy on an intermittent basis, with treatment focused on her continuing marital difficulties (including periodic concerns about her husband's drinking), her depressive symptoms, and concern about Tony.

After consultation with the clinical team, the intake worker recommended that an individual psychological assessment be done covering academic, intellectual, perceptual-motor, and personality factors. Marital and family assessments were also recommended, but Mrs. B. indicated that her husband would not cooperate. Mrs. B. consented to allow her individual therapist to provide information to the Institute.

Psychological Testing Results

In general, Tony's attitude toward the psychometric testing was positive, although he used the testing situation as an opportunity to make a "pass" at the female psychometrist. He was especially pleased that the assessment took place during school hours.

Tony's self-report on his study habits confirmed what both his mother and teachers had reported, namely that he was not actively using effective study habits. One of his current teachers commented: "This student seems intelligent, but lacks mental discipline to complete assigned tasks. He is friendly and agreeable but enjoys his own interests more than school tasks." A second teacher noted: "Tony is a very self-centered individual, without any apparent concern for others or how they feel about him. At the same time, he does things to attract attention—carrying a loud radio around with him, running a remote-controlled model auto around the school grounds, etc. He also seems to think he'll be able to get by in life without much effort."

On the Mooney Problem Checklist (High School Form), Tony circled relatively few problems that troubled him. He had some concerns about whether he could get a job in his chosen vocation. He perceived himself as lazy and careless, felt restless in class, admitted that he was behind in school and weak in spelling, couldn't seem to keep his mind on his studies, and said he was worried about exams. More revealing were his final comments at the end of the form: "School is school; my private life is private. They don't mix!" He also indicated that he was not interested in talking to someone about any of the problems he had checked.

Tony's drawings on the Bender-Gestalt Visual Motor Test did not reveal signs of perceptual-motor difficulties, but rather reflected signs of impulsivity, lack of adequate anticipatory planning, and difficulty with affect.

On the Wechsler Adult Intelligence Scale-Revised (WAIS-R), Tony obtained an overall IQ in the high end of the average range. There was a significant difference ($p = .05$) between the verbal scores and visual-perceptual performance scores, in favor of his verbal scores.

His verbal score on the WAIS-R was in the above-average range (84th percentile). However, there was considerable variability within his verbal scaled scores, ranging from a very low score on a test of general factual information (9th percentile), to high scores on a test of judgment, common sense, ability to evaluate social situations and use past experience (91st percentile), as well as on a test of logical, categorical, abstract thinking (84th percentile). Given his previous history of school difficulty, including difficulty concentrating, poor self-discipline, and lack of effort and increasingly spotty attendance, it is not surprising that his general factual information was the lowest verbal score.

His performance score on the WAIS-R was in the middle average range and the scatter among the various subtests was not significant. All performance scores were solidly within the average range.

Overall, Tony's intellectual functioning is predictive of academic performance about the same as that of his same aged peers. He should also be able to perform verbal tasks somewhat better than tasks involving visual-motor abilities. Since Tony's academic performance had been significantly below that of his same aged peers, factors other than intellectual capacity were considered.

Two objective personality tests were administered, the Minnesota Multiphasic Personality Inventory (MMPI) and an earlier version of the Achievement Motivation Profile (AMP) (Friedland et al., 1996). The MMPI was administered and scored using adolescent norms because at the time of Tony's assessment the MMPI-A had not yet been published.

Tony's MMPI results corresponded to a 4-9/9-4 profile. Overall, Tony's profile reflected someone who was willing to admit to minor faults and possessed a good level of ego strength with sufficient personal resources to deal with problems. The profile reflected someone who was not satisfied with his current life situation, and/or may have learned to adjust to a long-term dissatisfying situation.

The most common reasons for referral for such adolescents are interpersonal behavioral difficulties and truancy. Such individuals tend to make a good first impression, initially revealing only their pleasant, active, outgoing, and energetic nature. Yet, they do not like authority or rules and may act against such authority. They tend to be defiant, disobedient, and impulsive, and do not use good judgment to solve their difficulties.

They typically have a sufficient amount of available energy, which is channeled in nonconstructive or dysfunctional directions. They describe themselves as daring, energetic, adventurous, active, argumentative, and sociable. Such adolescents also show a history of smoking, drinking, and may abuse drugs. They value wealth and material possessions. If they appear "down" or depressed, these periods tend to be short-lived and may even be a superficial external response designed to manipulate others. They also tend to blame others for their difficulties and may experience difficulties in sustaining intimate relationships. They are described by others as narcissistic, egocentric, self-centered, selfish, and demanding. Their social patterns include early and active dating, and they value sexual activity highly.

Some antisocial activity is predicted from this profile (e.g., stealing, lying, and cheating), as well as some involvement with legal authorities (e.g., the police and the courts). The most probable diagnosis based on the MMPI profile is CD.

Tony's Achievement Motivation Profile (AMP) (Friedland et al., 1996) confirmed the MMPI findings, portraying him as an underachieving youngster with a very low need to achieve in school and very poor study habits. His anxiety and depression scores were average, indicative of little admitted internal stress. He exhibited extremely low patience, elevated resistance to authority, and low personal diplomacy scores, all of which are predictive of interpersonal difficulties. Together, these scales point to a diagnosis of either a CD underachiever or Oppositional Defiant Disorder underachiever.

Two projective personality tests were administered, The Thematic Apperception Test (TAT) and the Rorschach Inkblot Test. On the TAT, Tony tried again to impress and "test" the female psychometrist. He was expansive and animated and generated a great deal of detail in a somewhat exhibitionistic manner. The following are three examples of Tony's TAT stories:

Card 1: "A young boy is contemplating a violin which rests on a table in front of him" (Murray, 1971).

This boy's name is John. His mom always wanted him to play in the orchestra and he's sick of it! One day, he got very mad at his mother and he chucked the violin at the wall and broke some of it. Now he's looking forlorn. *(Examiner questions for outcome.)* His mother makes him take up the tuba—a sturdy instrument.

Card 3: "On the floor against a couch is the huddled form of a boy with his head bowed on his right arm. Beside him on the floor is a revolver" (Murray, 1971).

This is another tragedy. How can I turn it into a comedy? I can't do it, damn! This guy is a husband; he has a family and kids. The only problem is that he is an alcoholic. After a couple of years, the wife and kids can't handle him, so they leave. He takes the bottle of scotch and throws it on the ground and it shatters. He is all dejected, sitting on the ground crying. *(Examiner questions about outcome.)* The wife and kids come back to him when they find out he stopped drinking. I had to get a happy ending in there—it was starting to get depressing.

Card 16: Blank Card

The title of this story is: "The Takeover"! All the kids have come to school on Monday, and they have a plan. They throw the teachers out of school—no, wait, I've got something better. They place all the teachers under suspension. They round them all up in the first period, and make them sit in the auditorium all day long. The students take over and play Rock n' Roll over the PA into the auditorium and break all the rules just for the sake of breaking them. At the end of the day, they escort the teachers to detention. They carry cars to the football field filled with whipped cream and put the keys in a locked trunk. They pour booze into the teachers' staff room sink and take the coffeepot. The police surround the school and let them go at 5 P.M., which is a reasonable hour. The homework for the teachers will be to copy out the Bible ten times for the next morning or else the students will boycott again. *(Examiner questions for affect.)* All the teachers are feeling brokenhearted and go home and resign! The school gets a whole new set of teachers with fair rules and the school proceeds in a much happier fashion.

Tony revealed a number of themes, issues, and needs through his TAT stories:

- Needs to minimize certain feelings (e.g., frustration, hurt, disappointment, sadness).
- Needs to maximize certain feelings (e.g., instant and permanent happiness).
- Needs to impersonalize and/or trivialize interactions between people, portraying transactions in a gamelike quality.

- Needs to minimize the degree of effort and self-discipline required to problem solve and succeed by creating instant, magical, effortless outcomes.
- Views independent action as threatening the status quo of the family, implying a trap between the status quo and change.
- Portrays people in stereotypic and simplistic ways.
- Simultaneously needs and mistrusts females, reflecting powerful ambivalent feelings.
- Identifies with father, although this is *not* generalized to other male authority figures.
- Needs stimulation, even to the extent of increasing risk of self-destructive outcome.
- Needs to defeat and punish many in authority positions, reflecting anger and underlying sense of powerlessness.
- Needs to impress people, depicting self as a macho male hero, also reflecting an inner sense of powerlessness.

The Exner (1986) scoring system was used to analyze Tony's Rorschach protocol. His responses reflected a cognitive laziness and a careless, simplistic integration of his perceptions of the environment. Tony was inefficient and at times irrelevantly sensitive to detail. When he did respond affectively, Tony's reactions frequently were intense, with little or no cognitive controls. Tony's primary defense appeared to be intellectualization, which was effective in protecting him from material that might be problematic if consciously felt.

Tony's perspective on interpersonal relationships tended to be superficial and guarded. Apparently he does not directly experience the manifest need for interpersonal closeness. The Rorschach results also reflected an individual with considerable internal personal resources who has a tendency to be somewhat rigid and inflexible in his approach to the environment. He tends to set unrealistically high goals and may experience considerable personal frustration when he is not able to attain his goals.

The Semi-Structured Diagnostic Interview

No single test finding should result in a diagnosis. The cumulative records of content, attitude, and interactional process from the interview, combined with test results and other information, provide the diagnostic database.

The Semi-Structured Diagnostic Interview for Underachievers (Mandel & Mandel, 1995; Mandel & Marcus, 1988) was conducted by a male clinical psychologist. The entire transcript from the interview follows. Editorial comments are interspersed throughout to highlight issues of content and process. The inquiry covered five major areas of functioning, as follows:

1. Nature of academic difficulties and attitudes toward and perceptions of school.
2. Client perceptions of family members and family relationships.
3. Quality and nature of involvement in peer relationships.
4. Client self-perceptions, including issues of mood.
5. Client perceptions about and attitude toward the future.

Throughout the remainder of this text, *I* will refer to the Interviewer and *S* will refer to the Student. Comments about the transcript are identified as notes.

I: I think we told you what we would be talking about in this interview. Basically school, friends, family, yourself, and the future. Okay? *(Client nods his consent.)* I'm going to write some things down since it's easier to remember. First of all, what courses are you taking right now?

S: Right now? English, Math, Science.

I: English, Math, Science, that's it?

S: Yeah.

I: Okay. What grade for English? I don't mean what mark, but grade.

S: Grade Ten, Advanced—all the way!

Note. Courses at Tony's high school were divided into Advanced (University Prep), General (College Prep), and Basic (low skill).

I: Okay, how are you doing in each one?

S: English, not very well. But I think I'm going to do fairly well on the exam because I picked up *Caesar's Commentaries* and I found out from some guys who had Mrs. Peach last year that if you read *Caesar's Commentaries* and pull stuff out of it on the exam that she tends to throw marks your way.

I: So it's not an absolute requirement?

S: No, she just says it's a good book to read. And if you read it, she gives you a lot of bonus marks for it.

I: Okay. You just found that out recently?

S: Yeah.

I: How long have you been in that course?

S: Well, I've been in the course since September. But I found out that she gave you a lot of bonus marks just recently.

I: Question: Did you have any quizzes or tests in that class between September and December?

S: It's only on the exam you can pull those marks.

I: Oh! Okay. But you still haven't answered my original question about English.

S: *(Smiles)* You mean about how am I doing?

I: Right.

S: *(Smiles)* Not well!

I: Not well?

S: *(Smiles)* You want an average roughly where my mark is?

I: *(Acknowledging smile)* Approximately, yeah.

S: Okay. We're talking 35%.

I: Okay. Now you're saying that with the exam that's going to change?

S: It should change.

I: What do you think it should change to?

S: Realistically, I think about a 47. And if I get a 47 she'll probably chuck it up to a 50.

Note. The cavalier exchanges continued. The client admitted that he was hedging his bets in English. He will put in only enough effort required so that the teacher will "chuck" his final grade up to a pass.

I: Okay. What was it that contributed to the 35 so far?

S: Not doing the work, putting off stuff and then realizing, my God, I've put it off too long, it's due today! And then handing something in that's just quick, like fast.

I: Is that something that you tend to do in most subjects or just in English?

S: *(Chuckles)* I tend to do that in a lot of subjects.

I: So that's known as a basic style, a basic method of operating.

S: Oh yeah! *(laughs)*

I: Okay. Now, think back some time between September and December, think back to an assignment that you may have been given in English. She hands it out or talks about it. What do you do?

S: For instance, she gives a paragraph. Like we'll read something or talk about something, and then she'll say, give me a paragraph on this topic and make it ten to twelve sentences.

I: And it's due by?

S: Usually it's due by tomorrow. So what I'll do is, I'll sort of kick it around.

I: What do you mean by kick it around?

S: Sort of kick it, think about it, you know.

I: Like how?

S: I'll think about basically what I should write, stuff like that.

I: How and where do you do that? Do you do it at home?

S: I usually do it at home. I think about it. And I said well, I could do it this way, I could do it that way. Then the telephone rang, so I went and answered the phone, talked on the phone for about an hour. Then I had to flip my tape, so I flipped my tape; wanted a smoke, so I went out and had a smoke; came back, sat down, thought about it. Said, ah, fuck it!

I: Then let it go?

S: Then I let it go!

Note. Procrastination is part of Tony's approach to schoolwork. Incidentally, putting things off is common to all underachievers. What is significant here, however, is Tony's cavalier attitude about procrastination.

I: All right, then what happened next day?

S: Well, the next day in the morning I got to school early, I sat down, wrote what I thought about the night before, handed it in. So, it wasn't exactly what you'd call a very hot essay.

I: Right, it wasn't well thought through. You hadn't had time to rewrite what you had written.

S: No, it *was* well thought through, it was just full of grammatical mistakes, spelling mistakes, and it wasn't done neatly. But, it was thought through okay. Now, if only I hadn't been lazy enough to do it the night before and then rewrite it.

I: So you're saying the content of it . . .

S: Wasn't bad.

I: It wasn't as bad as 35%?

S: It was a solid B.

I: *(Incredulous)* Are you saying you went from a potential solid B, to a solid 35 because of spelling mistakes and sloppy grammar?

S: Yeah.

I: Wait, no, no. Are you serious? It's hard to believe that.

S: Yeah. Like Mrs. Peach, my English teacher is really strict on the paper being perfect and clean-cut, clean, neat final draft.

I: *(Sarcastically)* Son of a bitch! So in other words. . . .

S: What a difficult teacher! *(Laughs)*

I: So she's a stickler for neatness, organization, right?

S: *(Pauses)* No, I can't blame it on Peach, because all teachers expect that. But still, that's a teacher's right. I should have sat down the night before and I should have wrote it once, kicked it around.

I: Okay, question: Looking back at it now.

S: *(Laughs)* Yeah, I do this every year. I even know I'm doing it!

I: Right, so you're aware of it.

S: Oh, yeah. It's too easy to do anything about it.

I: So you're saying, well, maybe next time things will be a little bit different.

S: No, I'm looking ahead and saying, well, you know what? Ten bucks says I'm going to do the same damn thing!

I: Oh, okay. Right. And it sounds, Tony, that you're basically operating the way you would like to operate.

Note. The interviewer was willing to suspend judgment about Tony's perspective and point out its logical extension. Then Tony quickly sensed this, and responded.

S: Oh! Okay. That's sort of right and sort of wrong. I have been operating like that ever since sixth grade, even before. And sure, it would be nice if I sat down and did some work and it would be good. And I don't really like operating like this, but I'm just too lazy to actually do it.

I: Too lazy?

S: To actually do it.

I: The way you said that you'd think that laziness is genetic.

S: Oh, no! My dad and mom both work like fanatics.

I: *(Somewhat sarcastically)* If it's not genetics, maybe it's nutrition? Maybe you don't get the right food to eat.

S: Oh, I eat like a horse; steaks, filet mignon, a liter of milk each meal. And my mom is always shoving a salad at me every day.

I: Okay, so it's not heredity, it's not nutrition. Are you into heavy drugs?

S: No. I haven't had . . . *(Pauses and smiles)* Well, okay, I drink beer, but never had any illegal substance besides the fact that I'm under age. And I don't drink excessively.

I: In other words, you're not into marijuana, you're not into hash, coke, heroin?

S: No, I've never had, period!

I: So, it's not drugs?

S: Nope.

Note. The interviewer has been able to elicit some information about drugs. The extent of his drinking is an issue but it was not pursued at this point in the interview. Given the emerging impression about Tony's personality, it is reasonable to suspect some substance abuse. Yet, the original issue that triggered the present focus was Tony's attitude toward and methods of dealing with school. The interviewer chose to maintain that focus.

I: Okay, let's see. It's some evil force that is taking you over.

S: *(Laughs heartily)* Oh, I wish! Oh! That's it! I wish!

I: *(Assuming the client's voice)* "I went to see Dr. Mandel and he said that it's an evil force and there's nothing we can do about it." *(Laughs)*

S: Jesus, that's good! Can I use that?

I: *(Smiles)* I'm sure you will!

S: More than likely! *(Laughs)* A demon inhabited my body!

I: Right. But it was a demon of laziness.

S: A demon of laziness that's been around since Greek times. How do you think Caesar was assassinated? He was too lazy to get off his duff and organize his troops, that's why.

I: Laziness to you means what? Define laziness.

S: Laziness would be procrastination, would be knowing you've got something to do, realizing you've got to get it done.

I: You might just even start it?

S: *(In a sarcastic tone)* Sometimes I even get this stuff down on paper, which is rough!

I: *(Smiles and replies in a sarcastic tone)* Sounds dangerous!

S: Yeah, it's getting into the danger zone. Then I just sort of say, oh what the hell! Got to make a phone call or something. And then I sort of drop it.

Note. There was a mutual unstated acknowledgment that Tony's commitment to schoolwork was limited at best and that his discomfort with this state of affairs was also low. The interviewer chose to make these explicit.

I: Okay. The thing that strikes me though about the way you're describing it is that you don't seem that unhappy.

S: Okay. I don't seem unhappy. But hey, school's just a temporary social problem, right? *(Laughs)* It stops me from playing pool, all right? It takes up my time.

I: So what you're saying is you're really not doing well at school but at the same time you're not that uptight about it.

S: I'm not! I haven't changed in ages. I've been a lazy bum for years. Every year the same thing happens. Report cards come in with 40 and my mom says, "You failed! You're going to have to do it again. I'm upset! You're grounded! Blah, blah, blah, blah." Then, nothing happens.

I: You mean you don't end up getting grounded?

S: Oh, I get grounded for a few days.

I: So it's no big deal?

S: It's not anything major.

I: It's very interesting. You're saying something else now. If your mom treated you differently, you would change.

S: If she said that I couldn't go out until my grades came up, if she said I couldn't use the phone, I'd put my ass down on that chair so fast you wouldn't even see me make it from here to my room!

I: That is a fascinating assumption you're making.

S: If you're forced to work, you're forced to work. You have to.

I: So your poor showing in school is based on something that your mother's not doing?

S: *(Hesitates)* I see, now I'm pushing the blame off on my mom.

I: That's what it sounded like.

S: Yeah, I know. I don't really want to . . .

I: *(In a nonjudgmental tone)* What you're saying is, you can't change or won't change, or both.

S: No, I'm saying that I don't *need* to change! I can get away with being what I am.

I: Oh, okay. And that's okay because the way you are is fine?

S: Except for the fact that I'm failing.

I: Well, yeah, but that's small potatoes. In almost all other areas of your life, you think you're doing fine.

S: Yeah, socially I'm doing great.

I: And if your mom would just change a couple of things about the way she operates with you and school, you'd start to do something in school.

S: If my social life was indefinitely suspended, that would make a *big* difference on my grades!

I: Why do you think your mother has not come up with that solution a long time ago?

S: I think she's given up hope that I can change.

I: You mean she believes that no matter what she does, it's not going to make any difference.

S: Yeah. Right. If she took out my entire life, especially my social life, I'd change.

I: Are you serious? It's that simple?

S: Oh yeah. I think that would work fine.

Note. Tony has shown an ability to engage with the interviewer, a reasonable level of ego strength, as well as an ability for insight, all of which are positive prognostic indicators. However, he has also shown a great deal of externalization (including a willingness to admit it when confronted), as well as a low level of discomfort and no inclination for change unless forced to by someone else.

From a diagnostic perspective, the details are probably less important than the style with which they were presented. The manner reflects attitudes, perceptions of relationships with others, and a pattern of social interaction. In fact, the interviewer may well be advised not to accept as fact all details presented by this client.

I: *(Pauses)* Okay. Let's go on to some of the other school subjects. Let's get an idea of math. How are you doing in math?

S: Math—I'm doing good in it this year, actually. Better . . . *(Tony looks at the interviewer's face, hesitates, and laughs.)* Okay, sorry.

I: Tell me again what better means. Better means better than before, but what was before?

S: Better means that last year I had about 40. This year I'm going to pull off about 55–60.

I: How come? Your mother has not taken away your social life. How come you've gone from 40 to 55 or 60?

S: Well, one of my best friends is tutoring me and he really makes it interesting. Like, we'll sit there and have a smoke. And not only that, I'm going to a tutoring center for math which is costing my parents a fortune. I've got reports from there. They just phoned saying that I was God's gift to math.

I: You may be doing fine there, but in terms of your grade in math, it appears that you may already be an angel, but not yet God. *(Tony laughs)*

Note. The interviewer confronted Tony in a humorous manner on the student's self-aggrandized evaluation of his recent math performance. Such confrontation is not typical in diagnostic interviews with most types of underachieving students but may actually enhance the relationship with a CD underachiever. The interviewer has challenged some of what Tony presented, but has done so without judging him. This avoids the buildup of negative transference, challenges Tony to "improve" his delivery, and invites continued discussion.

S: Yeah *(laughs)*. Well it improved. In Grade Nine, I had a 25% math average.

I: How come?

S: It's pretty hard to think about. Thinking about math at night is great, yeah. I can solve this problem by doing x, y. And then in the morning when I go to do it, I've got four pages of math! I know the formulas, but still can't get it all done!

I: Oh, is that the issue of not enough time to do something?

S: Oh, yeah. That applies everywhere.

I: Right. But you're saying that it's not so much that you can't understand the math.

S: Oh no. In ninth grade, I did dick all, I did nothing! The last month of classes I read a *Star Trek* novel. My teacher said, "Listen Tony, you're failing; don't even bother. Just bring a book to class." And I did!

Note. Tony has confronted the interviewer with his lack of commitment to school. The interviewer decided to reconfront Tony on his position by extending Tony's position to its logical conclusion.

I: Question: How old are you now?

S: Seventeen.

I: Why are you still in school?

S: *(Hesitation; laughs)* Because you've got to be in school!

I: No you don't. You're over sixteen—you could be a free man right now.

S: Yeah, but I'd end up with a $2 an hour job.

I: No, the minimum wage in Canada is around $5.

S: Okay, but that's still diddly squat. *(Laughs, and waits expectantly for a reply)*

I: Listen to your logic. I'm going to present it back to you.

S: *(Leans forward in chair, and smiles)* I know, it's going to sound bad.

I: You're telling me that the reason you're still in school is because you don't want to end up with a shitty job. In other words, "Education leads to a better job." And that's the main reason why you're sitting in the classroom, as you put it, doing dick all!

S: *(Laughs)* Right. But see, eventually, I'm going to get all my courses. You've gotta!

I: No you don't. I don't understand this! What do you mean, you gotta? You can sit there and nothing will happen.

S: It's proof. I've got Grade Nine English. Sure it took me two shots at it, two and a half, three shots at it. But I got it!

I: Oh, yeah, eventually! Oh, wait! Now I think I've got the method.

S: Sooner or later I'm going to get them all!

I: Now I'm beginning to understand why you're operating the way you are. Maybe that's the answer. Maybe what you really want is to go as slow as possible.

S: That's a pretty fair assumption, I suppose.

I: In other words, you're willing to continue traveling.

S: Oh yeah!

I: But you want to go in slow motion.

S: Oh yeah! As long as I don't have to work too hard to get there.

I: Right.

S: I'll get there. Like, if I've got to climb a mountain, hey, I'll go three, four feet a day. It's hard work climbing a mountain; hard work doing math.

I: You're saying it's hard work doing anything in terms of school.

S: Actually, it's hard work doing anything that isn't recreational. So I take it slow.

Note. Tony has shown an ability to use metaphors, a relatively sophisticated cognitive procedure. It is a positive prognostic indicator for certain forms of treatment. Because this is a diagnostic interview, no further confrontation on this issue is necessary at this time. The interviewer has obtained a clear statement from Tony about the student's perceptions and methods of dealing with his school situation. He quickly completes the inquiry about school.

I: Okay, what's happening in science?

S: Science? Doing okay, which means *(laughs),* no . . . Actually, I just handed in an awesome project so I guess I'm doing okay. I'm at 50. Fifty is fairly guaranteed, more than likely higher.

I: Fifty is fairly guaranteed, more likely higher?

S: *(Smiles)* Yeah, more likely higher than 50, maybe even a 55. For me that's pretty high because I never do any work.

I: That's the point. So it's not that you *can't* do it. It's that you *don't* do it.

S: Yeah. Exactly.

I: Got it! *(Pauses)* Okay. Let's leave school for a while. You mentioned that your social life is both in good shape and an important part of your life. If I were to ask you to think of one close friend, and if I were to go up to that person and say, "Tell me what Tony's like?" what do you think they would tell me?

S: Okay. They'd say, I'm a nice guy, I can be counted on when it's really necessary, although if it's a minor thing, I don't get that involved. But if it's necessary he jumps in. They would also say that you have to get past his front. He goes with this front of the 200-pound ignorant guy, but once you get past that he's not like that at all.

I: Would they tell me what you were like once someone got past the front?

S: Oh, they'd basically say that I'm just an average, a run-of-the-mill nice guy and that I know when to keep my mouth shut.

Note. From a projective perspective, the question has elicited valuable information. Tony has admitted to throwing up a facade, something which he had done from the beginning of the interview. But by his own admission, he is not the type of person to freely admit things. Tony divulged and to some extent seduced the interviewer into seeking further clarification, and in so doing, has created another opportunity to "test" the interviewer.

I: Okay. *(Pauses)* Now, do you think that description that your friend gave is accurate? Do you think that captures some important things about you, about the kind of person you are.

S: Yeah, I mean, my friend and I are really tight. We really know each other well, although if I were to give it, I would throw in that I can be quite immature some times.

I: Oh! In what ways?

S: Like, sometimes I can act like a real child. I can go off and do something that is really stupid.

I: Okay. Give me an example of something you might have done that is really stupid.

S: Today is a beautiful example! Classic! I skipped once before in my life—once! *(A look of disbelief crosses the interviewer's face.)* Only one class and lunch! Today, I skipped my second class. I said to my friend: I don't want to go to class. He goes, "You got your work done?" I said, yeah. He goes, "Why don't you want to go to class?" I go, we got a supply teacher and we'll do diddly anyway. So what did I do? I took my project, put it in the teacher's mailbox. Well, I gave it to a friend to give to the teacher actually. It's guaranteed to get to the teacher. And then I went down to the cafeteria, sat in the cafeteria and read my *Caesar's Commentaries,* played a bit of cards, and went home, then picked up my sister and brother, and got a ride home from mom.

I: That's an example of something stupid? So it's not really a big deal. I mean, cutting class for your mom might be a big deal. For you, was it a big deal?

S: I felt so bad I even told my mom about it! And I phoned my dad and said, "Dad listen, the school might be phoning and saying that I skipped last period. I confess!" And I want to tell you that confessing is something I don't do!

I: Generally, you keep your mouth shut?

S: Oh yeah. Real good! If you can get away with it, shut up.

I: Is that a philosophy that you are using now, today, in this interview?

S: *(Smiles)* I use it all the time.

Note. Tony's example of something "stupid" was inconsistent in its seriousness with the buildup he had created. The interviewer was aware of this gap and mildly confronted the client. This served a dual purpose. It allowed the interviewer to examine Tony's reaction to mild confrontation and permitted the interviewer to "inform" Tony that not everything that had been presented had been blindly accepted. The interviewer chose to move on.

I: You mentioned your sister and brother, you picked them up. Tell me a little about them.

S: They're both younger than me.

I: What kind of person is your sister?

S: Ah, she's pretty good. She's cool actually. This you *can't* tell mom, cause I'm not allowed to smoke in the house. But whenever I'm babysitting my sister and I know my mom will be away for a while and she won't smell it, I smoke in the house. My sister's really cool. I said, "Don't tell mom, right?" She goes, "It's okay, don't worry." She's really cool. Me and her get along. I take her skating, you know.

I: How is she doing in school?

S: Oh, she's acing, the kid's a whiz. The teachers love her. In fact they invited her back to her old school. When she left they said she could come back any time. They love the kid. This kid is an A+ student.

I: Okay. And what about your younger brother?

S: He's okay too, although he always wants to hang around with me, and I don't want him to as much.

I: How come?

S: Because I don't want him to see me doing some of the things I do with my friends.

I: Like what?

S: Oh, just things. Besides, he slows me down. But he's okay, generally. He looks up to me a lot.

Note. Tony has hinted at activities he does not want either his brother or the interviewer to know about. What the interviewer is left with is Tony's admission about unspecified but by implication potentially problematic activities. This information is significant in developing a diagnostic impression.

I: How's he doing in school?

S: Average, I guess. His marks are going down a bit and mom's beginning to worry. She thinks I'm a bad influence on him.

I: What do you think she means by a bad influence?

S: I think she means my attitude about school.

I: Only about school?

S: No, probably about my smoking too.

I: Anything else?

S: *(Smiles)* Not that she knows about!

I: Okay. Has she talked to you about it?

S: Ya.

I: And?

S: And what? She talks too much anyway. She should mind her own business.

I: Sounds like she upsets you a bit.

S: Ya, but it passes quick.

I: Could we just spend a little more time talking about your parents? *(Tony nods his approval.)* What kind of person is your mom?

S: She's a perfectionist. Actually she's her own worst critic. She has to do it perfectly or she's upset with it.

I: Does that bother you?

S: Yeah, when she wants *me* to do better.

I: Is she laying some of that perfection on you?

S: Oh, no. But she's heavy into perfection. If she does something and it's got a tiny little flaw, watch out. She wails, "What am I going to do? What am I going to do?" But she's lightened up a lot.

I: Can you give me an example of how it might affect you?

S: Like, last year I wasn't allowed out past 11 o'clock. Now, if I'm going somewhere on a Friday night, she'll say, 12 o'clock and I'll say 1 A.M., and she'll say okay.

I: And generally speaking, are you the kind of guy, when you say you're going to be back around 1 you will?

S: *(Smiles)* Well, I usually get in sort of close to the time. It's just a few times I've been real late. But I had someone call for me. See, I've always got some legitimate reason for being a little late anyway. Because I know if I have a good reason she'll let me out the next time.

I: You said you had someone call for you. How come you didn't call?

S: I was a little "under the influence."

I: Want to tell me about it?

S: *(Firmly)* No!

Note. Tony had shown some irritation and overt resistance to the interviewer for the first time. There is tension between Tony and his mother both about his school performance and his negative influence on his younger brother. There is also a question about substance abuse.

I: *(Pauses)* Okay. What about your dad? What kind of a guy is he?

S: Oh, my dad's pretty right on. He's a bit distant, he's *(hesitation)* . . . my dad's hard to describe. My dad can be really cool for certain things and he can be just plain . . . I don't know . . . at other times . . . *(hmm)*.

I: Meaning what?

S: *(Hesitation)* Like for certain things, talking about cars, talking about guns, stuff like that, he's great. But I would never talk to him about a personal problem. No way!

I: How come?

S: Because he just doesn't like talking about things like that.

I: Can you tell me a little about his moods?

S: Well, most of time he's okay. Every once in awhile he needs to unwind.

I: And how does he do that?

S: Has a few beers.

I: Would you say he drinks too much at times?

S: No, cause he never drives when he's loaded.

I: Has his drinking affected you or others in the family?

S: Not really. We just work around it. Besides, it doesn't happen that often anyway.

I: How about the relationship between your mom and dad?

S: It's okay when they go off and do their own thing. But sometimes when they're together things heat up a bit.

I: Heat up a bit?

S: Well, not really anything heavy. Mostly shouting.

I: Anything else you can tell me?

S: No.

I: How does it affect you?

S: I don't let it.

Note. Tony was willing to admit some things about his father and his parents' relationship but limited the disclosure. The interviewer returned to a previous theme.

I: I see, okay. You said that you wouldn't turn to your dad if you had a personal problem. Would you talk to your mom?

S: *(Incredulously)* Are you joking?

I: Okay. So neither of them, then. So who would you turn to for a personal problem?

S: To my best friend, Sue, who's living about 140 miles from here now.

I: Just moved recently?

S: Yeah, just two months ago.

I: Do you miss her?

S: Oh, yeah! I could trust her with my life. She came here for the holidays. But I'm going to go down there on my break if my parents will let me, but I don't think so. I just skipped, so I'll probably be grounded. But because of exams we have the Friday off and Monday off, and I'm going to see if I can go down. And Sue's mom loves me. I have an open invitation whenever I get a couple of days off to come on up. So that's not too bad.

I: Could you tell me a bit more about your relationship with Sue.

S: *(Smiles)* Well, we have great sex together. She thinks I'm really great. *(Pauses)* She's right, you know.

I: I'll take your word for it for now. Is sex the basis of the relationship?

S: Sex should always be the basis of a male-female relationship, don't you think?

I: Well, it depends. But you haven't answered my question. What is the relationship with Sue like?

S: It's like it is. We enjoy each other's bodies. She has a great body.

I: What kind of a person is she?

S: Cooperative.

I: Cooperative?

S: Ya, she does what I want.

I: How serious is the relationship?

S: Not really, at least not from my side. But I do enjoy her company.

I: Okay. What sorts of things do you and your friends do together?

S: We hang out.

I: And when you hang out, what happens?

S: Not much.

I: You sound like there are things you could talk about but you've decided not to. Is that accurate?

S: Yeah.

I: Any particular reason why?

S: I've already told you, I know when to keep my mouth shut.

I: But why would you need to do that?

S: Take my word for it.

Note. Tony has cut off discussion of peer relationships or activities. Further, there is an implied threat that to pursue the topic at this time would risk the embryonic assessment relationship. The interviewer chose to shift topics.

I: *(Pauses)* Okay. Let's talk a bit about the future?

S: I want to be a cop.

I: Really! Very interesting. So you're seventeen now. When would you like to move in that direction?

S: Twenty would be nice. Twenty-one is age-maximum to get into the police academy.

I: Really? You know pretty definitely then, you're fairly clear. Any particular level of police work?

S: Okay. There are two things I'd want to be in. I'd like to be in narcotics, a lot of undercover work. I can handle that, dressed in cool clothes and have the gun and the badge still with you, right? Be a cop and still looking cool. Or, catching con men, going after con men.

I: Oh, you mean like going after embezzlers?

S: Yeah. Where you have to beat people at their own game. I wouldn't mind being a kiddy cop actually. They go to schools and talk about drugs. They bust kids with drugs, which I like. I love busting people for drugs because I hate drugs. I hate them! Anybody who takes drugs should be busted.

I: What about somebody who sells?

S: He should just be shot! Simple as that!

I: *(Smiles)* Okay.

S: My first goal when I become a cop is to go bust this dealer at school, Samuel the Mule. I'd like to bust his ass down to the floor, lock him up and throw the key away!! I'm going to sit outside his house in the cruiser and the minute he comes out, I'd grab him. "I have reasonable suspicion. Get up against the car. You're going *down!*"

Note. The excitement of the "chase" was an important element in Tony's career aspirations. Also, Tony presented a somewhat exaggerated and intense negative reaction to those who sell drugs but was careful not to mention his own drinking habits. The interest in law enforcement as a career is not unusual for CD underachievers.

I: What is it about police work that you think really turns you on?

S: The pay's good. Well, it pays fairly well. And besides, you can't get a speeding ticket. *(Interviewer smiles.)* It's true! I was talking to a cop this summer. I said, I want to be a cop. And he goes, "There's a lot of good points." I said like what? And he goes, "This is off the record right. All you have to do if you get a speeding ticket is to show your badge and it's sort of unwritten that the cop won't show up." Besides that, I could handle riding a big huge Harley 45 all day.

I: Okay. You're saying there are a number of possible advantages.

S: Oh yeah. Like, have you ever seen the coffee breaks cops take? They sit there for hours! It's great!

I: *(Smiling)* Okay. So I guess you're saying that it won't be any different from school.

S: No! It would be perfect! If I was a kiddy cop that would be great. Oh, I love to bust kids with drugs. Take them *down!* Catching con men that would be fun because you have to beat them at their own game. You have to think like them. I'm good at thinking—I just don't like to apply it! *(Laughs)*

I: How much have you checked into becoming a cop?

S: Oh, I've talked to a lot of cops. I know pretty basically you have to have Grade 12 education. That's the stumbling block. *(Interviewer smiles and Tony reacts.)* There you go. See, I have three years. I've got to get my Grade 12 in three years. *(Tony begins to laugh.)*

I: How many credits do you need to get your Grade 12 diploma?

S: The hell if I know, a bunch!

I: You know what I hear?

S: Okay. I think it's 26 credits to get into the force. But I don't know what an average diploma is going for. I don't know if it's more or less. I know you need 26 to get into the force.

I: You know what I hear? *(Assuming the client's voice)* "Harv, I don't know what a diploma is going for these days. It's like, well, a few years ago it was 26 credits, but you know Harv with inflation it's probably about 32 now."

S: *(Joins in the fun)* It's the Communists! Communists are behind the inflation. Anyway, I hate Communists. Put them all on Baffin Island and nuke them.

I: You have some fairly strong attitudes and very strong opinions, including what you want to be when you grow up.

S: I'm never going to grow up.

I: What you really want to be is a non-grown-up cop.

S: Yeah, that would be good. Oh, it would be beautiful!

I: So what's going to hold you back from being a cop?

S: Not getting my Grade 12 in time. That's a bitch, isn't it?

I: So school could possibly hold you back?

S: Um, yeah, that's the big one really.

I: You could do it if you actually sat down.

S: I don't know. It's kind of rough. I'm pretty far behind but . . .

I: You *really* want to become a cop so much that you are doing what you need to do to get there?

S: I got *everything* except school! I've done *everything* except school!

I: Yeah! You're the right height.

S: I'm the right build, I've got volunteer work—I was an Air Cadet. That sounds good, doesn't it?

I: Great.

S: And I'm getting my FAC (Fire Arms Certificate).

I: Excellent!

S: *(Laughs)* All I need to do now is finish my education.

I: It's the only thing that's holding you back from being independent, from being a cop.

S: That's a scary thought. Out in the world with all the Communists. Wow! It's a scary thought! *(Laughs)*

I: So, the plan you've developed is basically to go slow, still holding on to a dream that you have, never questioning the fact that you may screw up the dream by going slow.

S: Yeah, that's a pretty good assessment. I know I've got to get there by the time I'm 20.

I: What do you mean, you have to?

S: If I don't get there by the time I'm 20, I don't get into the police academy.

Note. Tony had presented the possibility of not fulfilling his career aspirations in a nonchalant manner. The interviewer reflected this by minimizing the consequences of such an occurrence.

I: Are you telling me that you really care about being a cop?

S: Yeah. I just don't want to do school to get it. I'm trying to work around that. I'm looking for ways to buy, barter, or steal a diploma.

I: Right.

S: But they're not working though.

I: That's really too bad. So you're trapped in a very difficult scene. You want to do as little as possible but you've got to stay there because you're going to need that piece of paper for what you want.

S: Oh yeah! If I could get that piece of paper with a signature and blank, and fill it in, now that would be beautiful! Unfortunately, those are pretty hard to come by, especially authorized ones. Yeah, I'd kill somebody for it.

I: Okay. But you haven't looked. You haven't tried to set it up that way. What you've done is, you've stayed in limbo . . .

S: Hoping, somewhere, by the time I get . . .

I: With the emphasis on *hope.*

S: *(Laughing)* I pray every night!

I: Maybe you should pray to become a cop.

S: No, no. Faith is bullshit, to put it basically. I believe in what I can see, hear, feel, taste, and touch.

Note. Tony has stated his philosophy succinctly. He believes in tangibles and in the here and now.

I: There are several questions I'd like to ask you. Sort of a shift in gears.

S: No problem.

I: Tell me about your moods.

S: Oh, I'm not that moody. If someone crosses me I get pissed off. Other than that, I'm pretty even.

I: Do you ever get sad?

S: Sure, sometimes. Like when I split up with one of my girlfriends. But it doesn't usually last that long.

I: Could you estimate how long is typical for you?

S: You mean from ditching my girlfriend?

I: Yeah, although I though you said splitting up. Now it's ditching.

S: Well, actually, no one has ever dropped me. I've always dropped them.

I: And have you felt any sadness or something else during that time?

S: Just a little, for part of a day maybe. Then I'm off again.

I: Off again?

S: You know, moving on!

I: Talking about moving on, is there anything about you that we haven't talked about that's important?

S: Sure. Lots of things.

I: Like what?

S: Like the guys I move with.

I: Tell me a bit about them.

S: *(Smiles)* It's just that we do a lot of things together, know what I mean?

I: Not exactly.

S: Well, I can't say much more. I'd thought you'd get it.

I: Do you mean illegal things?

S: I think I'd better shut up right now.

Note. For a moment, problems with peer activities arose again. Tony offered little additional information, but the earlier theme remained the same.

I: Okay. I think I've got somewhat of a picture of what's going on. We can stop at this point.

S: *(Somewhat surprised)* That's it?

I: That's it for now. Do you have any questions or comments about what we've talked about?

S: No, except that went fast. It was pretty good.

I: Okay. We'll be calling you in about a week to set up an appointment for a feedback session. At that time, I'll meet first with you and then with you and your mom to share the results of the assessment. At that time I'll tell what I think and you'll have a chance to react to the findings and recommendations.

S: Okay.

Throughout the diagnostic interview, the interviewer maintained a non-moralistic attitude in response to Tony's comments. The interviewer did not condone Tony's opinions, behaviors, and perceptions and suspended his own personal moral reactions in order to gather information. Even though the interviewer had not pursued all important leads, Tony had revealed a great deal. Among other things, he divulged his need for immediate gratification, his lack of commitment to school, some limited insight about his family issues, the gamelike quality of his interpersonal relationships, his intellectual ability, sense of humor, curiosity about and willingness to deal with conceptual and abstract issues, his superficial relationships with female peers, his secretive activities with male peers, and his seductive manner of withholding information. He did not exhibit signs of continuing sadness, although he clearly had some conflict regarding family relationships. His closing comments reflected his comfort with the interviewer and some sense of surprise about the direction the interview had taken.

Reaching a Diagnostic Impression

To reach a working diagnosis, it is helpful to consider a number of guiding diagnostic questions.

- Has the student stolen material goods (e.g., shoplifting) or forged documents (e.g., admit slips for school absences) more than once? *Answer:* No direct evidence, but strong possibility exists.
- Has the student run away from home overnight more than once? *Answer:* No.
- Has the student lied regularly? *Answer:* Evidence of selective reporting and lying reported by mother.
- Has the student cheated (e.g., on exams)? *Answer:* No direct evidence, but admission of potential.
- Has the student set fires deliberately? *Answer:* No.
- Has the student been truant from school regularly? *Answer:* Student's self-report is negative, but school and mother report consistent truancy.
- If the student is working (e.g., part-time) has the student been truant from work regularly? *Answer:* No.
- Has the student engaged in breaking and entering behavior (e.g., into a house, car, school building)? *Answer:* Again, no evidence, but suspicion by both police and school authorities.

- Has the student destroyed the property of others? *Answer:* No.
- Has the student been physically cruel to animals? *Answer:* No.
- Has the student coerced someone else into sexual activity with him or her? *Answer:* No.
- Has the student provoked or initiated fights with others? *Answer:* Yes, although the extent of the pattern is unclear.
- Has the student typically used a weapon in these fights? *Answer:* Yes.
- Has the student engaged in any illegal activities in which others have been confronted against their will (e.g., extortion)? *Answer:* No evidence, although suspicions expressed by mother, school authorities, and the police.
- Has the student been cruel to others? *Answer:* Some evidence of bullying behavior.
- Has the student abused drugs (legal or illegal)? *Answer:* No direct admission, but mother reports that Tony is smoking cigarettes and drinks beer regularly.
- Has the student regularly shown a lack of remorse or concern for the rights or feelings of others? *Answer:* Yes.
- Has the student regularly blamed others for his or her own actions (e.g., externalizes blame)? *Answer:* Yes.
- Has the student consistently shown a poor ability to tolerate frustration or delay gratification? *Answer:* Yes.
- Has the student exhibited provocative recklessness in his or her dealings with others (e.g., playing chicken)? *Answer:* No direct evidence, although reports from mother point to Tony's general reckless attitude and love of high-risk situations (e.g., driving his motorcycle at high speeds, etc.).
- Has the student shown the signs of Attention Deficit/Hyperactivity Disorder? *Answer:* No direct evidence, although some question about the source of Tony's distractibility remain.
- Has the student experienced rejecting, neglectful, or inconsistent child rearing practices? *Answer:* Yes, there are clear signs of inconsistent parenting.
- Has the student experienced harsh parental discipline, physical or sexual abuse, and/or frequent changes in parental figures? *Answer:* No direct evidence, although Mrs. B. reports that her husband's approach to child-rearing and disciplining is much harsher than hers.

- Has at least one parent shown a persistent pattern of antisocial behavior and/or been diagnosed with an Antisocial Personality Disorder? *Answer:* Mr. B., needs to be assessed. There are hints of a paternal APD, including substance abuse, but no direct evidence.
- Does the student associate frequently and repeatedly with a delinquent peer group? *Answer:* Probably, especially given Tony's hints of illegal peer activity, but the actual facts remain unclear.

Tony's academic history, family dynamics, psychological test results, previous assessment findings, and diagnostic interview all point to a diagnosis of childhood-onset Conduct Disorder. Several additional diagnostic possibilities should be considered. It is highly probable that Tony has a specific spelling skill deficit, which may or may not reflect a learning disorder. Diagnostic tutoring could determine to what extent this is a legitimate learning disability or due primarily to Tony's lack of commitment to the learning process.

Several areas need further exploration. These include family variables such as marital problems, Mr. B.'s alleged alcohol abuse, and a more thorough exploration of Tony's peer relationships. Mrs. B. reported that her daughter was doing well in school, although she worried about Tony's influence on her younger son.

Feedback of Results

At the feedback session, both Tony and his mother accepted the results as an accurate portrait of relationship and academic difficulties. Tony was intrigued by the way in which behavioral predictions were based on test and interview findings. These predictions were presented without moralizing, although the dangers were described. Tony's mother admitted that the predictions coincided with her own fears about Tony's future.

In addition, the assessor discussed "information gaps" that he believed were important to pursue, including facts about male peer relationships. Tony's mother admitted that she had difficulty accepting some of Tony's male friends and was worried about their negative influence on her younger son. When pressed, she reported that Tony and his male peers had been detained several times by the local police, once on suspicion of B and E (breaking and entering). In addition, the police were concerned about various weapons (e.g., hunting knives) that they had found in the neighborhood. Tony minimized both examples, saying that they had done nothing wrong. The proof, he said with pride, was that they had never been charged.

Mrs. B. also mentioned that school authorities had contacted her because of their suspicions about Tony's illegal extracurricular activities, including his presence in restricted school areas, and missing school lab equipment during a time when Tony and several of his friends had been present. As with the police, school authorities could not substantiate their suspicions. Tony proclaimed his innocence again, disdainfully dismissing the allegations as part of a campaign to get him.

An offer of ongoing counseling was made and Tony accepted, mainly as a way of getting his mother off his back. Continued individual academic tutoring was also recommended. As well, permission was granted for continuing and regular contact with Mrs. B.'s individual therapist, the school, and the tutoring service.

Risk and Protective Factors in Case 1

It is fair to conclude that Tony's long-standing impulsivity, poor concentration, and the problems in his family have had a cumulative and long-term impact on his school achievement. What risk factors contributed to Tony's CD underachievement? Early parental discord and discrepant child-rearing approaches played a role. As well, Mr. B.'s alcohol abuse not only contributed to the parent management discrepancy, but also modeled acceptable male behavior. Tony did not think he had a drinking problem, but his mother and teachers were worried that it was gradually getting out of control.

Mrs. B.'s depression should also be considered a risk factor, in that it may have frequently deprived her of the energy she needed to be more effective as a parent. It may have also have had an additional impact on Tony, as he grew up in an environment of sadness.

Childhood behavioral patterns such as oppositionality, distractibility, and poor impulse control contributed to decreased learning, which fed Tony's negative attitude toward school. Tony's poor spelling skills also may have contributed to less than predicted performance in a number of school subjects, including English, history, geography, and foreign languages. These entrenched early family and internal influences were magnified during adolescence through negative peer influences and escalating conflicts with authority.

But were there any protective factors in Tony's case history? Yes, and they may have played a significant role in diminishing the impact of the risk factors. Pregnancy, delivery, and developmental milestones were all normal. There were no obvious early signs of a learning disability.

TABLE 2.1   Summary of Risk and Protective Factors in Case 1

Risk Factors (in Elementary School)	Protective Factors (in Elementary School)
1. Impulsivity	1. Normal pregnancy and delivery
2. Poor concentration in school	2. Normal developmental milestones
3. Parental conflict	3. Verbal IQ > performance IQ
4. Discrepant child-rearing practices	4. Early school success
5. Paternal substance abuse	5. Persistent seeking of professional help
6. Maternal depression	by mother
7. Academic skill deficits	
8. Some early peer rejection	

Tony's WAIS-R verbal-performance score discrepancy in favor of the verbal explains to some extent why Tony had been able to progress academically throughout elementary school. His early school success may have contributed to some early positive psychological growth. His verbal intelligence may have acted as a protective factor, mitigating against the earlier development of academic underachievement.

His mother's early and continuing concern for her son, reflected in her persistent requests for professional help, also may have acted as a protective factor. Although the therapy he received did not prevent an escalation of the CD pattern, we do not know how much more severe the pattern would have been without treatment. And we do not know whether Mrs. B. would have been able to sustain herself to the same degree as a mother without her own individual therapy.

The overall pattern of individual, family, peer group, school difficulties, and community difficulties are characteristic of CD diagnosis. But the evidence points to a moderate CD. This is reflected by the fact that both the school and his mother view Tony as an underachiever with behavior problems, rather than as an out-of-control delinquent who happens to be underachieving academically.

Table 2.1 provides a summary of Tony's risk and protective factors.

Case 2: Adolescent-Onset CD Underachievement

Reason for Referral and Developmental History

Sam is a 16-year-old male, Grade 11, high school student from an intact family. His parents have been married for 18 years. Sam's father works as a manager in a small business firm and his mother is a civil servant. Sam's 12-year-old brother is doing well academically. Over the past 3 years, the family has experienced several major changes, including medical problems.

Sam's parents have been concerned for several years about his increasing school truancy and deteriorating school performance and his escalating overbearing, bullying, intimidating behavior aimed at both his parents and his brother. Parents report that Sam shows little respect toward his teachers. They are also concerned about Sam's experimenting with alcohol and other drugs, and are worried about the allure of money-making possibilities connected to selling drugs.

Sam's father did not enjoy school when he was a youngster, admitting that he could have done much better, but was too easily distracted. In contrast, his mother enjoyed school, even though she too could have done much better in high school, preferring to socialize much of the time. Once she graduated from high school, Mrs. S. performed extremely well academically in college.

Sam's parents report that his developmental milestones were normal. Although active as a youngster, Sam was not described as hyperactive, nor was there a concern at any time during his childhood or early adolescence about attentional problems.

Sam's early schooling was nonproblematic. A Grade 5 progress report contained a number of complimentary teacher comments: "Although Sam is often a quiet and reserved student, his participation in class and group activities is always positive and on target. He is responsible about completing his work and putting his best foot forward." The teacher was very pleased about his academic progress in spelling, creative writing, math, and French vocabulary.

Positive teacher comments continued through Grade 7. With the exception of Physical and Health Education where he scored in the 60s, Sam obtained marks in the 70s and 80s, with a foreign language mark in the 90s. For the first time and in spite of his acceptable academic performance, some teachers began to express concern about his social choices, as in the following teacher comment on his final Grade 7 report card: "Sam has done very well academically this year. He is organized and complete in his assignments. He must pay attention to due dates and work consistently toward them. Socially, I think Sam is learning a lot about appropriate friendships and how to balance classwork with friendships."

In his first year of high school (Grade 9), Sam's average dropped to 63%, with marks ranging widely (55% to 80%). His first semester Grade 10 average was 65%, with one failure, and some teachers commented on his escalating absences from class. He averaged 51% in the second semester of Grade 10, having barely passed most of his subjects. The final report card noted a total of 51 class absences and an interview with a school counselor was recommended. At the time of the current assessment, Sam was enrolled in three courses, all of which he was failing. Teacher comments included concerns about 35 absences and incomplete homework and assignments.

In summary, Sam had performed well in elementary and junior high school. His marks began to decline significantly in high school, at least in part due to attendance problems, social involvement with peers, and lack of follow-through on homework and assignments.

Psychological Test Results

On the Wide Range Achievement Test (WRAT3) Sam's skill levels in word recognition (88th percentile) and spelling (81st percentile) were well above scores obtained by most high school students his age, while his math score was in the average range (55th percentile). It appears that Sam's academic skill levels, therefore, at least in the areas tested by the WRAT3, do not appear to be a major contributing factor to his poor academic performance.

On the WISC-III Sam's verbal score was at the 63rd percentile. He exhibited moderate variability across the verbal scale tests and did not show specific strengths or weaknesses (he was generally average). However, Sam's performance score was at the 4th percentile (borderline range). In addition, there was substantial variability across the performance scale tests. Significant relative weaknesses occurred on perceptual tasks which demanded visual alertness, visual recognition, and visual identification (attention to visual detail). In addition, in comparison to same-aged peers, Sam showed relative weaknesses on tasks which tapped anticipation of consequences and temporal sequencing, interpretation of social situations, planning, perceptual organization, and visual-motor control.

Sam's overall IQ score was at the 21st percentile. The discrepancy between the verbal score and performance score is statistically significant, occurring in only 1% of adolescents his age. Sam's overall IQ was adversely affected by his very low scores on the performance tests of the WISC-III. Although Sam's *verbal abilities* are in the average range, his *nonverbal reasoning abilities* were significantly below average. He performed much better on items tapping verbal comprehension skills than he did on tasks requiring perceptual organization. The ability to attend to, concentrate on, and manipulate numerical material was much better than his scores on visual-perceptual organization tasks. His information processing efficiency was significantly below his verbal comprehension skills.

In addition to the verbal and performance scores, other scores from scales were calculated and analyzed. Bannatyne factors of verbal conceptualization (50th percentile), sequencing ability (37th percentile), and acquired knowledge (63rd percentile) were all in the average range. However, spatial ability was at the 9th percentile. As well, Sam's Index Scores in processing speed (18th percentile) and perceptual organization (6th percentile) were well below average.

Two verbal WISC-III tests, arithmetic and digit span, have been used as a Freedom from Distractibility Index. Both of Sam's scores on these tests were in the average range. Interestingly, both of these tests tap concentration with aurally presented tasks (auditory stimuli). When items were presented in this manner, Sam did not exhibit any problems with distractibility.

Several important findings emerged from Sam's WISC-III profile:

- His average verbal score on the WISC-III is predictive of at least average school marks, provided there are no other interfering factors. In fact, in Sam's case other significant factors could account for his poor academic performance.
- The WISC-III performance scores point to a significant visual perceptual learning disability. In other words, visual perceptual and/or motor deficits should be considered as significant contributors to Sam's academic underachievement.
- Sam's average verbal skills probably have masked his poor visual-motor processing skills in his earlier schooling, and parents and teachers may have concluded that he is fully capable of performing adequately without any special assistance.
- Based on the WISC-III results, it is predicted that Sam would experience great difficulty when material was presented primarily or

exclusively through visual input (e.g., solely on a blackboard, or when he is asked to read silently).

The unanswered question at this point in the assessment was how did Sam manage to achieve in elementary and junior high school with this perceptual difficulty?

On the Bender-Gestalt Visual Motor Test, Sam was able to reproduce the overall designs accurately. However, several behavioral tendencies emerged during the task. Sam's designs were consistently smaller than the original drawings and only filled one half of the page. Both of these tendencies are reflective of emotional constriction or guardedness. Also, even though Sam captured the overall gestalt in his drawings, several were incomplete or lacked closure, reflecting poor attention to detail and follow-through. Sam does not appear to experience visual perceptual *distortions,* but specific behavioral tendencies emerged that are predictive of academic difficulty.

The Achievement Motivation Profile (AMP) (Friedland et al., 1996) is an objectively scored personality test that taps achievement motivation, inner resources and interpersonal characteristics, work habits, and career interests. Sam's scores on the AMP validity scales indicate that he tended to downplay his strengths and to be self-critical, perhaps measuring himself against very high standards.

Individuals with similar AMP profiles describe themselves as performing academically below their potential. They tend to have trouble working consistently on academic tasks. They do not experience a strong inner drive to achieve academically and often have difficulty maintaining a higher level of motivation. They do not place much value on performing better than others. Such individuals also do not have clear goals and because of this may find themselves following the goals of others.

Individuals with this profile exercise less initiative and are not consistent in their use of specific plans or strategies for achieving goals or meeting deadlines. They also prefer to work alone rather than as part of a team. Although individuals with this profile exhibit an outer sense of self-confidence, they tend to feel discouraged or frustrated when faced with problems or difficulties at school, at home, or in the community (e.g., on a job). They tend to experience tension or worry in many situations and have difficulty relaxing. They also tend to become impatient and are easily frustrated.

Interpersonally, such individuals are usually introverted, even though they perceive themselves as sociable and outgoing in some situations. They perceive themselves as less assertive or less direct in expressing themselves, but also believe that they are at least as diplomatic as most others their age.

Individuals with this profile report that their unhappiness, worry, impatience, and poor work habits tend to interfere with school success.

Sam's self-portrait on the AMP is that of a low achiever or underachiever who is experiencing both internal and interpersonal difficulties. His motivation to achieve academically is low and his poor work habits are predictive of continued low achievement.

Sam's MMPI-A profile was valid and reflected someone experiencing a great deal of stress and having trouble managing his life. Individuals with similar MMPI-A profiles have problems with impulse control. They exhibit low frustration tolerance, and their need for constant stimulation often causes them to act recklessly or irresponsibly at times. They get involved in conflicts with authority at home, at school, and in the community.

Individuals with this profile are described as uninhibited and self-indulgent, with an exaggerated sense of self, irritable, moody, agitated, and overactive. When problems arise, they are likely to blame others for their problems. They also tend to be mistrustful of others.

The types of problems adolescents with this profile report include stealing, shoplifting, lying, property destruction, and general oppositional behavior. Furthermore, most of these behavior problems occur in more than one setting (home, school, community). Their behaviors tend to escalate when in the presence of like-minded peers.

Most teens with this profile also report school difficulties, including underachievement, low expectations about achievement, dislike of reading or study, and difficulty getting started and completing projects. They tend to have histories of truancy, school suspensions, negative attitude toward school, as well as some anxiety or fear about attending school. They report symptoms of anxiety (e.g., tension, worry, and sleeping difficulties), along with symptoms of sadness or depression, somatic complaints, and concerns about their health. From their perspective, the only positive aspect about school for these teens is that they can mingle with their peers.

In the area of interpersonal relationships, teens with similar MMPI-A profiles have the ability to charm, even con others. They may be sociable and outgoing at times, but tend not to be open and honest in their relationships, especially with adults.

On the MMPI-A, Sam reported a great deal of tension and conflict within his family. He perceives them to be angry, jealous, and faultfinding, and reports that there are increasing arguments between him and his parents and between his mother and father. Because of his poor impulse control, Sam may even find that some of these family tensions may spill over into other areas of his life (e.g., taking some of his frustrations out on others in school). Teens with this profile also report serious problems with risk-taking behavior involving alcohol and other drugs. They usually belong to a peer group that uses alcohol and/or drugs.

The results of the MMPI-A profile point to a comorbid or combination diagnosis, including Conduct Disorder, possible mood disorder (e.g., cyclothymia), drug involvement, and poor academic achievement.

Because the MMPI-A is long, self-administered, and tedious, the examiner was able to observe the way in which Sam coped with a prolonged reading task. He persevered throughout, taking only a short break, which is testimony to his constructive motivation during the assessment. Much more important, however, was the system he adopted to complete the test. Quite early in the test, he began reading each item aloud. This helped him stick with and better understand each item. In other words, he used *both visual and auditory "channels"* to maximize his ability to complete the test. It was a strategy even he himself was not conscious of, but which he immediately acknowledged when it was described to him. Intuitively, Sam knew that if he silently read the material, it would dramatically slow his processing speed. In other words, Sam had devised a coping strategy to work around his visual perceptual learning difficulty. There are some profound academic implications of this finding for Sam.

The Multiscore Depression Inventory (MDI) (Berndt, 1986) screens for affective, behavioral, and cognitive components of depression. Sam's overall MDI score and specific MDI scale scores indicate that he is suffering from specific affective, behavioral, and cognitive symptoms of depression. Specifically, he scored at the 99th percentile on the pessimism, learned helplessness, and effectiveness of thinking scales. The sad mood scale was at the 96th percentile and the instrumental helplessness (being treated unfairly by others) at the 93rd percentile. These mood problems also contribute to his poor academic performance, because they decrease the probability that Sam will persevere when faced with academic difficulty.

The individual diagnostic interview confirmed much of what has already been reported. Several additional issues emerged, including Sam's ambivalence about school. He is torn between the "street smart" lifestyle and finishing high school. He is much more interested in applied or practical educational training (e.g., at the community college level) versus pursuing a university-bound educational program, and judges his current high school as not meeting these practical needs.

He expressed some career interests, such as becoming a policeman or learning to rebuild engines, but has spent little if any time researching what he would need to do to actively pursue these interests. In addition, when asked to discuss some of these interests in greater detail, Sam tended to give up quickly or claim that he really didn't care. It was fairly obvious, however, that he does care and wants to be successful. His denial was merely a way of saving face in front of others and protecting himself from his own private tendency to be self-critical.

Sam was not forthcoming about the extent of his drug involvement, although he was willing to admit that he has been and may still be involved with drugs. He was also willing to admit regular involvement with a deviant peer group, although he also pointed out that he has a number of friends who are not into drugs or antisocial behavior. In fact, he offered that in order for him to be academically successful in the coming term he would have to affiliate more with this latter group. It appears that Sam spends a great deal of time with a select group of peers, both at school and in the community. He influences them and they influence him to cut classes and spend time at community hangouts (e.g., coffee shops).

In discussing his family, Sam talked about conflicts between him and his parents, between him and his brother, as well as between his mother and father. He claims that he is the "black sheep" of the family and is both the target of criticism as well as the victim. He did not take much responsibility for any of his contributions to these tensions. He alluded to some sporadic physical intimidation within the family.

The interviewer tested Sam's ability and willingness to engage in counseling. Although cautious at first, Sam was willing to admit that he needed some help in organizing his life and in learning how to protect himself from doing things that would get him into difficulty. However, whoever works with him will have to deal with Sam's oppositionality, his distrust of adults, his tendency to test limits, externalize blame, and withhold vital information.

Reaching a Diagnostic Impression

To reach a working diagnosis, it is helpful to consider a number of guiding diagnostic questions.

- Has the student stolen material goods (e.g., shoplifting) or forged documents (e.g., admit slips for school absences) more than once? *Answer:* No direct evidence, but strong possibility exists.
- Has the student run away from home overnight more than once? *Answer:* No.
- Has the student lied regularly? *Answer:* Evidence of selective reporting, and some outright misrepresentation of facts.
- Has the student cheated (e.g., on exams)? *Answer:* No direct evidence, but admission of potential.
- Has the student set fires deliberately? *Answer:* No.
- Has the student been truant from school regularly? *Answer:* Yes.
- If the student is working (e.g., part-time) has the student been truant from work regularly? *Answer:* No.
- Has the student engaged in breaking and entering behavior (e.g., into a house, car, school building)? *Answer:* No.
- Has the student destroyed the property of others? *Answer:* No.
- Has the student been physically cruel to animals? *Answer:* No.
- Has the student coerced someone else into sexual activity with him or her? *Answer:* No.
- Has the student provoked or initiated fights with others? *Answer:* Yes, both within the family (e.g., with brother) and in the community, although the frequency and extent are not clear.
- Has the student typically used a weapon in these fights? *Answer:* No.
- Has the student engaged in any illegal activities in which others have been confronted against their will (e.g., extortion)? *Answer:* No.
- Has the student been cruel to others? *Answer:* Yes, via bullying and intimidating behavior, including threat of physical violence (both inside and outside the family).
- Has the student abused drugs (legal or illegal)? *Answer:* Yes.
- Has the student regularly shown a lack of remorse or concern for the rights or feelings of others? *Answer:* Yes.

- Has the student regularly blamed others for his or her own actions (e.g., externalizes blame)? *Answer:* Yes.
- Has the student consistently shown a poor ability to tolerate frustration or delay gratification? *Answer:* Yes.
- Has the student exhibited provocative recklessness in his or her dealings with others (e.g., playing chicken)? *Answer:* No.
- Has the student shown the signs of an Attention Deficit/Hyperactivity Disorder? *Answer:* No.
- Has the student experienced rejecting, neglectful, or inconsistent child-rearing practices? *Answer:* No.
- Has the student experienced harsh parental discipline, physical or sexual abuse, and/or frequent changes in parental figures? *Answer:* No, although there has been some admission of infrequent physical abuse within the family.
- Has at least one parent shown a persistent pattern of antisocial behavior and/or been diagnosed with an Antisocial Personality Disorder? *Answer:* No.
- Does the student associate frequently and repeatedly with a delinquent peer group? *Answer:* Yes.

Sam's academic history, family dynamics, psychological test results, previous assessment findings, and information gleaned from the diagnostic interview all point to a comorbid diagnosis of adolescent-onset CD underachievement, anxiety, sadness, coupled with a specific visual learning difficulty. He did not exhibit any signs of CD, affective problems, or academic underachievement in childhood. His family situation had been stable until about 3 years ago.

Feedback of Assessment Results

Sam and his parents were present at the feedback session. Both parents were amazed at the finding of a visual-perceptual learning difficulty and wondered why this problem had not been detected earlier in Sam's school career.

Sam offered a plausible explanation. He had gone to a private elementary school where class size was small relative to a public school. In addition, he remembered that because his school projects had required teamwork, he had always arranged for his friends to do most of the reading, while he took responsibility for other aspects of the projects. He also mentioned that his friends always gave him the notes they took during class, which he copied. Thus, in a private school environment, Sam was able to adapt well to his visual learning difficulty.

In contrast to his experiences at the private elementary school, he remembered that he began having some academic trouble in the public junior high school. These early behavioral difficulties escalated in high school. Sam attributed the change in his academic performance to two factors—the changed school structures in his public high school and the influence of some peers who, he admitted, were trouble seekers. Sam's parents also admitted that tensions and conflicts had escalated at home because of health and financial changes in the past 2 or 3 years.

His academic skills were at least average, a testimony to positive early schooling experiences and a supportive home environment. Although Sam had begun to underachieve and exhibit CD tendencies by junior high school, he was troubled by these changes, as evidenced by his inner tension and sadness. In high school, he was unable to perform academically, and gradually gravitated to a high-risk peer group in which drugs were available and antisocial behavior common. He gained some sense of self-respect and success as a member of these peer groupings, which for him stood in marked contrast to his sense of failure in school. Yet he also maintained some positive peer relationships with achieving adolescents.

Assessment recommendations included alerting the school to Sam's learning difficulty so as to arrange for special education assistance, arranging for a drug screen to ascertain the type and extent of Sam's drug involvement, providing individual counseling for Sam focused on developing greater self-control and more constructive options, and providing parent management sessions, with a focus on the tensions between parents as well as several family sessions to highlight the family tensions and potential for physical violence.

Sam's parents agreed to follow up on all the suggestions. Sam was hesitant about going into counseling and wanted to know more about the counselor he would be seeing before committing himself to the process. He seemed relieved to know that there were specific reasons for his difficulties in class when material was presented primarily in visual format.

A follow-up three weeks later revealed that Sam's mother had already alerted the school about the findings of the psychological assessment. School personnel were more than willing to offer appropriate special education assistance, and in fact, were somewhat embarrassed that they had not detected any of the learning difficulties revealed by the assessment. One example of a learning strategy they thought would be helpful was to have Sam use taped books from the English course so that he could listen and read the required materials at the same time. In addition they offered to have the school psychologist explain Sam's learning difficulty to his teachers and develop specific teaching strategies for each course.

In addition, the drug screen had been arranged. Several individual therapists had been contacted and discussions were underway about Sam's treatment. Mr. and Mrs. S. were following up on a lead for parent and marital therapy. Despite family health and financial concerns, the parents were mobilizing to address many of the issues raised by the assessment findings.

Risk and Protective Factors in Case 2

What were the risk and perpetuating factors in Sam's life? They involve a school change and exposure to high school structures that made it much more difficult for Sam to avoid the consequences of his learning difficulty. In addition, increasing parental tensions about financial and health concerns added to daily parental and family conflicts. The negative influence of a new peer group cannot be overstated.

And what protective factors were at work? Sam had experienced solid beginnings within his family, at school, and in the community. He had been able to achieve in elementary school and develop reasonable peer relationships, some of which continued into his adolescent years and remained after he transferred from the private to the public school system. And even though this protective family factor had diminished somewhat within the past 3 years, it was evidenced again in the organized and rapid manner in which the family responded to the assessment findings and recommendations. In addition, Sam's own willingness to admit his sadness and inner tension to those who may be able to help him should be considered an internal protective factor.

In addition, the reaction of school personnel to the uncovering of a learning disability was very positive. It is possible that the negative chain reactions that had built up at school over the past 3 years may begin to change somewhat as a result of hearing about the findings of the psychological assessment. The Learning Disorder, which was one factor contributing to underachievement at the high school level, may now become less of a risk factor because of appropriate educational programming.

Table 2.2 summarizes Sam's risk and protective factors.

TABLE 2.2 Summary of Risk and Protective Factors in Case 2

Risk Factors	Protective Factors
1. Change to public high school (larger class size)	1. Normal pregnancy, delivery
2. Parental financial & health problems during Sam's adolescence	2. Normal developmental milestones
3. Acceptance by deviant peer group in high school	3. Private elementary school with small classes diminishing impact of LD
4. Substance abuse	4. Functional child-rearing practices
	5. Reasonable peer relationships in childhood
	6. Internal sadness; willingness to accept professional assistance
	7. Mobilization by mother of school resources
	8. Willingness of school to modify academic program based on identified LD
	9. Verbal IQ > performance IQ

Chapter 3

Treatment

> If the therapy goals are to make the psychopath into an upstanding
> citizen who will care about others, feel what others feel, and feel
> guilty when he hurts someone, the therapy is doomed to failure.
>
> DOREN (1987, P. 168)

Generally, the targets of intervention have been the acting-out student
and his or her parents. Treatment goals include improved management
and child-rearing skills in parents as well as decreased disruptive behavior and improved academic achievement in the conduct-disordered child
or adolescent. The focus of this chapter will be on outpatient or inpatient
treatment programs and research studies. Programs for dealing with Conduct Disorder within the school will be reviewed in Chapter 5.

One of the characteristics of antisocial children and adolescents (and
adults too, for that matter) is that they tend to act precipitously (with high
impulsivity) and/or react automatically (due to negative attributions).
Even if they had more effective cognitive processing, however, many
would not have the social skills necessary to implement their revised cognitions.

It is not a coincidence, therefore, that among the many treatment approaches, three predominate: Parent Management Training (PMT), Cognitive Skills Training (CST), and Social Skills Training (SST). All are
rooted in a developmental framework and learning theory and derive
largely from research findings on the etiology of the disorder. But as Forehand and Long (1988) have stated, "A clear treatment of choice for acting out or antisocial behaviors has not emerged" (p. 134).

Two notes of caution seem warranted. First, the most severely behaviorally antisocial children and their families tend to drop out of treatment. Forehand, Middlebrook, Rogers, and Steffe (1983) reviewed 45
studies of PMT and found that in half, the dropout rate averaged 28%. A

few studies report dropout rates as high as 80%. This leaves outcome statistics unrepresentative and therefore suspect.

Kazdin (1990) examined the characteristics of families with antisocial children who dropped out of treatment and found that the children exhibited more severe antisocial behavior than those who remained in therapy. In addition, the dropout mothers reported greater stress precipitated by their acting-out children, by their own problems, and as a result of the cumulative negative impact of life events. In contrast, the families who remained in treatment were less socioeconomically disadvantaged. If Kazdin's findings can be generalized, it means that treatment outcome statistics have been based primarily on less severely antisocial children and their less dysfunctional and/or disadvantaged families.

The second limitation of treatment studies in this area is that follow-up has typically been limited to one year. Long-term impact is rarely studied. Nevertheless, "A small number of carefully evaluated programs provide promising evidence that positive changes in antisocial behavior can be brought about at the child and family levels" (Dumas, 1989, p. 197).

PARENT MANAGEMENT TRAINING

more for young kids

Most parent management training (PMT) programs have been geared to parents of disruptive preadolescents, including preschoolers, and often provide a major part of the program in the home. This training targets behavior problem children by teaching their parents ways of changing dysfunctional parent-child interaction.

This is accomplished by teaching parents to systematically identify and observe disruptive behaviors. Social learning principles are taught that parents are expected to implement (McMahon, Forehand, & Griest, 1981). Debriefing of daily problematic events and discussion of alternative parenting strategies are integral to these programs. Once behaviors in the home have changed for the better, some PMT programs shift the focus to the child's dysfunctional behavior outside the home (e.g., school, community).

Outcome studies of PMT (Kazdin, 1987a; McMahon & Wells, 1989; Miller & Prinz, 1990; Patterson, Dishion, & Chamberlain, 1993; Peed, Roberts, & Forehand, 1977) provide evidence of improvement at treatment termination and up to one year following cessation of treatment.

For example, Strain, Steele, Ellis, and Timm (1982) tracked parents and children for up to 9 years posttreatment. At follow-up, teachers rated the children as similar in their behavior to nonproblematic peers. Forehand and Long (1988) tracked families from between 4 and up to 10 years posttreatment. They too found that the treatment and control groups did not differ up to 10 years after termination of parent training. Parent management training had brought the once disruptive behavior into the normal range, where it remained for a significant period.

What is encouraging about long-term PMT follow-up research is that gains typically have been maintained from between 1 to 4.5 years after treatment (Baum & Forehand, 1981). These changes in the identified patient are also paralleled by positive changes in siblings (Humphreys, Forehand, McMahon, & Roberts, 1978) and parents and their marital relationship (Brody & Forehand, 1985; Kazdin, 1985; Mullins, Quigley, & Glanville, 1994).

Yet these improvements have not been observed in the most severely antisocial youngsters treated with PMT. Often the treatment problem with these children is lack of parent cooperation.

It appears that long-term positive impact of PMT is lessened as a function of several factors. Wahler (1980) and Wahler and Dumas (1987) reported that although they found similar gains as a result of PMT, at follow-up the increases had disappeared. Almost all the families in these studies were on welfare. In contrast, in the study by Baum and Forehand (1981) where gains had been maintained, only one family was on welfare. Families under great socioeconomic stress and/or isolation appear to have difficulty in maintaining PMT gains posttreatment (Dumas & Wahler, 1983; Wahler, 1980; Wahler & Dumas, 1987).

Is there any way of predicting outcome in parent management training? Routh, Hill, Steele, Elliott, and Dewey (1995) found that mothers who scored as insecure on the attachment measure showed a strong relationship between initial referral intensity score and outcome intensity score. This same relationship did not hold for those mothers who initially scored as secure on the attachment measure. In other words, it is possible that degree of attachment security may predict outcome in PMT for mothers of conduct-disordered children.

Several researchers have compared the effectiveness of different types of parent-training programs. Webster-Stratton (1984) compared the results of 9 weeks of individual therapy for mothers, with 9 weeks of group therapy (videotape modeling) for mothers, with a no-treatment control group. All parents had a conduct-disordered child. Compared with the control group, Webster-Stratton reported significant changes in maternal attitudes accompanied by significant changes in the disruptive behavior of the children for both treatment conditions at one-year follow-up.

Webster-Stratton (1989) expanded her comparisons to three parent training approaches. Each parent had a disruptive child between the ages of 3 and 8 years. The first training group was led by a therapist and included the use of videotape and group discussion (GDVM). In the second group, there was no therapist and the videotape was administered individually (IVM). The third approach used group discussion without videotape or therapist (GD). All treatments produced significant reductions in disruptive child behavior, increases in prosocial activity, and a decreased need for spanking. While IVM was the most cost-effective, GDVM produced the best outcome.

Webster-Stratton (1990) evaluated the effectiveness and client satisfaction of the three types of parent training one year after termination. Both fathers and mothers in all three treatment conditions reported high levels of satisfaction. Parents expressed a preference for therapist-led groups. There were also some differences between mothers and fathers in the ease with which they learned new parenting strategies.

Griest and Wells (1983) recommended an expansion of the parent management training model, calling their broader approach Behavioral Family Therapy (BFT). They drew a parallel between the disruptive child's difficulties at home, at school, and in the community, with parental difficulties at home (child management and marital problems) as well as in the community (e.g., with relatives, social agencies, their child's teacher). Griest and Wells went beyond teaching parents adequate child management techniques and addressed parent perceptions of the child, especially if these perceptions were faulty.

They also recommended dealing with certain psychological parent variables, especially maternal depression and marital conflict, as well as targeting nonproductive relationships between parents and the community. Griest, Forehand, and Wells (1981) found that pretreatment of parental depression was a significant predictor of lack of compliance with a 2-month follow-up request. In addition, McMahon et al. (1981) incorporated the teaching of general social learning principles to parents as part of PMT's focus on child management. Their study demonstrates the superior impact of the combined approach over the more basic program.

In their review, Miller and Prinz (1990) concluded, "Discussion of personal and marital distress and parental expectations can facilitate familial and child outcomes. Such expansion promotes more cooperation and follow-through on child-management interventions" (p. 297). There has been some clinical concern that improvements in the home resulting from PMT may be accompanied by simultaneous increases in disruptive behavior in school. In a well-designed study, Breiner and Forehand (1981) found that this did not occur.

Several researchers have examined the interaction across research instruments used to measure outcome in PMT. In their study, Forehand, Griest, and Wells (1979) found that observational data, parent-generated data, and questionnaire data all reflected positive change as a result of PMT. Yet these measures were not significantly correlated with each other. These findings point to the importance of collecting outcome data across a number of variables, in a number of ways, and from a number of sources.

Although PMT has been shown to be effective when used with parents of preadolescents, Weathers and Liberman (1975) found that in-home contingency contracting was not effective with families of delinquent adolescents. They also reported a dropout rate of approximately 80%, and caution about the use of a single treatment technique in dealing with these difficult adolescents and their families.

What are the critical components of PMT? Forehand and Long (1988) postulate that the therapist must be knowledgeable about social learning principles, have good training, and believe in the approach. The parents must have opportunities to observe behavior and practice interventions (didactic teaching alone is insufficient), learn how to provide positive attention for appropriate behavior, uncover and modify their own antecedent behaviors that trigger their child's reactions, learn the principles of effective disciplining, and use problem-solving throughout the process.

Because many PMT studies do not distinguish between disruptive children with CD and Oppositional Defiant Disorder (ODD), and lump them under a disruptive or behavior problem rubric, it is often difficult to discern the exact sample composition. Parent management training is effective for parents of preadolescents with Conduct Disorder. Is it also effective with preadolescents with Oppositional Defiant Disorder? Wells and Egan (1988) compared two types of treatment for ODD: Social learning-based parent training (SLPT) and systems family therapy (SFT). "Results showed that SLPT was more effective than SFT in reducing the primary symptoms of Oppositional Disorder" (p. 138).

COGNITIVE SKILLS TRAINING

As mentioned earlier, disruptive children and youth tend to act impulsively, often following automatic and rapid hostile attributions. Cognitive skills training (CST) is designed to get the child to examine his or her *thought processes* and how these lead to problematic reactions. Participants are taught the principles and techniques of behavioral analysis, including self-monitoring, self-evaluation, and self-reinforcement. Typically, a self-management course consists of 10 one-hour sessions and participants are expected to choose disruptive behaviors they wish to change.

Many of the earlier studies used CST to target hyperactive or impulsive rather than antisocial behavior. A problem with much of the research on impulsivity in children is that the term is used for a wide range of conditions—attentional problems, behavior problems, non-self-control, aggression, and so on (Baer & Nietzel, 1991). Further, in a meta-analysis of 36 outcome studies, these same researchers found that many children labeled as impulsive fell within one standard deviation of the norm. They were identified as impulsive through a range of procedures, but they did not in fact differ from most "normal" children: "The normative comparisons highlight the importance of using clinical samples in treatment outcome research" (p. 409).

One of the earliest studies of *cognitive self-instruction* ("talk to yourself") was used to assist impulsive children develop greater self-control (Meichenbaum & Goodman, 1971). Gains in self-control were maintained at a one-month follow-up. Chandler (1973) used CST with delinquent youngsters, aged 11 to 13. The training consisted of 10 half-day small group sessions. Chandler found that CST produced significantly increased perspective-taking in the treatment group, and these changes were maintained at an 18-month follow-up. Synder and White (1979) reported similar results using a cognitive self-instruction treatment. Several researchers have used CST with predelinquent and delinquent youth (Brigham, 1989; Gross, Brigham, Hopper, & Bologna, 1980; Brigham, Hopper, Hill, deArmas, & Newsom, 1985) and report significant changes in targeted behaviors.

Camp, Blom, Hebert, and van Doorninck (1977) found that their *"think-aloud"* cognitive self-control training program for aggressive 6- to 8-year-old boys was successful. Brown and Greenspan (1984) also reported significant gains as a result of school-based *social foresight training* for high-risk adolescents.

Lochman (1985) held group sessions for aggressive boys (mean age = 10.3 years) and focused on deficiencies in their social cognitive skills. Lochman also varied the length of treatment to assess the impact of longer (18 sessions; Anger Coping Plus Goal Setting [ACGS-18]) versus shorter treatment (12 sessions). The boys were trained to take another's perspective, to increase awareness of their own physiological reactions when they got angry, to mediate automatic aggressive responses through cognitive self-talk, and to implement alternative problem-solving strategies. Longer treatment was significantly more effective than shorter intervention.

Guerra and Slaby (1990) attempted to alter aggression in incarcerated adolescents using 12-session *Cognitive Mediating Training* (CMT). These adolescent offenders showed decreases both in their endorsement of beliefs that supported aggression as well as in actual aggressive behavior. They also showed an increase in solving social problems. Interestingly, the extent of changes in aggressive behavior were directly related to the extent of changes in the beliefs that supported aggression.

In general then, CST produces improvements in antisocial behavior, but these changes may not be enough to result in normal behavior in severely acting-out children and youth.

SOCIAL SKILLS TRAINING

Although there are many variations of social skills training (SST), all focus on getting the child or adolescent to think about how to approach any potentially *problematic social situation.* The treatment is provided in offices, clinics, and hospital inpatient and outpatient programs.

Children are taught the specific steps in constructive problem solving and are provided structured situations in which to practice these principles, often through modeling and role playing. Specific skills are targeted, including carrying on constructive conversations, receiving and sending complaints in a nondestructive manner, dealing more effectively with anger or rejection, and dealing productively with authority figures.

The overall aim of this training is to provide the child or adolescent with practical, self-help, problem-solving skills that can be used long after treatment termination. Anticipating problems, predicting reactions, and internalizing self-help skills are methods to achieve these goals. Insight into self often emerges, but it is not the primary aim of treatment.

Some of the earlier studies reported that initial gains were not maintained over a long period (Spence & Marzillier, 1981; Thelen, Fry, Dollinger, & Paul, 1976). But other outcome studies of antisocial children and adolescents have shown that this treatment approach significantly reduces aggression and other acting-out behavior, with older children appearing to benefit the most (Baer & Nietzel, 1991; Durlak, Furhman, & Lampman, 1991; Ollendick & Hersen, 1979).

Kazdin, Esveldt-Dawson, French, and Unis (1987a, 1987b) compared the impact of problem-solving skills training (PSST), nondirective relationship counseling, and a contact control group in inpatient children, aged 7 to 13 years. The PSST group showed significantly lower antisocial and disruptive behavior, both at home and at school. They also showed greater increases in prosocial behavior.

In a later study, Kazdin, Bass, Siegel, and Thomas (1989) compared two SST treatment conditions (25 sessions of either SST with no practice or SST with in vivo practice) and a no-treatment control for severely antisocial children, aged 7 to 13 years. He found that both treatment conditions produced behavioral improvements at home and at school, and these were maintained at a one-year follow-up. One strength of this study was that the severity of the deviant antisocial behaviors was great enough to have warranted hospitalization. Thus, the most severely antisocial children were included in the study, unlike many other outpatient studies in which the most deviant dropped out of treatment.

Chalmers and Townsend (1990) instituted a 15-session *social perspective-taking* program for delinquent adolescent females in residential treatment. Social skills were taught that included role playing of predictable problem situations. When compared with a control group in a physical fitness program, the treatment group exhibited increased prosocial behaviors, as well as significantly higher scores on measures of interpersonal problem solving, empathy, and willingness to accept differences in others.

Overall, social skills training has been effective in reducing many of the social interaction problems for which it was designed. As Kazdin (1993) pointed out, however, even with these changes, the treatment group behaviors were still outside the normal range. One reason for this is that many of these programs have included the most severely disturbed children.

FAMILY THERAPY

Functional Family Therapy (FFT), a particular type of family therapy augmented with social learning principles, has been used successfully in the treatment of 13- to 16-year-old delinquents (Alexander, 1973; Alexander, Barton, Schiavo, & Parsons, 1976; Alexander, Holtzworth-Munroe, & Jameson, 1994; Alexander & Parsons, 1973, 1982). Conceptually, problems are examined for the functions they serve, and treatment strategies incorporate PMT principles. Important components include improving content and affective communication, negotiation and problem solving, and structures that delineate the rights and responsibilities of each family member.

Parsons and Alexander (1973) reported significant gains for their modified family therapy approach compared with client-centered and psychodynamic family therapies, and a no-treatment control. At follow-up (6–18 months), the delinquency recidivism rate was about half that of the other three groups. Klein, Alexander, and Parsons (1977) found that the court referral rate for siblings was significantly lower as well over a 3-year follow-up period.

While these results are encouraging, Dumas (1989) noted that they are based on data from one set of treatment families and will need to be duplicated in other settings. Further, "This approach makes extensive use of social learning and cognitive (negotiating, problem solving) principles. While this offers a breadth usually not found in other approaches, it raises questions of treatment specificity" (p. 212). Components of a number of approaches were reflected in the program.

Using a variation of PMT, Sayger, Horne, Walker, and Passmore (1988) tested a 10-session social learning family therapy model for families with aggressive children. Significant changes occurred in the children's disruptive behaviors both at school and at home, and measures of family functioning also improved (e.g., cohesion, empathy, problem-solving effectiveness). These gains were maintained up to one year after treatment.

OTHER TREATMENT APPROACHES

Howell and Enns (1995) described a cognitive-behavioral program based on principles of *relapse prevention* (Marlatt & Gordon, 1985) that targeted high-risk adolescent juvenile offenders. These adolescents, aged

14 to 18, had been sentenced to secure custody in a behaviorally focused treatment hospital. Those who volunteered for the program were involved in multiple treatment activities, including individual and group therapy, social skills training, school, occupational therapy, and a substance abuse group. Helping the youngsters understand the chain of events, thoughts, and affective reactions that preceded their antisocial behavior and getting them to develop more functional coping strategies were major components of this high risk recognition program.

Some programs have combined treatments in unique settings. For example, Kirgin, Braukman, Atwater, and Wolf (1982) compared a *group home "teaching-family" approach* (Achievement Place) with group home treatment to juvenile delinquency. Differences were reported in favor of the "teaching-family" approach reflected by court and police files, records of criminal conduct, and the percentage of youth involved in these behaviors. Also, the greater the degree of client and teacher satisfaction with the program, the lower the rate of alleged problem behaviors.

Davidson and Wolfred (1977) evaluated a *community-based* residential behavior modification program for predelinquents. Although desired changes in behavior occurred during the program, they were not maintained at follow-up. Fleischman and Szykula (1985) reported success when they implemented a social learning treatment for aggressive children at a community family teaching center.

Some of the early interventions for antisocial youth involved streetwork programs with community gangs. These typically included group programming (dances, athletic events, etc.) and individual counseling. Klein (1969) reported that such programs often had the opposite effect than was intended. Delinquency rates went up and consisted of more high-companionship offenses especially for those aged 12 to 15 years. The programs had inadvertently increased group cohesion but had not provided alternatives to deviant group involvement. This was also found more recently in a school-based Guided-Group Interaction (GGI) program for delinquents (Gottfredson, 1987), and reported as well by Feldman (1992).

However, a large-scale study ($N = 700$) by Feldman, Caplinger, and Wodarski (1983) provided insight into the key ingredients of a successful community-based intervention program for antisocial youth (ages 8–17). Factors that were predictive of successful outcome included using experienced group leaders, ensuring heterogeneity of group composition by including both antisocial and non-antisocial youth in each group (thereby decreasing the numbers of antisocial youth in each group), offering a multiactivity program with discussion sessions, athletics, arts and crafts, and community fund raising. In addition, behavior modification proved more effective than group psychotherapy.

Another type of treatment for antisocial behavior involves placing youngsters in *environmentally challenging settings.* For example, Kelly and Baer (1971) compared recidivism rates of delinquents who had attended Outward Bound schools with those who were dealt with routinely through the court system (e.g., probation, parole). At one-year follow-up, recidivism rates were 50% lower for the Outward Bound participants, although factors such as number of court appearances, number of parents at home, number and type of offenses had an influence on outcome. The researchers recommend a physically challenging program for those teenagers who appear to be reacting to an adolescent crisis rather than for those with a history of characterological defect.

Specific techniques have also been recommended in the treatment of delinquent adolescents. These include reframing and paradoxical instruction, aimed at overcoming resistance to treatment (Kolko & Milan, 1983; Mandel, Weizmann, Millan, Greenhow, & Spiers, 1975).

Pharmacotherapy has also been used in the treatment of CD. Campbell and associates (1995) monitored the effectiveness of lithium with 52 highly aggressive and explosive CD children (mean age = 9.4 years). The medication was helpful and rated more effective than the placebo.

TREATMENT COMBINATIONS

Kazdin, Esveldt-Dawson, French, and Unis (1987a) compared a combination of SST for children aged 7 to 12 and PMT for their parents, with a control group. Children in the control and treatment groups participated in a brief inpatient hospital program. The combined treatment group showed significantly lower rates of aggression and acting-out behavior, which were maintained at a one-year follow-up. Kazdin (1992) and Kazdin, Siegel, and Bass (1992) compared the effectiveness of SST, PMT, and a combination of these treatments in 97 CD or ODD children, aged 7 to 13. Outcome at a one-year follow-up showed that the combination treatment was more effective than either approach alone.

In a more recent study, Kazdin (1995a) highlighted the importance of using different outcome measures that tap different sources of information. In a study of 105 conduct problem children (mean age = 10.3 years),

Kazdin examined the outcome of problem-solving skills training and parent management training. He found that, as predicted, more serious dysfunction within the child, in the parents, and in the family at the onset of treatment was related to poorer outcome, as measured by parents, but *not* as rated by teachers. In other words, different measures produced contradictory findings. Was treatment successful or not?

Lochman and Curry (1986) compared two forms of cognitive-behavioral treatment. The first was an interpersonal cognitive problem-solving program (anger-coping), the second was a combined approach involving anger-coping followed by self-instruction on impersonal problem solving and school tasks. Results showed that both treatment conditions significantly increased on-task classroom behavior, reduced aggression (as rated by parents), and increased self-esteem.

Dadds, Sanders, Behrens, and James (1987) described the changes that occur in parent-parent interactions during a sequential treatment program involving child management training (PMT) followed by *partner supportive training (PST)*. During PST, parents were taught to listen more and to question and provide feedback constructively. Prior to treatment and during PMT, husbands and wives engaged in negative interactions, especially while their child was disruptive. Yet, despite these aversive exchanges, most were able to utilize the trainings to implement more effective child management structures. Once PST began, the negative parent exchanges decreased and problem solving increased.

Rossman and Knesper (1976) described an inpatient program for disruptive adolescents. In the initial stages of treatment behavioral techniques and structures are used to interrupt the cycle of disruptive behavior and negative interactions with staff. As antisocial behaviors decrease, *psychodynamically oriented treatment* is offered.

Ulrici (1983) reviewed the impact of behavioral and family interventions on recidivism of juvenile delinquency. She found that studies which used only behavior modification principles changed targeted antisocial behaviors effectively but did not reduce recidivism. Family therapy in combination with behavioral intervention was successful in reducing antisocial behaviors, but "only when overall aspects of the family system were addressed" (p. 25). Either family therapy alone or in combination with behavioral interventions produced equally effective outcome.

Several programs have expanded to a broadly based multisystems approach. An example is Multisystemic therapy (MST), which focuses on home, school, peers, and community influences (Henggeler & Borduin,

1990). Economic assistance, child care, employment counseling, along with more traditional components such as marital counseling are examples of this expanded focus. In their review, Miller and Prinz (1990) concluded, "Parental implementation of child-focused interventions will be enhanced only after efforts are made to alleviate a variety of basic family needs and to strengthen a family's acquisition of resources across multiple domains" (p. 299).

Wells and Faragher (1993) reported on the outcome and 1- and 2-year follow-up results of 165 adolescents treated for 4 months in an inpatient unit for Conduct Disorder and emotional disorders. The program components consisted of individual and group therapy, art therapy, group sociodrama, and social skills training, as well as community-based activities (e.g., community meetings, camping). In addition, the teens attended an in-unit school. Overall, 74% of the adolescents who completed the program were rated as improved. Program dropouts were more likely to be female, "with a presenting history of significantly more running away, truancy, taking overdoses, aggressive and manipulative behaviour, and impulsive behaviour" (p. 351).

Short and Shapiro (1993) and Webster-Stratton (1993) independently reviewed many of these intervention approaches, especially those that targeted young behavior problem children. They concluded that early intervention both at home and at school and involving teacher, parents, community agencies, and young behavior problem children reported the greatest success.

TREATMENT MANUALS

One of the more interesting developments in the field of CD treatment is the publication of a number of program "guides." These manuals include approaches that use:

- A dynamically-oriented model (Kernberg & Chazan, 1991).
- A cognitive-behavioral model (Feindler & Ecton, 1986; Horne & Sayger, 1990; Kendall & Braswell, 1985, 1993; Padawer, Bupan, & Kendall, 1980).
- Parent training models (Barkley, 1987; Forehand & McMahon, 1981; Kozloff, 1979).

- A problem-solving model for teachers of behavior problem children (Kendall & Bartel, 1990).
- A behavioral self-management model (Brigham, 1989).
- A behavioral social skills training model (Michelson, Sugai, Wood, & Kazdin, 1983).
- A competence-based therapy for young children and their parents (Strayhorn, 1994).
- A problem-solving communication training program (Forman, 1993; Robin, Bedway, & Gilroy, 1994).
- A social skills training model (LeCroy, 1994b).
- A cognitive-behavioral anger control training model (Feindler & Guttman, 1994).
- A multimodal treatment model (Glaser & Horne, 1994).

Not only do these manuals offer valuable practical information, but they provide a greater degree of specificity about the components of treatment. This will allow others to more accurately replicate and evaluate research findings.

CHARACTERISTICS OF EFFECTIVE THERAPISTS

Are there any therapist characteristics that appear to be correlated with increased probability of success with CD children and adolescents? Although some research has been conducted in this area, the answer is based mainly on clinical impression.

It appears that an effective therapist is accessible, has a sense of self and boundaries, is willing to be informal without losing professional stance, exhibits warmth and is able to understand the client's predicaments and patterns (Persons & Peplinsky, 1966), is willing to confront dysfunctional behavioral patterns in an invitational way, is able to help the client define alternative goals to current self-defeating ones, is active and directive, is able to see through the client's manipulations (Suedfeld & Landon, 1978), and is able to set and abide by clear and reasonable limits. "Therapeutic modesty is a prerequisite . . . . Therapeutic omnipotence, even enthusiasm, may lead to severe disappointment for both patient and therapist. Some individuals do benefit from treatment; many do not" (Strasburger, 1986, p. 194).

KEY ELEMENTS IN SUCCESSFUL TREATMENT

A number of theoretical, structural, and process issues are uniquely relevant to psychotherapy with adolescent CD underachievers. If incorporated, they will increase the probability of positive outcome. The most successful outcomes come from those that incorporate the following 11 treatment principles.

1. *Intervene as Soon as Possible.* There is strong evidence that the longer treatment is delayed, especially for the childhood-onset CD type, the lower the probability of positive change. Without active and early intervention, the behavioral stability coefficient is very high (Loeber, 1982; Olweus, 1979, 1980; Reid, Baldwin, Patterson, & Dishion, 1988).

2. *Incorporate Differential Antecedents by Type.* The second principle addresses the need for differential treatment structures depending on the type (e.g., childhood-onset CD). For the antisocial disruptive *child,* intervention into family processes is indicated. For the acting-out disruptive *adolescent,* treatment must incorporate the realities of decreasing family control and increasing physical mobility, greater potential for negative peer influences, and expanded community temptations.

3. *Target Perpetuating Intrapsychic Components.* This principle involves increasing success by targeting specific components of the disorder within the individual. Dodge, Price, Bachorowski, and Newman (1990) found that those diagnosed with CD often perceive hostile intent in others, especially when the social cues are ambiguous. Examination of hostile attributions should be included in any treatment for Conduct Disorder.

4. *Target Resources and Perpetuating Systems Components.* To increase treatment success, treatment programs should integrate resources in the family, community, and peer group, as well as target perpetuating family and extrafamilial factors (e.g., dysfunctional parenting skills, depressed or antisocial parent, delinquent gang influences).

5. *Take an Active Rather than a Passive Role.* Most treatment approaches require that the change agents be active and directive, especially in the early phases of treatment. Passive therapists are seldom successful with CD adolescents or adult psychopaths (Persons & Peplinsky, 1966).

6. *Use a Multimodal Treatment Team Approach.* Because of the need to address a range of issues, successful treatments have used more than one change agent across various settings (e.g., school, mental health

practice, community organizations). This has also been found to be true in the treatment of antisocial adults where multimodal, reality-oriented, cognitive-behavioral team approaches are most often associated with better treatment outcome (Doren, 1987).

7. *Establish Focused, Practical, and Attainable Goals.* Most programs specify clear, circumscribed goals that are also practical. These goals target a decrease in disruptive behavior as well as the gradual substitution of gratifying nonaggressive prosocial behavior.

8. *Solicit Accurate and Detailed Information.* Successful treatment approaches always include accurate information. Sometimes this information can be obtained from the student or parent, but other sources of information (e.g., school reports, court records, assessment reports, etc.) should be used.

9. *Exercise Reasonable Limits to Confidentiality.* Although not explicitly stated, it appears that most successful treatment programs for disruptive youth place limits on confidentiality. Treatment effectiveness seems to be enhanced by regular sharing of developments across the "treatment team."

10. *Incorporate Structures to Increase Attendance.* Because predictions can be made about attendance problems, a number of structures have been devised to enhance attendance. These include home visits to explain the program, incentives for participation, frequent reminders about upcoming sessions, and tracking families that move frequently (Capaldi & Patterson, 1987).

11. *Use Multiple Data Sources in Outcome and Follow-up Research.* Outcome measures should generate data from the child, family members, teachers, and community sources (e.g., court and/or police records). Further, follow-up should be extended beyond the traditional 6-month or 1-year period. Research reports should also include a clear statement of attrition rates and a comparison of those who dropped out of treatment or follow-up.

SUMMARY

A number of treatment approaches and structures have been utilized with antisocial children and adolescents including individual, family, group, and residential therapies. Approaches have used dynamically oriented, behavior, and cognitively oriented therapies, social skills training, pharmacotherapy, parent management training, systems community-based programs, and various combinations of these approaches.

Overall, outcome research has shown that it is possible to decrease disruptive and problematic behavior by intervening both on parenting processes and on the student's behavior. Gains have been sustained up to one year in most studies where positive change occurred. It is also true that those children with less disruptive behaviors show the greatest and longer lasting gains and that the younger the child at time of intervention the better the long-term outcome. It also appears that simultaneous and/or sequential multiple interventions produce the best results (Brandt & Zlotnick, 1988; Dumas, 1989; Kazdin, 1985).

The treatment of Conduct Disorder has several unique aspects. To maximize outcome benefits, treatment programs must become multimodal, with teams whose members specialize in program components (e.g., SST, PMT, community agency involvement). In addition, developmentally based sequential treatment programing, focusing first on one or two areas (e.g., child management at home and maternal depression) and expanding to others when appropriate, likely will become commonplace in the future.

An important finding is that any group therapy program should consider whether to make group membership homogeneous with respect to antisocial behavior. Research findings point to the value of group heterogeneity as well as including normal children or adolescents. In addition, the issue of coed membership has yet to be researched, although a viable hypothesis would be that groups consisting of both male and female, problem and nonproblem adolescents would fare better at outcome.

Major concerns in the field include the high dropout rate from treatment, which limits generalizability of results, the scarcity of well-designed comparative studies, the heterogeneity of disorders as reflected by a range of terms used (e.g., delinquent, antisocial, conduct disorder, disruptive, aggressive), and the scarcity of long-term follow-up data. As Kazdin has pointed out (1995b), we need well-tested treatments and combinations of treatments with well-trained therapists, with specified replicable procedures using well-defined subject samples, with adequate follow-up using multiple measures.

Other unique aspects of work with Conduct Disorder include confidentiality, coordination of professionals and parents, and transference and countertransference reactions. Thus far, much of the research reviewed here has focused on home, clinic, hospital, or community-based settings. School-based programs for CD underachievers will be presented in Chapter 5. In addition, a case history that highlights many of these treatment issues will be presented in Chapter 6.

Chapter 4 includes a review of the literature on prevention studies. There is much to be learned from these programs and outcome findings.

Chapter 4

Prevention

For a number of reasons, Conduct Disorder makes an ideal target for
prevention science.

REID (1993, P. 245)

DISTINGUISHING PREVENTION FROM TREATMENT

It is Reid's (1993) contention that despite limited treatment success, we
have learned much about the risk factors, mediators, symptomatology,
and course of Conduct Disorder. Behavioral problems show up at home,
school, and in the community (e.g., with delinquent peers). Many adults
in divergent roles and responsibilities confront these problem behaviors.
As Reid has stated: "Because there is evidence for both intraindividual
and social-interactional antecedents for the disorder, it should be possible to develop and test theory-based prevention strategies that target
either individual characteristics of the child . . . or the environment . . . ,
or both" (p. 246).

Treatment programs for disruptive behavior generally have met with limited success for several reasons. The first is that many disruptive children
do not receive assistance early enough (Hawkins, Catalano, Jones, &
Fine 1987; Schweinhart, 1987; Wilson, 1987). And by the time they finally
do, behavioral patterns are well entrenched. In fact, for the childhood-onset
type, delaying intervention reduces the chances of successful clinical intervention in adolescence. Early intervention is almost always less time
consuming, less costly, and leads to more positive outcome.

Second, most treatment programs report relatively low rates of patient
compliance, reflected in poor attendance and high dropout rates. On the
other hand, most prevention programs do not report high rates of noncompliance, in part because primary prevention programs often target
infants and young children. Young mothers with at-risk children often

welcome support and their infants or toddlers are small enough to be physically controlled and psychologically influenced.

Third, to increase the chances of success, programs must address as many of the risk factors as possible. Chapter 1 contained a review of these major factors, including heredity, neuropsychology (e.g., perseveration of response), cognition (e.g., negative attributions of others' intentions), comorbidity (e.g., depression, ADHD, ODD), family characteristics (e.g., poor child-rearing and supervisory practices, marital dysfunction), delinquent peer influences, community factors (e.g., lack of attachment to community institutions), and global contributions (e.g., violence in the media). To address most of these factors requires coordination of both professionals and programs (teachers, parents, therapists, law enforcement officers, recreation club leaders, etc.). This is easier to accomplish with younger children. Comprehensive integration of organizational structures for treatment of CD in adolescence is difficult and seldom attained.

In general, however, there has been a much greater investment in treatment programs for delinquents than for the prevention of disruptive behavior. Why? First, proving the efficacy of preventive programs requires a long-term financial commitment, because often the benefits are not seen immediately. Second, it is often hard to estimate the cost-effectiveness of some prevention programs. Third, there is enormous pressure to allocate funds for treatment programs to help antisocial youngsters because they are causing major difficulties at home, at school, and in the community.

Ideally, funds should be committed for both treatment to change already entrenched behavior and prevention to decrease the incidence of the disorder. Regrettably, the political realities often demand different priorities: "My thoughts about primary prevention programs in delinquency tend to be pessimistic. Unless the larger political, organizational, economic, and social issues are addressed we will make small headway" (Leitenberg, 1986, p. 329).

Adding to the complexity of the study of prevention are the different types of prevention. *Primary prevention* targets those who, although at risk for a particular disorder, have not yet developed the problem. The goal is to forestall the disorder by targeting risk factors, thereby reducing their potential harmful effects. *Secondary prevention* targets those who have already begun to show symptoms but who have not yet developed the full-blown clinical condition.

PREVENTION PROGRAMS

Defining Outcome Criteria

One research difficulty is that effectiveness criteria are often vague and vary across studies. Partly in response to the disappointing results on delinquency prevention, the American Psychological Association established a task force in 1988 to gather information on *effective preventive programs* for many disorders across the life span (Price, Cowen, Lorion, & Ramos-McKay, 1988). Successful delinquency prevention programs had to meet a number of criteria, including adequate research design and follow-up.

Reid (1993) accurately points out that even in programs that report positive outcome in one setting, the results often do not generalize to another setting. This is most likely because not all antecedents for CD make the same contribution across all settings. Therefore, prevention programs that target single or limited factors will likely not produce the optimal preventive impact.

Several excellent reviews of prevention models and programs have appeared recently (Coie & Jacobs, 1993; Price, Cowen, Lorion, & Ramos-McKay, 1989; Reid, 1993; Zigler, Tausig, & Black, 1992). The professional community has begun to identify well-designed and successful prevention programs and uncover key elements that they share (Dryfoos, 1990). These reviewers summarized the criteria used in identifying children at risk for disruptive behavior and CD. Zigler, Tausig, and Black (1992) pointed out that the power of prediction that these criteria have lies in their interaction and not in any single factor.

This chapter will examine the structures and outcomes of a number of these programs. Frequently used effectiveness criteria in prevention studies for at-risk children and adolescents include:

- Significantly higher school attendance rates and improved behavior compared with the control group as reflected in teacher behavior ratings, school marks, school files, and so on.
- Significantly lower prevalence of antisocial behavior at home compared with the control group as reported by parents.
- Significantly lower prevalence of antisocial behavior in the community compared with the control group (e.g., lower arrest and fewer

criminal charges as reflected in court records and community reports).

* Significantly lower prevalence of self-reported antisocial behavior compared with the control group.
* Significantly lower prevalence of substance abuse compared with the control group as reported by drug testing, parent, and teacher reports.

Identifying At-Risk Children Prior to Birth

The *Family Development Research Program (FDRP)* at Syracuse University (Lally, Mangione, & Honig, 1988) targeted a group of high-risk pregnant single young women. These mothers-to-be were poor, had not completed high school, had substandard work histories, and in many cases had been arrested for a variety of offenses. Their unborn children were presumed to be at considerable risk for disruptive behavior problems.

After the program had begun, a matched control group was established. The program structure included regular and continuing assistance to both mother and child. Mothers received help with nutritional information, child-rearing education, and advice and practical suggestions about utilizing community agencies effectively. Infants received gradually increasing day care throughout the preschool years at the University Children's Center. In a 10-year follow-up, the experimental group exhibited significantly less frequent and severe delinquent behavior. In addition, the mothers who had participated in the FDRP had developed higher achievement expectations for their children and were prouder of their children's accomplishments than were the control group mothers. The researchers also examined the court costs at follow-up incurred by children in the experimental and control groups. The difference was approximately $1,800 per child (significantly lower societal cost incurred by those children in the FDRP).

A similar preventive effort, the *Yale Child Welfare Research Program (YCWRP)* was reported by Provence and Naylor (1983). Health-care professionals regularly visited the homes of poor mothers for the first 2½ years of their children's lives. As in the Syracuse Program, assistance covered health checkups and education, practical suggestions about food and shelter, and planning for both mother and child. Compared with a matched control group at the 10-year follow-up, YCWRP mothers had completed more education and most had become self-sufficient financially. They had continued to utilize community resources more than the control group mothers to their child's and their own betterment. Researchers estimated a savings of approximately $1,100 in remedial and legal services for each child per year in the prevention program.

At the University of Rochester, a *Nurse Home-Visitation Program (NHVP)* identified poor, young, or single pregnant women and provided prenatal and postnatal medical appointments and home visits by nurses for a period of 2 years following birth. Findings were similar to previous studies, with one notable addition. For those families in the NHVP, there was a significant decrease in documented child abuse and neglect (Olds, 1988; Olds, Henderson, & Tatelbaum, 1986).

Identifying At-Risk Children in the First Year of Life

Gutelius, Kirsch, MacDonald, Brooks, and McErlean (1977) reported positive results in a long-term prevention program for poor African American adolescent mothers and their infants in the Washington, DC, area. By age 6, at-risk children in the control group were involved in significantly more disruptive behavior and their mothers exhibited less effective discipline and supervision of their children than was the case for the experimental group.

Many of the basic tenets of prevention theory were embedded in the structures and programs of *Head Start.* Parents were assisted early in child-rearing practices, in dealing more effectively with community institutions, and their children were exposed to programming for cognitive, emotional, and social competence. Longitudinal studies of the impact of this preschool program point to long-term benefits, including academic success and absence of delinquent behavior (Copple, Cline, & Smith, 1987; Price et al., 1989).

The *Houston Parent-Child Development Center (HPCDC)* provided a similar 2-year preventive program for 12-month-old infants from poor Mexican American families (Johnson, 1988; Johnson & Breckenridge, 1982). In addition to the activities described in the Yale and Syracuse prevention programs (e.g., 25 home visits per year, health and parenting support, English language classes, half-day nursery during the second year), this program involved the fathers and siblings through weekend workshops. A follow-up when the children were between 8 and 11 years old (Johnson & Walker, 1987) revealed that those who had participated in the preventive program exhibited significantly less aggressive, disruptive, hostile behavior. They also showed greater consideration of others, had a significantly smaller chance of being referred for special services, and scored higher on certain cognitive skill measures.

Identifying At-Risk Children and Youth

In 1981, the *Seattle Social Development Program* was initiated (Hawkins, VonCleve, & Catalano, 1991; Hawkins & Weis, 1985). Their primary prevention model dictated a comprehensive multiprogram approach that addressed family, school, peer group, and community influences. Results have been encouraging although questions have been raised about the comparability of the control and experimental groups (Zigler et al., 1992). At-risk children from Grades 1 through 4 were enrolled in the program, and evaluated in Grade 5. Significantly lower delinquency rates were reported for the experimental group.

One prevention program is unique both because of its target population and long-term follow-up (Berrueta-Clement, Schweinhart, Barnett, Epstein, & Weikart, 1984; Berrueta-Clement, Schweinhart, Barnett, & Weikart, 1987). The program was designed by the *High/Scope Education Research Foundation* and became known as the *Perry Preschool Project.* This program targeted African American preschoolers who were at risk for school failure and intellectual retardation. Experimental and control group assignment was random. The program included up to 2 years of intensive academic stimulation, home visits by teachers and active participation by parents in monthly small group meetings. Children were followed to age 19, and the results point to better academic achievement, graduation rates, and employment levels. In addition, the experimental group produced significantly lower arrest rates and in general were charged with less serious crimes. This study will be reviewed in some detail in Chapter 5.

One of the largest early prevention studies was conducted in Canada by Cunningham, Bremner, and Boyle (1995). These researchers screened over 3,500 families and obtained teacher and parent ratings to identify youngsters at risk for disruptive behavior disorders. The outcomes of parent training were examined under two treatment conditions and a no-treatment control group: *large group community-based* versus individual clinic-based versus the controls. Because of the large sample size and participation rate, the researchers were able to ensure pretreatment equivalence across all groups. The results pointed to significantly greater behavioral improvements at home for the community-based parent training groups. The improvements were maintained at a 6-month follow-up. The cost-effectiveness analysis showed that community-based programming with 18 families/parent training group produced a sixfold savings over clinic-based individual parent training.

The *Conduct Problems Prevention Research Group* includes a number of social scientists: Karen Bierman (Pennsylvania State University), John Coie and John Lochman (Duke University), Ken Dodge (Vanderbilt University), and Mark Greenberg and Robert McMahon (University of Washington). They have developed and researched the *FAST Track Program (Families and Schools Together)*. Based on a developmental model and results from previous prevention research, the FAST Track Program develops competence in parents and at-risk children, and integrates school resources with family-based preventive interventions. Their aim is the prevention of behavioral problems, deviant peer relationships and poor academic performance. They are among the most active researchers in the field of prevention and their work has been reviewed in many sections of this manual.

J. H. Wehby, K. A. Dodge, E. Valente, and the Conduct Disorders Prevention Research Group (1993) reported the results of using direct observation of structured and unstructured activities with Grade 1 children who had been identified 15 months earlier while in kindergarten: "Results of this study suggest that children identified as high risk at kindergarten demonstrate difficulties one year later in their interactions with teachers and peers when compared to a low-risk group" (p. 67).

Lochman and the Conduct Problems Prevention Research Group (1995) reported on a screening program prior to entry into school for children with behavior problems. Multiple-gating was used, in which both teacher and parent ratings of 382 children were used in the two-step screening process: "The 2-step screening system was found to effectively predict negative behavior outcomes over 1 year later, although some false-positive and false-negative predictions were evident" (p. 549).

Shinn, Ramsey, Walker, Steiber, and O'Neill (1987) studied at-risk Grade 5 students in Oregon. These researchers used a composite antisocial score to identify at-risk subjects. Information included behavior observations in the home, interviews with the child and teacher, peer ratings, and scores on an aggression scale (based on parent and teacher ratings). The

Grade 5 control group was similar ethnically and socioeconomically. A sequential cohort research design was used; a year after the initial at-risk and control group data were collected, similar measures were used on a second distinct but demographically similar cohort. Results from both samples were consistent.

Compared with normal groups, at-risk children spent less time on academic tasks and more time involved in negative peer interactions (both initiated by at-risk children as well as aimed at them by peers), were rated by teachers as poorly skilled socially, had behavioral problem reports in their school files, and were much more likely to have been involved in special education programs. In addition, during recess normal children were much more involved in structured games and other activities. The results of this study indicate that by Grade 5, children at risk for antisocial behavior can be identified by examining their school behavior. Many researchers would claim that these children can be identified well before Grade 5.

Some prevention programs that reported early success later reported that improvement rates were not maintained at follow-up. For example, Davidson and Wolfred (1977) found that behavior modification initially produced decreases in delinquent behavior. At follow-up, however, there were no behavioral differences between the predelinquent experimental and control groups. The socially desirable changes that occurred while the children were in the program did not generalize.

Researchers at Michigan State University (Davidson, Blakely, Redner, Mitchell, & Emshoff, 1985) selected college student volunteers to meet individually for 6 to 8 hours a week for 18 weeks with a court-referred antisocial youngster who had committed crimes against people and/or property. Follow-up results 2½ years later showed a significant reduction in the recidivism rate as well as in number of police contacts.

A Canadian study targeted the *unemployment* rate among at-risk youth (Hiew & MacDonald, 1986). The assumption behind the program was that continued unemployment was a major risk factor in the development of delinquency in at-risk adolescents. Job interview skills were taught and rehearsed with the aid of videotape simulations and 2 months after securing a job group members were compared with a control group. Significant differences were obtained in favor of the experimental group. The authors emphasized the importance of practical life skills in changing delinquency probabilities.

Identifying At-Risk Siblings

Some prevention studies have targeted the *siblings of children at risk* for CD. Using a tripartite model of prevention, Klein, Alexander, and Parsons (1977) assessed the impact of treatment on the identified delinquent (38 male and 48 female delinquents, aged 13–16 years), family members, and siblings in a Utah program. *Tertiary prevention* was targeted on treatment process changes in the family, *secondary prevention* was focused on changing the delinquent's behavior, and *primary prevention* was aimed at decreasing the probability of antisocial behavior in siblings.

In a 3-year follow-up, the no-treatment control families reported a 40% rate of court contacts for siblings, whereas those families enrolled in a short-term behavioral family systems approach reported a 20% rate. Two other treatment approaches (Rogerian family and eclectic-dynamic) produced 59% and 63% sibling rates respectively). In other words, the use of a short-term behaviorally oriented family systems approach can have preventive impact for at-risk siblings.

Community-Based Prevention Programs

Single event or limited programs, such as dances, meetings, or sports events, do not have any effect on delinquency rates (O'Donnell, Manos, & Chesney-Lind, 1987). But programs that target unemployment and skills needed to enhance employability of at-risk youth do have an impact (Hiew & MacDonald, 1986; O'Donnell et al., 1987). Aside from the individual benefits of enhanced skills and self-esteem, employment programs probably also decrease the cohesiveness of deviant groups (O'Donnell et al., 1987).

The *Boys Clubs of America* implemented a delinquency prevention program for high-risk adolescents called *Target Outreach*. Individual relationships, combined with linkages to club activities and community organizations, and a data-based tracking system have resulted in 39% of participants improving their academic performance. The recidivism rate for graduates of the program as measured by reinvolvement with the juvenile justice system is only 7%.

Many other local programs target at-risk children and youth (Davidson & Redner, 1988; Feldman, 1988). The most successful provide a range of services (e.g., academic tutoring, crisis intervention, recreation). Successful prevention programs for at-risk youth all offer a stable adult relationship as a cornerstone.

KEY ELEMENTS IN EFFECTIVE
PREVENTIVE PROGRAMS

All preventive programs share a common aim: to intervene so as to change a highly probable negative developmental outcome. As the preceding review demonstrates, preventive programs have produced positive outcomes. But these benefits are not always sustained, especially in programs of short duration, narrow focus, and limited intervention. Continued intervention might enhance these benefits. But it may also be true that intervention at a critical moment in an at-risk child's life may permit early success experiences for both parent and child and may prevent or retard the development of serious antisocial behavior. The following subsections summarize the elements that the most successful prevention programs have incorporated in their structures and interventions.

Identification of At-Risk Children

The most successful prevention programs identify at-risk children early, including some programs that target the unborn. As research uncovers other at-risk mediating factors we can look forward to an improvement in the identification process and a concomitant improvement in preventive programs. A general assumption in the field is that the earlier the preventive intervention, the better the outcome. Outcomes from preventive studies and treatment of older CD underachievers support this assumption.

Multimodal Intervention Programming
(Home-, School-, and Community-Based)

Because of the many contributors to CD, all successful prevention programs have a range of goals aimed at both parents and the at-risk child. Examples include in-home medical services, child-rearing and supervision training, skills training to maximize continued use of community resources assistance by parents, and early and continuing educational programs for preschoolers focused on skill acquisition and socialization. Schorr (1988) emphasized the comprehensiveness of these programs.

Reid (1993) pointed out that because not every antecedent for CD appears in every context (e.g., home, school, or in the community), prevention programs must access all important settings to effectively address all important antecedents. He recommends that parents learn about the dysfunctional social information processing that often triggers aggressive reactions in their children as well as learn how to monitor and track their child's peer relationships.

Coie and Jacobs (1993) and Reid (1993) recommend that schools implement academic intervention for at-risk youngsters (Slaven, Karweit, & Madden, 1989) and use social skills training principles inside the classroom. And because so much disruptive behavior occurs outside the classroom but on school grounds (Olweus, 1991; Walker, Hops, & Greenwood, 1981), Reid recommends that these same principles be incorporated into recess, field trips, and so on.

Involvement of Family Members

Many successful preventive programs reach out beyond the primary caretaker to include the other parent (if appropriate) as well as other siblings. This approach not only enhances outcome for the at-risk child but may benefit the other parent and especially other at-risk siblings. Some programs have even recruited successful mother "graduates" to assist the next generation of participants.

Involvement of Stable Adult Helper

The importance of having a stable (continuing) positive adult relationship for the at-risk child cannot be overstated. Although institutional coordination is important and skills training and opportunities for success are critical, there is no substitute for the pivotal, continuing, one-to-one adult-child relationship.

Short-Term Inoculation versus Long-Term Programming

Many of the early prevention programs were time-limited. They provided multimodal programming during the child's preschool years. There is increasing support for extending these short-term inoculation programs to address the changing needs of both parent and child. An example of this is the *Head Start Transition Project*, which continues its assistance beyond preschool. "Program benefits often 'wash out' after the intervention stops. Continuity of effort is very important" (Dryfoos, 1990, p. 146).

Use of Self-Help Support Groups

The value and increasing popularity of self-help groups has been documented over the past 25 years. Several successful preventive programs encourage the formation of self-help parent support groups. Group members share learning and provide support as they address similar problems.

Shifting Focus

The emphasis in all delinquency prevention programs is always first on parent and child (the early home environment). As the at-risk child enters public school, many successful prevention programs shift to contributing factors outside the family (e.g., teachers, social services in the community, after-school clubs with positive peer interaction and appropriate adult supervision).

Integrated Use of Community Resources—Precipitating Institutional Change

All successful preventive programs actively involve community agencies and professionals, including medical and allied health workers, social service/assistance school personnel, agencies at provincial/state and federal levels, churches, and recreation clubs. Often, a secondary purpose of such integration is the precipitation of institutional change to better meet the needs of at-risk children and youth.

Longitudinal Evaluation of Program Impact

Many successful preventive programs build in both outcome and longitudinal research. Often unexpected findings point to needed additions or modifications to the programs. For example, many programs report secondary gains by participants from home visits, including a decreased sense of isolation and increased sense of self-confidence beyond the targeted learning.

THE FUTURE OF PREVENTION RESEARCH

Research has demonstrated that prevention programs work in decreasing the symptoms of Conduct Disorder. However, there is some evidence that the generalizability of gains from one environmental context (home, school, or community) to other contexts is not high. Future prevention programs should target multiple contexts, with unique programming for each context. Another solution to this cross-context obstacle is for researchers from different prevention projects to *coordinate* their efforts, each examining different aspects of complex interactions (Reid, 1993).

Coie and Jacobs (1993) do not minimize the importance of the family and the individual in preventing CD, but they emphasize the need to test interventions in the broader context. They urge the broad implementation of preventive programming in the classroom using approaches that are already available (Werthamer-Larsson, Kellam, & Wheeler, 1991). They also recommend a national network of prevention programs. The knowledge is available to implement successful prevention programs and the research tools exist to improve them. Whether there is the national will to mount an aggressive prevention program is another question.

Chapter 5

Academic Underachievement and Conduct Disorder

> Although academic dysfunction is a risk factor for subsequent conduct
> disorder, the relation is not merely unidirectional.
>
> KAZDIN (1995, P. 53)

The links between disruptive behavior and poor marks in school are well
documented (Kazdin, 1987b; McGee, Share, Moffitt, Williams, & Silva,
1988). More recently, two partially independent behavioral subtypes have
been documented: inattention and hyperactivity, and aggression-conduct
problems (Hinshaw, 1992b). In this chapter, the focus is on the literature
about underachievement in relation to Conduct Disorder. The definitions
of underachievement, contributing factors, theoretical models, types of underachievers, long-term outcome, and the unique aspects of underachievers with this disorder will be addressed.

DEFINITIONS

While all definitions of underachievement reflect the concept of a gap between a student's potential and performance, many ways have been suggested to operationalize this definition (Hinshaw, 1992a; Mandel &
Marcus, 1988). *Subjective* approaches include parent, student, and/or
teacher ratings. Opponents of these methods point to biases from these
sources.

   Objective approaches typically use a standardized measure of potential
(e.g., IQ), which is contrasted with actual performance (e.g., school marks)
to determine if the student is performing significantly below what would
be expected given that student's potential. Opponents of these approaches

point to biases inherent in measures of potential (e.g., cultural, socioeconomic). This has led to the development of IQ test alternatives that are more culture-fair. For example, a test of nonverbal reasoning, the Matrix Analogies Test (Naglieri, 1985) has been used in the study of academic underachievement.

But there are other concerns. In measuring potential, what attribute(s) should be used (e.g., verbal or nonverbal; quantitative or linguistic or athletic or artistic)? There appears to be less controversy about which academic areas to assess. For the vast majority of studies, scores in reading and/or mathematics have been used. But even here, there is some criticism about biases in grading systems that may place some students at a learning disadvantage.

There is no perfect method of defining underachievement (or achievement for that matter). Each approach has its merits and drawbacks, some more serious than others. In this text, for purposes of simplicity, academic underachievement will be defined as a *significant* gap between a student's potential (however measured) and a student's performance (however measured).

This operational definition should not be construed as an avoidance of the difficulties of definition. In fact, the way underachievement is operationally defined has major implications for prevalence rates, remediation programs, and the inclusion of some students and exclusion of others. A study is now under way to explore the academic and clinical implications of using statistically based regression formulas versus self-defined underachievement (Fraser, 1996).

An implication of defining underachievement by statistical regression equation is that a group of CD underachievers will contain students with a wide range of intellectual abilities—gifted students as well as students who are intellectually average—all of whom are performing below statistical expectation. If the findings about the protective qualities of higher IQ in outcome as mentioned in Chapter 1 are valid, then any outcome research on these underachievers should separate out gifted and nongifted students.

RISK FACTORS

Research has consistently shown that intellectual capacity contributes only about 25% of the variance to academic achievement (Mandel &

Marcus, 1988). In other words, 75% of a student's final marks are due to factors other than intelligence. These include an adequate home environment, relevant school structures and competent teachers, challenging and rewarding peer relationships, a supportive community that provides opportunities for applying school learning, and a motivated student.

There are many reasons an individual with academic ability does not perform at a level commensurate with that potential. Broadly speaking, these can be divided into four types of risk factor: short term (temporary), long term (perhaps even permanent), external, and internal. Short-term factors can be external (e.g., disagreement with parents about curfew; absence of a favorite teacher because of the teacher's short-term illness) or internal (e.g., a student gets the flu and finds it difficult to concentrate). Long-term factors can also be either internal or external. External long-term factors may include parental divorce (Bisnaire, Firestone, & Rynard, 1990), extent of parental involvement and/or employment (Williams & Radin, 1993), or transfer to a new school (Felner & Adan, 1988). Long-term internal factors could include specific learning disorders, or a personality makeup that inhibits academic performance. These risk factors are summarized in Table 5.1.

Almost any factor may be short *or* long term. For example, experimenting with marijuana may result in some decrease in grades if the experimentation is periodic or occasional. On the other hand, usage that becomes extensive and frequent may result in a permanently lowered performance. Underachievement also may be due to a combination of internal and external factors, such as family dysfunction accompanied by ADHD in the student.

Mandel and Marcus (1988) reviewed the research on personality, family, peer, and school-based variables that affect achievement. Personality variables include intelligence, self-concept, cognitive style, attention and distractibility, affective factors, and behavioral tendencies. Family variables include parental and child-rearing factors, sibling characteristics, gender influences, family relationships, socioeconomic, and cultural contributors. The impact of peers has been implicated in the achievement process.

But these relationships are not as simple as once was thought. In a study focused on cultural influences on achievement, Steinberg, Dornbusch, and Brown (1992) found that in the United States, Caucasian youngsters "benefit from the combination of authoritative parenting and peer support for achievement, whereas Hispanic youngsters suffer from a combination of

Table 5.1   Examples of CD Risk Factors in Academic Underachievement

	Short-Term Risk Factors	Long-Term Risk Factors

External Risk Factors	School transitions (e.g., from elementary to junior high)
	
	Parent ill (acute)
	
	Concerns for friend in trouble:
	   friend suspended from
	   school
		School risk factors:
		  poor teaching
		  lack of discipline code
		  school in disrepair
		Family problems:
		  dysfunctional parenting
		  parental substance abuse
		  maternal depression
		Peer problems:
		  deviant peer affiliations
		  peer rejection

Internal Risk Factors	Student ill (acute)
	
	Nutritional imbalance (acute)
	
	Substance abuse (acute)
		Comorbidity
		  learning disorders
		  ADHD
		  substance abuse (chronic)
		Personality factors

parental authoritarianism and low peer support for achievement. Among Asian-American students, peer support for academic excellence offsets the negative consequences of authoritarian parenting. Among African-American youngsters, the absence of peer support for achievement undermines the positive influence of authoritative parenting" (p. 723).

The sex of the child may also have an impact on the achievement process. In reviewing annual academic performance records, Shaw and McCuen (1960) found that underachieving males began to produce significantly lower marks by Grade 3 and the discrepancy increased with each passing year. For girls, a significant gap appeared in Grade 9, although female underachievers had actually obtained higher marks up to Grade 6 compared with an achieving female control group. "Beginning in Grade 6 Underachievers began a precipitous drop in grade-point-average and remained below the Achiever group from Grade 6 through Grade 11" (p. 107).

Teacher characteristics and educational structures such as school board size, academic expectations, behavior codes, and quantity and quality of resources have also been found to have a major impact on student performance (Coleman & Hoffer, 1987; Stevenson & Stigler, 1992). The work of these researchers has been summarized by Mandel, Marcus, and Dean (1995): "Schools that demand and enforce high standards of student conduct, regular attendance and meaningful homework each night, that offer a challenging curriculum emphasizing the core subjects of English, math, science, and history, and have a dedicated teaching staff that communicates quickly with parents about potential problems, consistently produce students with academic skills approximately two full school years ahead of schools that do not" (p. 9).

In an earlier study in England, Rutter, Maughan, Mortimore, and Ouston (1979) had reached strikingly similar conclusions. They studied the structures and functioning of 12 high schools and related these to the behavior of students. Student variables included attendance, remaining in school, frequency of delinquent behavior, and marks. Rutter et al. (1979) found that school variables associated with positive student behavior included an academically oriented curriculum, greater teacher time spent in class preparation, appreciation and reinforcement by teachers of student accomplishments, holding students responsible for their behavior, maintaining the physical condition of school facilities at a high level (e.g., keeping rooms clean, repairing furniture), willingness of teachers to make themselves available to deal with student problems, and reasonable and consistent teacher expectations for student achievement.

A student's final marks depend on the interaction among many variables. But the actual risk of the development of underachievement is determined by the interaction of risk and protective factors. For example, any one of the family risk factors already mentioned for CD increases the likelihood of academic underachievement, and when many of these coexist, the risk dramatically increases. In addition, internal comorbid factors such as a learning disability or Attention Deficit/Hyperactivity Disorder (ADHD) will increase the probability of underachievement. Yet, this increased risk can be "neutralized." One way is by enrolling the student in a school with small class size, where more supervision by the teacher occurs (see Chapter 2: Case 2). Another is by the early detection of the learning disability so that prompt special education programs can be made available.

THEORETICAL MODELS OF UNDERACHIEVEMENT

Krouse and Krouse (1981) and McCall, Evahn, and Kratzer (1992) reviewed theoretical models of underachievement. There is overlap among theories, although each tends to emphasize certain contributors more than others. Some researchers tend to look for commonalities within the underachiever group and compare these to commonalities within the achiever group. Others differentiate within the underachiever group. Westman and Bennett (1985) postulate that underachievers wish to remain dependent to avoid issues of increasing responsibility and so do poorly rather than succeed. Others emphasize interactions among contributing factors. Krouse and Krouse (1981) describe how academic skill deficits in reading combine with difficulties in self-control and emotional problems to produce poor school performance.

Whitmore (1980) proposes that gifted underachievers operate using the social psychology principle of *comparison level for alternatives* (Jones & Gerard, 1967). In essence, this theory hypothesizes that a person tends to avoid unpleasant activities and approach personally rewarding ones. For gifted underachievers, the avoidance solutions vary widely, including immersion in sports, music, and/or social activities, becoming the class clown or disrupting the class in more serious ways such as engaging in antisocial activities, blaming the teacher or the school, and acting out the anger. All the while, academic performance suffers.

A number of researchers focus on the role of *attribution* in the development of decreased motivation to achieve (Carr, Borkowski, & Maxwell, 1991). According to this *metacognitive motivational model,* achievers have come to believe that their achievement is due to their efforts, whereas underachievers have come to believe that performance is based on externally controlled factors over which they have little influence. Even when underachievers succeed, they conclude that their achievement was due to external factors, such as luck. They conclude that there is no reason to work harder because the outcome is preordained. This in turn results in more failure and lowered self-esteem and motivation.

"The oldest and most comprehensive theory is the Developmental Theory Model (Roth, Berenbaum, & Hershenson, 1967), which Mandel and Marcus (1988) recently summarized" (McCall et al., 1992, p. 32). For these researchers, the role of personality dysfunction and motivation play a key role in understanding and treating underachievement. Personality results from the sum total of a person's life experiences and as such represents the interactive culmination of individual, family, school, peer, and societal influences. Underachievement is conceptualized as a sign or behavioral symptom that may have a range of underlying causes or combination of causes. Although avoiding responsibility may be a significant causal factor for one underachiever, attentional or impulsivity issues may be more critical for another. Further, these issues can be understood within a developmental framework. And just as the needs are different at each developmental level, the treatment implication is that no single remedial approach will be effective with all underachievers.

A body of research using a combination of concepts from the Developmental Theory Model and the *DSM-III-R* and *DSM-IV* (American Psychiatric Association, 1987, 1994) has resulted in the identification and treatment of seven major personality constellations related to academic underachievement (Mandel & Mandel, 1995; Mandel & Marcus, 1988; Mandel, Marcus, & Dean, 1995; Roth, 1970). Included in this research is the recent development of an objective personality test, the Achievement Motivation Profile—AMP (Friedland et al., 1996), which can identify underachievers and differentiate among them.

And complicating the theoretical issues is another question. Do underachievers exist as a separate entity, or are they indistinguishable from low achievers? Low achievers are students who do not show a gap between their potential and performance, but who are attaining the same marks as so-called underachievers. Some preliminary research by McCall et al. (1992) has explored this issue and the results are equivocal. A current study (Fraser, 1996) is exploring this question in greater detail.

There are very few well-developed theoretical models of underachievement. Research has been focused primarily on practical issues and has largely been data-driven rather than theory-driven.

TYPES OF UNDERACHIEVERS

McCall, Evahn, and Krazter (1992) summarized types of underachievement that have been studied. These include gifted versus nongifted underachievers (Whitmore, 1980), chronic versus situational (Shaw & McCuen, 1960), hidden underachievement (Shaw & McCuen, 1960), general versus specific underachievement (Whitmore, 1980), and nonlearners versus nonproducers (Kessler, 1963).

Mandel and Mandel (1995), Mandel and Marcus (1988), and Mandel, Marcus, and Dean (1995) have emphasized differences within the underachieving group using *DSM-III-R* and *DSM-IV* classification systems (American Psychiatric Association, 1987, 1994). Types included underachievers who were struggling with chronic anxiety (Anxiety Disorder), persistent sadness (Dysthymic Disorder), combinations of continuing anxiety and sadness (Comorbid), issues of personal identity (Identity Problem), those who were rebelling by opposing authority (Oppositional Defiant Disorder), those who exhibited poor impulse control and antisocial behavior (Conduct Disorder), as well as those who did not appear to have any personal, interpersonal, or academic skill problems, but who were underachieving nonetheless (Academic Problem).

Although much of this research has focused on differences within the underachieving group, recent research has also pointed to several commonalities across diagnostically different underachiever groups. Although Mahy (1994) found that differentially diagnosed underachievers produced unique AMP patterns, they all reported low scores on the achievement and work habits scales. This finding may explain some of the confusion in the field about whether there are distinct types of underachievers. The answer may be that all types share some characteristics and simultaneously differ on other specific dimensions. It may also explain why many parents label their underachieving children as "lazy and unmotivated," even though there are major differences among underachieving children. Parents may have focused on the lack of effort, on procrastination, and on poor study habits, and reached the conclusion that such behaviors reflect laziness and a lack of motivation.

Another commonality across all underachievers was reported by Tollefson, Hsia, and Townsend (1991). Teachers from elementary, secondary and postsecondary levels were asked to report on the types of excuses that their students typically gave for academic difficulties: "Analysis of teachers' reports indicated that students were most likely to attribute their academic difficulties to external, uncontrollable factors, whereas teachers tended to believe that the 'real' reasons for students' difficulties were internal and controllable" (p. 146). Most students in academic difficulty use externalization as a method of explaining their problems, independent of whether these external forces are the causes of their academic problems.

LONG-TERM CONSEQUENCES OF UNDERACHIEVEMENT

Is underachievement in high school predictive of future problems? In a well-designed 13-year follow-up of more than 4,000 high school students, McCall, Evahn, and Kratzer (1992) compared data from achievers, low achievers, and underachievers. At follow-up, these researchers found that both male and female underachievers had obtained significantly lower level job entry positions and had advanced more slowly than achievers. Thirteen years later, they held jobs of lower status and pay than achieving students with similar IQs. Male underachievers were 50% more likely to enlist for military service and underachievers were 50% more likely to divorce compared with achievers of similar IQ. And the picture is worse for those underachievers with large academic deficits: "Underachievers whose grades were substantially below expectations (e.g., two or three grade levels) did not catch up" (McCall, Evahn, & Kratzer, 1992, p. 141).

Do any underachievers eventually catch up? The answer is yes, but only a small percentage:

> If a youngster is underachieving by only a grade or so, comes from highly educated parents, and possesses the aspirations, expectations, and self-confidence for attainment, then complete catching up is possible, but not assured. Otherwise, it seems, underachievement is a relatively permanent characteristic. (McCall et al., pp. 142–143)

Unless there are strong protective influences, the odds against catching up are high. Interestingly, McCall and colleagues (1992) also found that some outcomes for *underachievers* were similar although not identical to those for *low achievers* (no discrepancy between IQ and actual poor grades).

PATHWAYS TO UNDERACHIEVEMENT

It has been well documented that juvenile delinquents as a group produce lower IQ scores than same-aged peers. This discrepancy is much greater for verbal IQ subscores and is seen most dramatically in aggressive delinquents (Quay, 1987). Nor can these differences be explained by such factors as social class or race (Hirschi & Hindelang, 1977; Wilson & Herrnstein, 1985).

The *differential detection hypothesis* (Hinshaw, 1992b) holds:

> It is not delinquency per se but rather detection and incarceration that are associated with lowered intelligence. In other words, much of our knowledge about delinquents is derived from "captive audiences" of acting out and disruptive adolescents, who as a group have lower verbal intelligence scores. But Moffitt and Silva (1988a) found that both adjudicated

delinquents and a severity-matched group of self-reported delinquents had comparably depressed IQ scores. (Hinshaw, 1992b, p. 134)

But does underachievement predict delinquency? As early as the end of elementary school, low grades significantly increase the probability of delinquency (Brier, 1995; Loeber & Dishion, 1983). And this relationship holds in males for both system-labeled and self-reported adolescent delinquents (Dishion, Loeber, Stouthamer-Loeber, & Patterson, 1984).

One problem with this conclusion is that hyperactivity confounds the picture, and it too is predictive of underachievement and delinquency. A study by Maughan, Gray, and Rutter (1985) sheds some light on this confound. They found that *some* reading disabled elementary school underachievers who were *not* externalizers (not defiant or impulsive or disruptive or aggressive or overactive) developed delinquent behavior in adolescence. The suggestion here is that for *some* children, "School failure may predispose to acting-out behavior. As is evident, causal pathways between domains may be variegated and complex" (Hinshaw, 1992b, p. 135).

Other studies point to the key role of ADHD in the development of serious academic underachievement in Conduct Disorder (Frick et al., 1991). This latter finding is especially true for childhood-onset CD underachievers. Under certain conditions, the emergence of Conduct Disorder precedes the development of academic underachievement, while under other conditions it follows. Hinshaw et al. (1993) conclude with some wise advice: "If the multiple paths to antisocial behavior are to be understood, the field must be cognizant of differing subgroups with divergent trajectories. Variable-centered predictive research strategies are quite likely to mask such relationships" (p. 43). A subgroup worthy of future research is that of CD underachievers whose verbal IQs are at least average and whose performance IQs are less than their verbal IQs.

According to Patterson and Dishion (1985), the development of conduct problems in adolescence has its roots in ineffective parent monitoring and poor academic skills. Patterson, DeBaryshe, and Ramsey (1989) proposed a general model for the development of CD underachievement:

As a first step, ineffective parenting practices are viewed as determinants for childhood conduct disorders. As a second step, the conduct-disordered behaviors lead to academic failure and peer rejection. These dual failures lead, in turn, to increased risk for depressed mood and involvement in a deviant peer group. This third step usually occurs during later childhood and early adolescence. (p. 329)

Dishion, Patterson, Stoolmiller, and Skinner (1991) reported that academic failure and peer rejection at age 10 were highly predictive of early and continuing involvement with delinquent peers. Therefore, existence of a delinquent peer culture interacts with these two precursors (ineffective parenting and poor academic skills) to dramatically increase the likelihood of delinquent activity. These findings have been recently confirmed by Dishion, Capaldi, Spracken, and Li (1995).

In an excellent review, Hinshaw (1992b) concluded that there is considerable overlap between underachievement and Conduct Disorder, but recent evidence points to a developmental course: "In early and middle childhood, the specific link is between hyperactivity-inattention and underachievement; aggression shows overlap with learning problems during these years chiefly through its comorbidity with inattention-hyperactivity (Frick et al., 1991). Yet, by adolescence, clear links have emerged between frankly antisocial behavior and variables related to verbal deficits and underachievement" (p. 149).

So, does academic underachievement lead to disruptive, aggressive, defiant, impulsive behavior? Is the converse true? Are both true? Do other factors produce both underachievement and antisocial behavior?

Tremblay, Masse, and colleagues (1992) addressed these developmental questions in their longitudinal study:

With regard to self-reported *delinquent behavior* at age 14, results indicate that the best model for boys was a direct causal link between Grade 1 disruptive behavior and delinquent behavior. Poor school achievement was not a necessary causal factor. As for *delinquent personality,* results indicate that, for both boys and girls, poor school achievement was a necessary component of the causal path between Grade 1 disruptive behavior and age 14 delinquent personality. (p. 64)

Tremblay et al.'s findings were recently supported by Fergusson and Horwood (1995):

A number of authors have suggested that school failure may lead to increased risks of delinquency. However, an alternative explanation is that the association between school failure and delinquency may be noncausal and arise from common antecedent factors which are associated with both increased risk of academic problems and increased risks of delinquency. These factors may include early disruptive behavior patterns and early childhood IQ which may act to make children vulnerable to increased risks of early academic problems and later delinquency. (pp. 184–185)

Fergusson and Horwood (1995) generated a series of structural equation models to test the relationships among CD, ADD, early IQ, academic achievement as measured at age 8, and the subsequent development of adolescent delinquent behavior in a large sample followed for between 10 and 13 years. They found two very different developmental sequences:

- *Sequence A.* Early behavior problems (by age 8) predicted later delinquency, but were *not* predictive of academic achievement in high school.
- *Sequence B.* The presence of ADD and lower IQ (measured at age 8) were predictive of lower academic performance in high school but were *not* predictive of adolescent delinquency.

In clinical practice, children and adolescents who exhibit mild to moderate antisocial behavior are often brought for professional help by their parents, who define the presenting problem as academic underachievement. Those who exhibit severe antisocial behavior are referred because of their behavior problems. The presenting problem and reason for referral may differ in less severe and more severe CD underachievers. In addition, it is likely that those with a milder form of this disorder may very well have a different verbal-performance IQ profile than those with more severe CD. This distinction undoubtedly impacts on choice of professional service sought by the parents of children with this problem.

SCHOOL-BASED PROGRAMS

The toll that these underachievers take on their teachers and peers has been discussed by Hazler, Hoover, and Oliver (1991), Pullis (1991). In addition, Short and Shapiro (1993) and McConaughy and Skiba (1993) describe the current educational controversy about how best to deal with CD underachievers. Should they be referred to special education programs as suffering from emotional and behavior disorders, or should they be excluded because their social maladjustment disqualifies them from special education programs? Should they be involved in regular classrooms or should they spend most of their time in suspension programs or alternative schools? Short and Shapiro (1993) suggest that such underachievers must be handled within the school structure and recommend the implementation of early prevention programming. They admit that such programming should include not just the school but families and community agencies in an integrated and multilevel prevention program. They also urge school psychologists to become more proactive in setting up programs and in intervening with families of conduct-disordered underachievers.

The issue of eligibility of these students for various school programs is further complicated by the possibility of comorbidity (Forness, Kavale, & Lopez, 1993; McConaughy & Skiba, 1993). McConaughy and Skiba (1993) recommend multimethod assessment because of comorbidity. In addition, they raise the intriguing notion that intervention programs in the schools for comorbidities need to be carefully planned and informed by outcome research findings. For example, using a given intervention approach with children with comorbid conditions may help both problems, or it may alleviate one condition while exacerbating the other one. They recommend that teacher training include new information about comorbidities and review the most helpful in-class procedures.

One of the earliest programs for CD underachievers was reported by Patterson (1974). He evaluated a combination of in-home parent management training and a classroom intervention program for conduct disorder boys. Outcome demonstrated significant gains both at home and at school. Similar gains were reported in a home-school motivational approach targeting disruptive classroom behavior and discipline problems (Ayllon, Garber, & Pisor, 1975). "The procedure consisted of linking the child's daily classroom behavior to consequences provided at home by the parents" (p. 616).

Programs to assist teachers with *classroom management* of disruptive student behavior have also been developed (Hops et al., 1978; Kendall & Bartel, 1990). The RECESS program (Reprogramming Environmental Contingencies for Effective Social Skills) is a behavior management approach for dealing with aggressive and socially rejected children. It was originally designed for children in kindergarten through Grade 3, and some aspects have since been tested cross-culturally (Walker, Retana, & Gersten, 1988). For example, the CLASS program (Contingencies for Learning Academic and Social Skills) has been tested in Costa Rica. CLASS is a comprehensive behavior management package consisting of the following components: (a) a response cost point system, (b) adult praise, (c) group and individual contingencies, (d) school and home rewards, and (e) behavioral contracting procedures. These procedures are applied not just in the classroom but for all school property. Positive outcomes for those students in the program have been reported.

Success from other school-based self-management behavioral programs for disruptive adolescents has been reported by Brigham et al. (1985). Some of these programs have a preventive focus (Hawkins & Lam, 1987).

As mentioned in Chapter 4, the Perry Preschool Project is unique both because of its target population and long-term follow-up (Berrueta-Clement et al., 1984; Berrueta-Clement et al., 1987; Schweinhart, 1987; Schweinhart & Weikart, 1988; Weikart & Schweinhart, 1987, 1992). The program was designed by the *High/Scope Education Research Foundation* and targeted 3- to 4-year-old African American children at risk for school failure and intellectual retardation. Experimental and control group assignment was random. The program focused on physical, intellectual, and social development, and was based on Piagetian principles. It included up to 2 years of intensive academic stimulation, home visits by teachers and active participation by parents in monthly small group meetings.

Children were followed to age 19, and the results point to better school attendance, academic achievement, graduation rates, and employment levels. Fewer children who participated in the program were found to be mentally retarded, and fewer ended up on welfare by age 19. The girls who were enrolled in the program also reported fewer pregnancies and births when compared with the no-treatment control. In addition, the experimental group produced significantly lower arrest rates and in general were charged with less serious crimes. In other words, this school-based early intervention program had accomplished one of its main goals, the reduction of significant risk factor for Conduct Disorder. In so doing, it had decreased the degree of academic underachievement in the treatment group.

The *Seattle Social Development Project* (Hawkins et al., 1992; Hawkins, Doueck, & Lishner, 1988; Hawkins & Lishner, 1987) was specifically designed to decrease the risks for Conduct Disorder. The program had a number of components, including school-based (in classroom), family-based (PMT), community-based (career counseling), and peer focused (SST). Among other things, the school-based aspect emphasized classroom conduct, involvement with peers who did not exhibit at-risk disruptive behavior or underachievement, and structuring teacher-student interactions to enhance bonding. Follow-up findings pointed to decreased truancy, theft, and alcohol use at Grade 5 for those youngsters who had participated in the program from Grade 1 through Grade 4. A more recent 6-year follow-up report (O'Donnell, Hawkins, Catalano, Abbot, & Day, 1995) continues to demonstrate the action of protective factors from this program. Compared with the control group, the intervention group showed greater commitment to education and participated more actively and constructively in school. Female students had significantly lower substance abuse rates and male students showed significantly better work habits and social skills than the control group students.

A number of programs have targeted *bullying* behavior in elementary school students, under the assumption that if unchecked, such behavior would lead to increased aggression and peer rejection, making the bully more prone to Conduct Disorder and underachievement (Pepler & Slaby, 1994). One such program is the *Earlscourt Social Skills Group Program (ESSGP)* in Toronto, Canada. It included school-based intervention for bullying behavior in aggressive youngsters (Pepler & Craig, 1993; Pepler, Craig, & Roberts, 1995; Pepler, King, & Byrd, 1991) as part of a multiple systems approach: "Eight basic skills are taught: Problem-solving, knowing your feelings, listening, following instructions, joining in, using self-control, responding to teasing, and keeping out of fights" (Pepler, Craig, & Roberts, 1995). The learning process in the classroom is also a target of this program through structures that enhance the generalization of social skills training (e.g., homework assignments, teacher involvement, teaching social skills to all students). In addition, parent management skills are enhanced through parent groups. At the end of the program, "a substantial proportion of the aggressive children were no longer rejected by peers and they were rated as less disliked by peers following social skills training" (Pepler, Craig, & Roberts, 1995).

Other school-based antibullying programs have also been reported (Pepler, Craig, Ziegler, & Charach, 1993, in press). To maximize effectiveness, these programs incorporate schoolwide implementation of an antibullying program, in-class focus on the issue for all students, parent involvement, and the targeting of aggressive students who bully their peers. More recently, there has been increasing concern about female CD underachievers, especially about the degree of aggression that many of these prepubescent and adolescent girls show (Pepler, 1995).

A nationwide antibullying and antiaggression program anchored in the schools of Norway was recently reported by Olweus (1991). Rules were developed to provide and enforce behavioral guidelines for unacceptable bullying and aggressive behavior in students. One aspect of these guidelines included active support for those children who had been targets of bullies. Parents were also informed of the purposes and structures of the program. Olweus reported at a 2-year follow-up that not only had bullying behavior been reduced by approximately 50%, but that other CD-related behaviors had also significantly decreased, including truancy, destruction of property, and theft.

In a review of the treatment of comorbid conditions involving academic underachievement, attention deficits, and aggression, Hinshaw (1992a) concluded: "Reducing problem behavior is not a sufficient intervention for youngsters with overlapping achievement and behavior problems; the promotion of academic success is critical for these children" (p. 899). He also concluded that academic programs that include extrinsic motivators, especially in the early phases, will increase their effectiveness. Direct intervention aimed at academic skill gaps in conjunction with treatment for disruptive behavior maximizes benefits.

SCHOOL STRUCTURES FOR CD UNDERACHIEVERS

Early research findings pointed to a relationship among school structures, achievement, and increased probability of delinquency (Elliott & Voss, 1974; Hirschi, 1969). Some school-based prevention programs have modified school structures to decrease delinquency rates (Kimbrough, 1985). Most of these changes are based on an assumption that greater attachment to school as an institution will decrease delinquency rates. Increased attachment is accomplished in a variety of ways:

- *Smaller class and/or school size,* or the setting up of a school-within-a-school to increase intimacy within a larger setting (Garbarino, 1980).
- *Interactive teaching* where performance is directly tied to small incremental rewards (Brophy, 1979).
- *Proactive management* by teachers to seek out problems in their early stages (Brophy, 1979).

- *Student team learning,* including older students teaching younger ones (Slavin, 1979; Slavin et al., 1989).
- *Greater student involvement* in classroom rules and discipline procedures (Wall, Hawkins, Lishner, & Fraser, 1981).
- *Experiential prevocational training* (Wall et al., 1981).
- Creation of a *supportive link* between front-line teachers and the school administration (Wall et al., 1981).
- Parent-training for *home-based teaching and monitoring* of schoolwork (Wall et al., 1981).
- *School Transitions Environmental Program (STEP)* (Felner & Adan, 1988).

Felner and Adan (1988) observed that changing schools, for example as part of a natural transition from elementary to junior high school, can trigger changes in achievement as well as create conditions for the reemergence of problem behavior in at-risk children. They developed the School Transitions Environmental Program (STEP) for minority students from poor socioeconomic families. STEP was designed to decrease the likelihood that school transitions would increase risk factors for these at-risk children. The two major components of STEP were (a) ensuring that the transition students would be connected with a developmentally stable peer group in the new school; and (b) assigning one teacher the multiple roles of administrator, counselor, parent contact, and academic resource, which ensured effective communication and allowed the transition student to bond quickly with an adult who could assist in "navigating" the new school systems. Those in the control group showed increased attendance problems, dropout rates, and placement in special education programs, and decreased marks when compared with the STEP students. Felner and Adan (1988) have extended this initial work to many other school settings and report similar positive results.

It is Kimbrough's opinion (1985) that positive outcomes in school-based prevention programs usually can be traced to two factors. The first is cooperative team learning practices, which appear to impact on achievement. The problem-solving components of the programs tend to decrease disruptive behavior. If supported by further research, the implication is that school-based delinquency prevention programs must incorporate changes in teaching methods (e.g., team learning) as well as provide youngsters with the cognitive and social skills necessary to implement changes in behavior, including academic achievement.

In addition, school-based crime prevention programs, including police in teaching roles and community youth development programs, have produced some positive results (Colorado Juvenile Justice and Delinquency Prevention Council, 1987). In general, the extent to which any of these programs impact on delinquency rates will depend on the degree to which the programs integrate school changes with family, peer, and community resources.

The *Positive Action through Holistic Education (PATHE)* program in North Carolina targeted both middle and high schools (Kimbrough, 1985). Staff, teachers, parents, and student representatives participated in decisions about policy and discipline. Team teaching by students was also organized. Interestingly, greater positive results emerged in the middle schools, where there were significant reductions in delinquency and suspensions. Perhaps there is a critical period when cooperative policy management and student team teaching have maximum impact on delinquency rates.

Programs for alternative schools (not simply alternative school programs) have been created to prevent delinquency. Gottfredson, Gottfredson, and Cook (1983) reviewed 17 of these alternative programs situated in high crime areas. The philosophy of these alternative programs was to encourage academic learning, while helping at-risk youngsters learn and practice prosocial skills: "The most successful programs had some of the following components: individual attention, peer counseling, cooperative arrangements between administrators and teachers, and intensity" (Dryfoos, 1990, p. 139).

Gold and Mann (1984) studied high-risk Grade 10 students in schools that served youth with disruptive and delinquent propensities. School structures were modified to encourage closer teacher-student relationships and more individual attention was provided. Most important, teaching staff commitment was high and turnover low. Gold and Mann report significant decreases in delinquent behavior in school, but not in the community. Perhaps by the middle of high school, the positive outcomes in a school-base program will not be enough to generalize to the larger community.

One school-based mental health prevention program has been ongoing for over 30 years: the *Primary Mental Health Project* (Kazdin, 1987b). At-risk young children (kindergarten to Grade 3) were identified by teachers. These children met regularly either in individual or small group training sessions with paraprofessionals. Recognition and understanding of affect and the importance of self-control were the main focus of these "training" sessions. Long-term outcome results clearly demonstrated decreased antisocial behavior among shy and withdrawn at-risk students. However, results have not been as positive among at-risk highly aggressive children.

A disconcerting study was reported by Henggeler (1989). Peer group counseling formed the basis for an approach entitled *Guided Group Interaction*. Even though the frequent group discussions consisted of confrontation of dysfunctional behavior and reward for positive actions, the negative influence of the high-risk peers dominated the results. This homogeneity of group composition has been raised before as an important contraindication for treatment.

Dryfoos concluded: "Current school practices found *not* to be effective in changing school misbehavior include suspension, detention, expulsion, security guards, and corporal punishment. Interventions of any kind that were exclusively concentrated on delinquents increased contact between like peers and increased delinquency" (Dryfoos, 1990, p. 146). The pervasive power of a deviant peer group can only be countered through integrating a range of structures, professionals, and programs. The school can play its part, but it must be part of a larger partnership involving family and community resources.

FUTURE RESEARCH

In some situations, academic underachievement precedes the development of Conduct Disorder, while in others it is a consequence of the development of the disorder. Many home, school, peer, and community factors impact the achievement process. Effective programs for these underachievers contain school-, home-, and community-based intervention components.

Research studies have tended to identify CD students without subdividing them according to severity of diagnostic criteria. Nor have researchers systematically identified in their sample descriptions the verbal versus nonverbal intellectual attributes in enough detail. They must begin to do so routinely and examine developmental pathways, risk and protective factors, response to treatment, and long-term outcome.

What about those underachievers who meet the diagnostic criteria at the less severe end of the behavioral continuum? How might they differ from those at the other end of the spectrum? They probably fit several of the following characteristics:

- Because they qualify for CD diagnosis based on less severe criteria, they are probably perceived by their teachers and parents as underachievers who happen to exhibit behavioral and impulse problems (CD underachievers), rather than as CDs who happen to be underachieving. Consequently, school personnel have probably not yet given up on the student, nor has the student necessarily been removed from the school system.
- They often have the requisite intellectual capacity to do much better, including at least average verbal intellect, which may act to increase teacher investment in them.
- Many have verbal scores on intelligence tests that are higher—often significantly higher—than their performance scores. This is in marked contrast to many of the research samples of Conduct Disorders in which significantly higher performance scores have routinely been reported.
- Frequently, they are fortunate enough to come from families and/or live in communities in which protective factors may decrease or at least delay the impact of risk factors. Some may be attending private schools, with low class size and closer teacher supervision. Others may live in communities where seriously deviant subcultures are small in number or more difficult to access. Still others may come from families in which the level of dysfunction and parental discord are less severe. In addition, family resources may act as a protective factor at least for a significant period, by shielding the youngster from more serious legal consequences of illegal activity.

In essence, the preceding characteristics provide for an expansion of the study of underachievement and Conduct Disorder. Most research has focused on youngsters from relatively "captive audiences" (e.g., mental health clinics, residential treatment, correctional facilities), where verbal IQ was almost always lower than performance IQ. "Studying multiple levels of a proposed risk factor is important to reveal the function (or relation) in a more finely grained fashion than the study of two groups (e.g., having the presence or absence of a particular characteristic)" (Kazdin, 1995b, p. 131).

Kazdin (1995b) discussed a number of important research issues as they pertain to the study of this disorder. He too highlighted the issue of heterogeneity within the *DSM-IV* CD diagnosis and the need for greater specificity in research. In addition, he also suggests expansion of the variables under study, to include among other factors, extent of prosocial functioning and intelligence levels. It appears possible to generate what Kazdin called a profile, and not just simply diagnose according to *DSM-IV* criteria. "For example, individuals can be assessed on a variety of domains such as parent and family functioning, peer relations, and neighborhoods. From the information, one might construct profiles of each case across multiple domains of their lives" (p. 126). This approach is illustrated with the two case histories in Chapter 2.

These same questions arise for female CD underachievers, and the answers will determine whether the same interaction of risk and protective factors produces similar outcomes. There is little information about the role of culture in this mix, although Steinberg, Dornbusch, and Brown (1992) have presented intriguing work.

One group which has received little attention is gifted CD underachievers. Are prevalence rates and sex ratios for gifted CD underachievers the same as for nongifted CD underachievers? Does giftedness influence the risk and protective factors that have already been identified for nongifted CD underachievers? Are the critical treatment components similar for gifted and nongifted CD underachievers? Initial findings in an ongoing study by Lacasse (in press) point to significant differences in prevalence rates in the two groups.

The next chapter includes the case history of a boy with childhood-onset CD underachievement. It will illustrate individual cognitively oriented treatment, will highlight many of the issues already raised, and will address critical treatment issues not yet discussed.

Chapter 6

Individual Cognitive Therapy
of CD Underachievers

> For therapy to be successful, the therapist must understand and be
> comfortable with the treatment of severe narcissism, which is both
> fragile and resilient.
>
> REID (1985)

As mentioned in Chapter 3, research points to multimodal team approaches as the most successful treatment for Conduct Disorder. These include parent management training (PMT), problem-solving skills training (PSST), school involvement, and peer group manipulation. In this chapter, an individual cognitively oriented approach is described that will provide a framework for treatment with these underachievers.

A number of treatment models of change have been proposed (Beitman, 1987; Prochaska, DiClemente, & Norcross, 1992). The approach in this chapter is adapted from a *four-stage therapy model* developed by Beitman (1987). As in any model, the four stages provide a guide to unfolding issues. In this model, the stages are Engagement, Identifying and Exploring Patterns, Change, and Termination. In practice, issues that appear in one stage may reappear in another, sometimes changed, sometimes not, because change evolves more in a spiral rather than in a lockstep linear fashion.

This cognitive therapy is predicated on a number of *assumptions:*

- A CD underachiever's automatic thoughts and actions provide clues about his or her maladaptive belief system.
- These automatic and maladaptive thoughts occur both in relation to school tasks and interpersonal relationships.
- These automatic and maladaptive thoughts trigger maladaptive behavior.

- Exploring the belief system provides an opportunity for change.
- CD underachievers can be taught to observe their maladaptive thoughts and actions (cognitive "crap detection").
- Behavioral alternatives are possible only when the dysfunctional cognitions are exposed.
- Cognitive "crap detection" can be practiced by the student during treatment and used long after treatment termination.
- Aside from the focus on cognitions, changes in therapy occur primarily because of the quality of the therapist-student relationship.

The *targets* of treatment are *academic underachievement* and *dysfunctional relationships*. Most CD underachievers discount the importance of the first problem and deny responsibility for the second. The goal of therapy is to confront each of these issues to increase the probability of change.

The stages of therapy will be elucidated through the use of extensive verbatim transcripts, liberally sprinkled with commentary. The reader will be drawn into the session-by-session variations and in this way will gain an appreciation of the issues, processes, successes, and missed opportunities. Several demographic identifiers have been changed, but the issues have not.

INDIVIDUAL COGNITIVE THERAPY: A CASE HISTORY

Stage 1. Engagement

Beitman (1987) listed a number of issues that must be addressed in the engagement stage, including trust, credibility, contracting, and motivation for change. In addition, it is important for student and therapist to develop reasonable and attainable treatment goals.

Fostering Trust

How does a therapist foster trust and gain credibility especially when most CD underachievers enter treatment because of pressure from others (e.g., family members, school, and/or the courts)? Unlike adults, these underachievers do not have to maintain a pretense of wanting to change. Some refuse to attend. In such cases, the therapist can act as a consultant to the parents, advising them on why and where to draw the line, how to shield other siblings from negative fallout, and how to protect family resources.

The primary responsibility for *attendance* lies with the parent, especially in the first session. But there are ways a therapist can increase the probability of continued attendance. For example, the therapist can tell the underachiever toward the end of the first session that the student's behavior is highly predictable but sadly self-defeating. The therapist can also suggest that there are less self-defeating ways of getting what the student wants, but for that to happen, further discussion would be necessary. If nothing else, this will raise the student's curiosity and tap into his or her enjoyment of interpersonal challenges. "This is accomplished in either or both of two ways: (1) through setting oneself up as someone the psychopath wishes to manipulate, or (2) by early confrontation of the client's verbalizations and behavior, with the idea of being perceived as playing verbal games that the psychopath will want to win" (Doren, 1987, p. 159).

Addressing Resistance and Passing Student "Tests"

Most CD underachievers wait for the therapist to raise issues. But some may be insulting, demeaning, and/or provocative early in treatment. This initial *passive* or *active resistance* poses a problem during the engagement stage. An example of such an exchange is contained in the following transcript of a bright 13-year-old. As before, *I* refers to the Interviewer and *S* to the Student:

S: You know, we've been talking about this shit too long. You're just like all the others my mom's taken me to. How's this going to help me?

I: You know Tom, you act like you don't want to be here.

S: You can bet on that, Jack!

I: Well, I don't want you to be here when you don't want to be here. So let's spend a few more minutes talking about this, and then if you want to leave, that'll be fine. I really don't want you to be unhappy.

S: Okay, but make it fast. *(Comment: Notice how it is still the therapist's responsibility to "fix" things for Tom.)*

I: It's just that you seem to keep getting yourself into jams, you seem to be shafting yourself on a regular basis.

S: *(Looks somewhat more interested)* If you mean that all the teachers in the school have branded me with a reputation, and no matter what I do I'm going to get it, you're damn right!

I: Well, that may be totally true and it may not be totally true.

S: You calling me a liar? *(Comment: A direct challenge—and a potential trap.)*

I: I'm saying I don't know the whole story and I probably never will.

S: But I can give you the whole story.

I: Actually Tom, you've missed the point.

S: What point? There was no point to this!

I: Actually, there is. And it's simple.

S: Shoot.

I: The point is that whatever the story or however it goes, you end up getting shafted. Now, if you want to keep getting shafted, we don't need to ever meet again. You're the expert on it.

S: Now who in their right mind would want to get shafted? I don't want to, but it's the teachers—they're out to get me.

I: As I said, maybe they are and maybe they're not. I just want to know if you would like things to change for you.

S: Damn straight I would.

I: We could spend this time trying to figure out ways for you to stop getting shafted and even get some of the things you want. Or, you could walk out of here now and keep on doing exactly what you've been doing, and I'll be able to tell your mother exactly what to expect in the future. The choice is yours!

S: Well, I'll stick with it a little while longer—today.

I: Okay, but you can leave at any time. Just remember—getting shafted is the key to all of this.

Although seemingly paradoxical, the therapist's willingness to say "good-bye" to the CD underachiever increases the chances of regular attendance. But why? The answer lies in an understanding of issues of control and transference reactions.

Transference Reactions

To some extent, the student's intimidation and manipulation are predicated on the assumption that the therapist, because of a strong commitment to provide help, will put up with a lot. Youngsters with Conduct Disorder perceive adults, especially those in the helping professions, as either targets to be manipulated ("patsies") or as threats to be avoided ("enemies"). They judge adults as either being for them or against them and have specific operational definitions for each of these conditions.

In the preceding exchange, Tom tested whether the therapist was his patsy or his enemy. But the therapist refused to be pegged at either extreme and in so doing expanded relationship options. He did *not* take the initial confrontation personally and hinted at a constructive "escape" from a self-defeating cycle, all the while leaving the decision (control) about attendance in the student's hands.

A predictable reaction of CD underachievers *(transference)* is their denial of the importance and/or value of education. They explicitly discount school, partly as a defense against increasing academic inadequacy and partly as a way of discounting the therapist's credentials. Understanding the CD underachiever's need to disparage the accomplishments of others while not taking the attacks personally will foster the therapeutic relationship.

Confidentiality

Most therapists would limit confidentiality for situations of self-harm or harm to others. For CD underachievers, the limits should be even wider because they have a tendency to report selectively, making it difficult to gain an accurate perspective. And because the disruptive behaviors occur at home, in school, and in the community, it is important that the therapist be informed about any changes across these settings from a number of adults. The structure of limited confidentiality conveys an important message to the student: Although responsibility for divulging material rests with the student, the therapist is part of a larger entity called "the team." Explicit limits to confidentiality are needed more for these students than for any other type of underachiever (Mandel & Mandel, 1995; Mandel & Marcus, 1988).

The following therapy excerpt reflects *contracting about confidentiality* with Steven, a 14-year-old male CD underachiever:

I: So, as I've said, I cannot promise you that I will keep everything we talk about just between you and me. First, if you are about to do something that will harm someone else or harm yourself, I will inform others. I will take some action to stop you. I will try to tell you in advance that that's what I'm about to do, but I may not always be able to get ahold of you. Do you understand what I mean?

S: *(Looking somewhat disconcerted)* Ya. But you don't need to worry about me harming myself. Not a chance!

I: I didn't think so but I did have to say it.

S: Ya, okay, but what if I know something that's really important, that you'd really want to know, but I decide not to tell you?

I: That's your choice. You can tell me or not tell me. Just know that if you tell me I may decide that it is important enough for other members of the team to hear about it.

S: What team?

I: That includes me, your parents, your teachers, the vice-principal and any other adult who is trying to help you. Now, for most things I won't need to tell people much of anything. But you know that I will be talking to some of these people from time to time and probably getting together too, although not as often. They'll probably be talking to me too if they need to.

S: Do I have any choice about this?

I: Good question. Actually you do.

S: Well, I don't see any!

I: You can decide to keep things to yourself. You probably won't get much out of these sessions, but that's your choice. So, if there's anything like what I've just mentioned that you might consider talking about, you have two choices.

S: Right. Either don't talk about it . . .

I: Right, or decide to talk about it, knowing that I may not be able to keep it confidential.

S: You really mean that I can just decide to clam up?

I: Sure. It's your choice. But if you decide to do that and there doesn't seem to be any point to meeting because we're really not talking about anything important, then I'll suggest to you and your parents that we not continue to meet.

S: Oh, so that's how it is—I talk or we stop meeting.

I: You know, you always put things in either/or terms.

S: Well, that's what you just said—either I talk or we don't meet.

I: What I said was that if you decided not to talk about anything important—like your problems in school or with your friends—then there's really no reason to meet.

S: So I can keep some things to myself.

I: I bet you will anyway.

S: You know it!

This is a fairly typical exchange for a CD underachiever. Most participate actively in "negotiations," searching for contract loopholes and therapist inconsistencies. Notice how Steven had already begun to test the therapist by alluding to important information while withholding the details.

But isn't this approach to confidentiality counterproductive? Wouldn't CD underachievers simply decide to "clam up"? Why would they tell any therapist about their more serious acting out? In almost all cases except for the most severe, CD underachievers can't wait to tell the therapist about their exploits. Their secrets emerge because they enjoy both impressing and intimidating the therapist with details of their "accomplishments." They are so trapped by their narcissism and need to impress others with their exploits and "scams" that they will generally be hard pressed to keep silent.

Countertransference Reactions

So far, this discussion has focused on predictable reactions of students in the engagement stage. What about predictable therapist *countertransference* reactions? Although many similar reactions can occur with other types of clients, the reactions generated in working with CD underachievers are usually felt intensely by therapists and may be experienced at any stage of treatment. Strasburger (1986) has summarized the most common countertransferences:

- Fear of assault or harm (due to stated or subtle hints).
- Fears of legal involvement (because of antisocial behavior, the likelihood of appearing in court as a witness is higher).
- Loss of professional self-worth and increasing sense of helplessness (e.g., about student's lack of improvement and escalating behavior).
- Sense of guilt (e.g., about having to take action against the student).
- Denial (e.g., minimizing the danger when it's really there).
- Rejection of the student (e.g., can be either overt, by acting so that student will terminate, or more subtle, such as resisting investment in the therapeutic relationship).
- Fear of rejection by the student (e.g., deciding not to take action because of an implied threat by the student to end the relationship).
- Hatred (generated because of constant client disdain of people).
- Anger (e.g., at having been manipulated or at having invested more than the client in the relationship).

The phenomenon of countertransference was originally viewed pejoratively; it was an aberration in the therapist, something basically wrong that had to be overcome. Current therapeutic technique, however, involves use of countertransference reactions as a part of the treatment rather than just things to be overcome. (Strasburger, 1986, p. 196)

King (1976) discussed a typical polar countertransference reaction in therapists of violence-prone youth: the desire to reject and/or punish, countered by identification with and the need to appease and rescue. King portrayed this as a constant battle in the therapist: "What he must guard constantly against are the twin lures in the dyad-system: attraction to unbridled power and helpless rejection in capitulation to an intransigent force" (p. 46). King also discussed a parallel reaction, what he termed the "counter-experience," triggered in teachers who have a violence-prone student in the classroom.

In addressing countertransference reactions in therapists dealing with adult antisocial personality disorder patients, Reid (1985) stated: "The therapist's feelings will vary with different patients' needs and with stages of treatment, but will include impulses to rescue, support, hurt, admire, identify with, or accept compliments from the patient" (p. 835). Antisocial children and youth trigger similar intense, often polar countertransference reactions in the therapist. These attractions and repulsions are both predictable and invaluable sources of information about oneself as a therapist and about the extent of the child's problems. "Being manipulated by a psychopathic client means that you have a potentially successful therapy in progress. The client is involved enough with you to have invested energy into your relationship. In so doing, he has exhibited his psychopathology" (Doren, 1987, p. 176).

Many therapists also report a sense of fascination with the tales spun by CD underachievers. The stories from such clients often have an outrageous and fascinating quality. Some shared enjoyment is reasonable, but it should never involve colluding with the client in the joy of having used others and it should not be mistaken for the real work that needs to be done in treatment.

Excessive identification with the client and unreasonable advocacy on behalf of the client in his or her battles against society are often signs that therapist wants more for the client than the client may want for him- or herself. The therapist has then become overinvested in a particular outcome. Most bright antisocial adolescents are quick to sense this and may use it to control the course of treatment.

Arguing over facts is another sign that therapist reactions have become counterproductive. In most situations, all the facts will never be known, partly because they may only be known by the student. Rarely is the treatment goal to get all the facts. The goal is to determine whether the pattern of dysfunctional behavior has again had negative personal consequences for the client (and others), and whether the client is interested in changing this outcome. "Rather the therapist should consistently focus on what the client could do that would likely be effective and useful in obtaining what he wants without destructive outcomes, and then 'challenge' all of the rationalizations the client has for maintaining his current set of behaviors" (Doren, 1987, p. 166).

From a countertransference perspective, the therapist will have to guard against manipulation or intimidation, but must also *not* permit this vigilance to interfere with opportunities for genuine involvement. The therapist will be confronted repeatedly by student actions and attitudes that are dramatically different from his or her own. This will produce polar reactions in the therapist—an intense desire to get the client to change versus tendencies to negatively judge and reject the client.

Confronting Motivation for Change

Most CD underachievers do not initiate discussions about their academic performance. They may focus on prejudices of teachers or school rules but will avoid issues of personal responsibility. How then does a therapist *confront the motivation* of these students? By raising the issue in a specific way. The following exchange was taken from an early therapy session with a 17-year-old CD underachiever named Tony who claimed he wanted to become a police officer:

S: Yeah. The only thing the police academy looks at really is my final senior year average.

I: Assuming that that's true, how are you going to do in spelling and grammar in English?

S: *(Laughs)* It'll have to be good in my senior high year.

I: Considering that you don't know how the hell you're doing now?

S: Yeah, that's a problem isn't it?

I: Not for me!

S: *(Laughs)* Oh, shit, yeah. I'll think of something when I have to.

I: Okay, so let's carve out the actual prediction about what's going to happen. You're going to hit your senior high year and you're going to be able to pull it together just like that. You're spelling is going to go up just like that *(snaps fingers)*. You're grammar is going to go just like that *(snaps fingers)*. And you're going to knock off grades just like that *(snaps fingers)*.

S: If I work now, yeah. If I do it just like that *(snaps fingers)*, fuck, no.

I: I agree. And you know something—I don't care if you do any more work than you're doing now, I really don't. *(Student looks surprised.)* Your mother cares, some teachers probably do, but I don't. All I'm interested in is shrinking the *crap gap* between what you say and what you do.

S: *(Grins)* Mm hm.

I: Okay. So, what you're telling me is very clear. Your senior year is going to be critical for you. I assume that means you plan to simply shift gears at the beginning of that year.

S: Right.

I: And you would like me to believe that your spelling and grammar problems, your math problems, and your behavior problems will all just disappear once you make up your mind to change.

S: *(Pauses, and smiles)* I doubt it. I don't think so.

I: Not unless you have some system.

S: Yeah. *(Laughs)* Which is called w . . . , wo . . . , wor. . . , work!

I: You got it. It's that ugly word again.

S: Yeah.

I: Okay. So, maybe you will be a police officer and maybe you won't.

S: Yeah.

I: And if you aren't, no big deal.

S: If not, I'll sell my dad's shop, which I'll inherit, for big bucks.

I: Okay. So there's no problem then?

S: Not really, no.

I: So in other words your life is going to be okay, no matter what.

S: Pretty much so, yeah.

I: Okay. So what you're saying basically is there are two reasons you aren't doing that much schoolwork right now. One, because you are not really that crazy about becoming a police officer. And two, because you're not really worried about your future. Your dad is going to take care of you.

S: Right.

I: So you've got a definite plan and you're following it.

S: *(Smiles)* And I'm getting away with it too, Harv.

I: And I don't see anything wrong with that, except for one thing: You're bullshitting other people. The only way that you can keep this whole thing going is to pretend.

S: Yeah.

I: Well, I've got two reactions to this. First, if you want to continue carrying out the plan, I think it's your choice. However, second, I have a choice too.

S: What do you mean?

I: Whether to continue seeing you and becoming part of the bullshit!

S: *(Smiles, and then frowns)* What do you mean, exactly?

I: What I mean is that I have a choice—to continue seeing you, knowing what your plan is. Your mom, dad, and the teachers all think you're getting professional help in counseling, when that's totally untrue. So the other choice for me is to tell your parents that I think you have a plan, that you're carrying it out, and that you don't plan to change.

S: Yeah, I see what you're getting at.

I: Okay. So there are no problems, and if there are no problems, why are *we* meeting?

S: *(Laughs)* Because I'm doing bad in school.

I: But that's not something *you* want to change. That's not a problem for you. It's a problem for your mother, for some of your teachers, but it's not a problem for you. Why don't *we* tell your mom and dad that you don't need to see me because you've decided either that you have no problems or that you really don't want to change. I'm not suggesting that we do it, I'm just proposing it, okay?

S: Cause then they'd say why.

I: And what would *we* say? What answer could we come up with?

S: Give me overnight and I'd come up with another con, but we can't go ahead and tell them the truth. That would fuck up all my plans.

I: So what are we going to do? If there's no problem and if there's nothing to work on, then why are we here? *(Tony laughs. The therapist* *assumes the client's voice)* "Harv, there's a very good reason, because you are now part of the con!"

S: *(Laughs)* That's right, every con has a different angle.

I: *(Assuming the client's voice)* "Harv, there's only one reason why I'm coming here."

S: Besides the coffee? *(Laughs)*

I: *(Laughs)* And besides the humor and challenge. The reason you keep coming here is very simple—other people will think you're trying to change.

S: Yup, that's the con.

I: That's right. And the only difference is that we're talking about it.

S: Shit, yeah, that throws a new light on things . . . . Well, I never really thought about it like that, like, my cons just come subconsciously.

I: That's because you're so polished! You are so smooth it's unreal! *(Laughs)* I am dealing with a black belt in con-artistry.

S: *(Beams)* Yeah, I guess that's exactly right.

I: And that's been your system and it's been there for a long time.

S: And it's worked!

I: Correct.

S: And even when it's failed, another scam covers it up again. Jesus Christ, this is fucking scary! *(Laughs)*

I: If you want that package, man, you got it. Don't change one thing. You have perfected the system.

S: *(Laughs)* Patent it, sell it. Tony's School of Con-Artistry is now open for applications. *(Laughs)*

I: Yeah. But what's the danger? Why would it scare you?

S: Whew. Because I never thought about it that way. *(Pauses; looks pensive).* So, I've not only been running the greatest con, I've been conning the con artist. I'm the world's only double con.

I: Yeah, you had two jobs. The first was on the world and that you've done with a certain amount of class and polish. But you also had to make sure not to spend any time thinking about it.

S: *(Laughs)* Yeah, then morals take over once again.

I: You've got it. Because if you actually slow down, there might be some things that you would begin to take a look at that you haven't till now.

S: *(Looking serious)* Like what?

I: *(Looks at his watch)* Oh, I see that our time is up for today. I'm not sure if we should meet next week.

S: I think we should. We need to discuss this more.

I: I expect that the next time we get together, you will have wiped all that we've talked about out of your memory bank.

S: *(Laughs)* You never know. Okay, until next week.

Tony was not quite as self-assured at the end of the session as he had been at the outset. His manipulative style had been exposed and Tony was uncertain about the resolution of a major issue: whether to continue the charade of treatment. The therapist had been able to engage Tony on the topic of motivation without condemning the client and without pressuring him to change. At the same time, the therapist was able to interest the student by uncovering a pervasive pattern—Tony's modus operandi. Meaningful engagement had begun in the relative absence of negative transference reactions.

Setting Mutually Agreed-On Goals

In the very next session, Tony initiated the discussion of scamming. He was clearly engaged. What remained was the setting of clear goals for treatment:

S: Whew! Man, that was a heavy, heavy session. I left and the next day I was just sitting on the bus going, whoa!

I: So you never expected we'd ever get to something like that.

S: No. Not to something that slick! I mean, you pull it off for eight years! The only thing is I've been pulling them so smoothly, people haven't even seen it! Jeez! *I* haven't seen it!

I: Well, my job is *not* to tell you what to be or how to be, but to hold up a mirror.

S: And say, lookie, lookie, hey, that's a new trick! *(Laughs and pauses)* And you know, last week, if I've had to, I've actually been sitting down at my desk working, doing all my work.

I: *(Looking and sounding somewhat suspicious)* Just because you took a close look at what you were doing to yourself, why would you decide to change?

S: Well, it was literally like the first time I'd been mentally punched. I mean, physically I've been knocked around. But mentally, I think that was the first time I'd ever been brought to a very sudden halt by a very large object! Or a very large concept, actually.

I: And the concept was what you were doing to yourself?

S: Yeah, and that's what scared me. Now whether this is going to keep up and whether I'm actually going to be a diligent student, or whether the scam is gonna slowly revert. Is it just a temporary reaction?

I: Yeah. Remember you once described one of your friends, a guy who was like you, but he was into serious stuff?

S: Yeah, sure. That was Tom.

I: Well, based on the way you described him, I believe that he is miles ahead of you in terms of the seriousness of his scams. He's probably into heavy drugs and stuff like that?

S: Actually, he sits up at night planning his scams.

I: Right, but there is a part of you that operates in some similar ways.

S: Oh yeah, there's no question about it. I've been running them for eight years, nine years?

I: Okay. But now, you really slowed down, just for a moment, maybe, but you've started to take a look at yourself.

S: Yeah. I've put it into neutral for a while.

I: Yeah. Now, are you worried that you may rescam?

S: Yeah. If for seventeen years I've been operating this way, there's no way I'm gonna change just like that.

I: That's correct. But there has been some change you're talking about.

S: You know, um, I think it's just sort of like the dinosaurs. They had to change or they would have died, and they didn't change, so they died. I think that's how I saw myself. I said, either I change just a little bit, or I'm gonna wind up like the dinosaurs.

I: Ah, you mean extinct?

S: Yeah. *(Pauses)* Now, whether of course, that means I just got to make my scams better . . . *(Laughs)*

I: So one possibility is that you haven't been as good at it as you could be.

S: Yeah. And just before I got myself plastered out of my mind, that's what sort of freaked me out. I was sitting there thinking: Have I changed, or is this just an involved and improved scam that I don't even know I'm pulling on myself?

I: So in a sense, two weeks ago you started to be a crap detector.

S: *(Laughs heartily)* I like that. Yeah, only this time on my own crap! Look, I was pretty sure that I was scamming a lot of people. But I didn't know I was scamming myself. That's what really freaked me out!

I: Well, you know, I bet that pattern happens in school, at home, with girlfriends, and with . . .

S: Probably. Actually, for certain. Exactly.

I: Well, we could spend some time looking at this more carefully and see how it has affected your life.

S: I know it has.

I: Or, we can stop meeting because you think that everything's really okay.

S: Na, let's look.

I: Okay. But the pattern probably shows itself not just in school.

S: Right.

I: Do you have any idea about why focusing on these patterns makes sense?

S: Well, some of the patterns I know about.

I: Right.

S: *(Pauses)* It's the ones I don't know about that I'd like to look at.

I: Good idea.

Why had Tony been so affected by the realization of the effectiveness of his "self-scams"? Most likely, it was the exposure of his own unconscious motives that had bothered him. This revelation raised the possibility that, contrary to his belief, not all of his behavior was under his conscious control. But was his dismay sincere? Was this simply another of Tony's manipulations?

Issues of trust and credibility, the establishment of ground rules, confronting treatment motivation, and the setting of goals are all part of the engagement stage of individual treatment.

Stage 2. Identifying and Exploring Patterns

Uncovering patterns is an important part of Stage 2, but not just because it provides a focus for treatment and opens up options for change. If done well, the search for patterns creates a challenge for the client. Will the therapist be able to discover patterns? If so, which ones? Are there any patterns of which the student is unaware?

Patterns of Manipulation and Impatience

Predictable patterns emerge in counseling CD underachievers. One has already been presented—the pattern of *manipulation*. A second pattern involves the choices made that lead to *immediate versus long-term* behavior. This is illustrated by the following exchange that occurred toward the end of a counseling session with Tony:

I: So what payoff or advantage is there to you in not doing the work?

S: I get a bigger payoff right now. Like, I get to laze around, to do whatever I want when I want to. It's just the shifting of the time of payments.

I: Shifting of the time of payments?

S: Yeah, you know that commercial. "You can pay me now or pay me later." Eventually I have to pay. Like up till now I've been pretty much operating from day to day.

I: That's probably how you operate in lots of ways in your life. It's more important to get a payoff now than for something later down the road. You want it up front. You want it now.

S: Yeah, right here on the table!

I: And my guess is, you probably even operate in relationships that way with people. That is, you'd rather have a good time now and screw what the consequences are later down the road.

S: I think that's dead on.

I: Okay. It's about the end of our session. Kind of an interesting chat.

S: Yeah, it's really amazing.

I: *(Smiles)* Okay. Interested in getting together again?

S: Yeah! Next week, same time?

I: Same time.

Patterns of Lagging Effort and Need for External Controls

Pattern search involves solicitation of details. At times, it may even appear that the therapist is getting "picky," always requesting more facts. These "facts" can include course requirements, exam marks, thoughts about the teacher, attitudes about male-female relationships, and perceptions about family arguments. The process of identifying patterns is not restricted to behavior. Exposing *thought patterns* is also critical, and it is only through facts that patterns emerge. An example of how Tony approaches his school responsibilities follows:

S: But that always happens to me. I start off strong and I slack off. I always make sure I got a little buffer there.

I: Like, how much of a buffer?

S: I was averaging about 70. Then it dropped; my midterm report card is where those two bad tests were—43 and 33. Right after those two bad tests, my midterm report came out and my average was 60. And then this test I got 50. So my average went down.

I: So, if you continue the trend, it will go down, down, down.

S: Yeah.

I: Okay, and you said earlier that you decided to bring it up? How did you decide?

S: *(Grins)* Well, Bill, my teacher, called me on the phone and said, "Tony, I'm afraid you're going to lose the credit."

I: But you knew that, didn't you?

S: Well, I didn't know how low my buffer had gone. I knew there was a buffer there, I just wasn't sure how much was left.

I: Right. So it took someone else to tell you? Is that a pattern?

S: Yeah. It happens all the time. So Bill said, "I'm afraid you're going to lose the credit," and I figured, well, I guess my buffer is pretty low, better restock it. *(Laughs)*

I: Now, what would have happened if Bill hadn't said something?

S: It could have been a problem.

I: Is this a general pattern?

S: Only for things I don't want to do.

I: Okay. So, assuming your teacher doesn't say anything, would that have been okay for you?

S: I would have lost the credit, I guess. But once he told me, I decided I couldn't lose the credit.

I: I don't get it. What's so important about that credit?

S: They'd throw me out.

I: You mean it would be bye, bye?

S: *(Laughs)* Yeah.

I: So if Bill hadn't said anything to you . . .

S: Yeah, but Bill is always telling me, always! He never fails.

I: You're lucky he's still alive. If he were in a car accident, your whole future would be going down the tubes!

S: *(Laughs)* I'd be in trouble, man.

I: Tony, what am I saying?

S: You're saying, what am I going to do when Bill isn't there?

I: Right! That's if you really care. Maybe getting kicked out of school is okay with you?

S: No. I don't want that.

I: Well, it could screw up getting into the police academy.

S: *(Reluctantly)* Yeah, I guess it could.

I: But if you really don't care about that, then there's no problem?

S: *(Somewhat dejected)* Right.

I: I guess you've got some choices you could make. Or, like with Bill, you could wait for others to tell you when it's getting shaky. Maybe you like to live that way.

S: Why would I want to live like that?

I: It can be kind of exciting, and besides, you can almost have your cake and eat it.

S: What do you mean?

I: Well, you can laze around for a long time and spring into action at the last minute.

S: But then it's really hard.

I: But changing the pattern will be really hard too.

S: Yeah, you're right.

The therapist has identified school patterns, including both the predictable slide in marks from the beginning of the term to the end, and Tony's need for external feedback about the dangers he was creating. In addition, the therapist was able to tie the consequences of the pattern to Tony's career aspirations. By exposing the pattern, the therapist has raised the question of motivation and options. Does Tony really want to change or merely maintain the status quo?

Patterns of Upping the Ante and Ambivalence

Often during the search for patterns (Stage 2), CD underachievers report a number of events. Typically, each succeeding story revolves around a slightly more serious problem. One purpose of these graduated stories is to gauge therapist values, beliefs, and *startle threshold*. This threshold is the point at which the therapist visibly reacts with, for example, noticeable surprise, curiosity, or fear. From a treatment perspective, each story contains a pattern that can be identified and confronted.

In the following example, Tony had already related two minor incidents and the therapist had commented about how nonproblematic they appeared to be. Tony then "upped the ante":

S: Okay. There was something else that happened this week. My friends and I all own pellet guns. You take your pellet gun and you go and tramp around by the Rouge River and you shoot at stuff—trees, rocks, you know. I said, listen, let's go shoot some fucking squirrels. So we went down. Now, this gets a bit tricky. There's a guy mowing his lawn, but he was behind a big fence, right, so he couldn't see us. And we figured the noise of the mower drown out the sound of the guns. So, anyway, we're sitting there—poom, poom, poom. I'd just finished nailing a squirrel, which by the way, is a federal offense.

I: Are you serious?

S: Yeah, it's a federal offense. Six months in the clink or a $2,500 fine, plus a criminal record.

I: Oh, so there goes the application to the police academy!

S: *(Laughs)* Yeah. Now of course, what are the chances of a couple of kids shooting pellet guns underneath the railroad bridge, with lots of dividers to hide them, actually getting busted? Zero! So, I figured we were safe. And I just finished knocking one down out of the tree. Then all of a sudden just after, my friend said, "Shit, that guy phoned the cops!"

I: But how did he know?

S: The lawn mower is off, man! Why would anybody turn off the lawn mower in the middle of doing the lawn? Two options: Either he had to use the john, or he got a phone call or something. But most likely, I really think he's called the cops. Right? Now, I knew visibility was out of the question because the fence was too high and solid. But still, cops were on their way! I could *sense* it. And we're sitting there with three fucking guns. I said, okay, I'm history! Right? At first my friend said, "That's bullshit man." And I said, I guess you're right. And then lo and behold, what do I see—Mr. Policeman walking down the embankment! Cops! Pow! Boom! Out of there! I took off and the cop was up on the Rouge River Bridge cutting across traffic. So I got away. And I went straight to my friend's house which is fairly close.

I: With the gun?

S: No, without the gun. My gun was, you know, I just "lost" it. That sucker went man! Like we had no qualms about losing something to beat getting busted.

I: I understand.

S: So, I lost the gun, whooo! Gord disappeared, whooo! But Sam's stupid, he kept his. Now I was out of there. I mean, I see a policeman, and I know he can fuck me for life. I'm history! I'm gone! Went to Gord's house and put the bike right in the garage. And I was wearing my green sweat top which is obvious, right?

I: Yeah.

S: The cop drives by, right? I'm just sitting there in the backyard and sat there, gasp, gasp, gasp, *(breathing heavily)* right? And about ten minutes later Gord and Sam arrive. And I go, what the fuck happened? You get popped? He goes, "No, but a cop pulled us over." And they had hid behind an embankment and the cop didn't see them with me. So, the cop pulled them over later and said, "What are you guys doing here?" And they go, "Well, we're just coming back from Beaverton, which is, like 600 feet away across the bridge. And Gord goes, "My chain fell off and I had to stop. So the cop says to Gord, "Lift up the back of your jacket." And he did what the cop had asked—Gord had ditched the gun, luckily. The cop didn't ask Sam to lift his jacket! What luck!

I: Right.

S: So the cop said, "Okay, fella, where do you live?" He told him—he didn't even write it down, right? Just let them go! So, they came back and we were freaking out. We stayed for awhile, talking about what had happened. I changed my shirt, left the green one at Gord's. Then we decided to leave, and guess what? We were walking along and a cop pulled us over and goes, "Have you seen a guy in a green sweatshirt on a bike?" Guess who laughs?

I: Yours truly.

S: *(Laughs)* No officer! So that's like the end of that, right? When we returned to the house, we burned it all under the house. Half an hour later, the same cop came by, because he had taken Gord's address down. "Just double checking," he said. "You said you were coming home and I just wanted to make sure you guys were here. And the guy looked around. He goes, "Do you own a pellet gun?" And they go, "No, our dads won't let us!" Okay, so he left.

I: What happened to the gun that Sam had?

S: I found out later that he ditched it just before the police stopped them on the road. So anyway, Maria, Gord's sister comes back and says, "How come you're in Gord's clothes?" And we all just laughed; she didn't understand. But it was really close! Close man, close! *(Pause)* It's these little things that make life interesting.

I: That makes life *interesting?*

S: See, the thing is, I didn't really think about it until after.

I: And what did you think about after?

S: Had I got caught, had I got a federal offense against me, then we're talking bye, bye police academy.

I: Right. I think there are at least two or three interesting things here. You didn't think about it until *after,* right? But that has to be the story of your life.

S: Yeah.

I: That's been your style. If you feel like doing something . . .

S: Do it!

I: And it's usually only later that you happen to think about it.

S: Yeah.

I: But you don't use your brain *before,* you use it *after.* You have devoted yourself to becoming a black belt in scrambling after the fact.

S: *(Laughs)* And every time I've gotten away with it! Well, almost every time.

I: Right, which is a very powerful incentive to keep operating that way. I mean, you'd be stupid to change.

S: Yeah, I've got a great track record, man.

I: That's right. The only concern I have . . .

S: If I run into a flat tire.

I: That's it. The law of probability says, keep on, keep on, keep on. Somewhere you're going to get shafted.

S: Yeah.

I: That's all. In other words, your string simply can't continue. But for you, I suppose that's a challenge. For you, the message is, let's see how long it can last.

S: Oh, Harv, I really didn't think I was going to get away this time. Cause those cruisers, I know what they have under the hood—a 440 heavy box. They're real fast, positive traction, they can handle a corner. Now if that cop hadn't been hung up in traffic, I think I would really have had to scramble. We're talking maximum overdrive!

I: Right. So one pattern is that you'd rather "do it" now, and scramble later. It's much more exciting that way.

S: Right.

I: Now, is there any other pattern in that story, anything else that's interesting for you?

S: I don't know. I just saw the scamming aspect of it. I didn't see anything else. Besides, I'd been there a thousand times before with the guns and had never seen a cop!

I: So are you saying that it was safe?

S: (Sheepish grin) Well, no, that's not exactly true now that I think about it. We usually go deep into the forest away from traffic and people. Geez, this time we didn't go deep into the forest, just stayed near the road and bridge. Mm . . . (Long pause) That's something else I hadn't thought about before. There are obvious ways of increasing the risks subconsciously without even knowing it!

I: So there are little things you do that open you up to greater risk as opposed to less. Sounds a little like you flirt with getting shafted.

S: (Pensive) It is, it really is if you think about it.

I: I guess that the chase is the whole game.

S: It's not the kill, it's the thrill!

I: Right! And you started off as the hunter and you ended up as the hunted.

S: And I could very easily have just stayed the hunter the whole time by just going down to the part of the forest where we usually gc to hunt. But the way I played it, it made it a lot harder to win.

I: Yeah. You set yourself up so that it was possible to lose. That's another pattern. Are you comfortable with it?

S: I wasn't then!

I: But are you now?

S: Sort of, but not really.

I: So you're torn?

S: Exactly. But I think I had better change. It's getting too close.

I: Right. You know what's interesting? Both of us need stimulation, both of us need a challenge. But I want a challenge without shafting myself. You want a challenge in which it is possible to get shafted.

S: Hmm.

Tony was struggling with his *ambivalence,* another predictable treatment issue for CD underachievers. They are often torn between arousal and boredom. They perceive arousal as inherent in high-risk situations and boredom as intrinsic to situations that require delayed gratification.

Patterns of Perception about Previous Treatment

Many CD underachievers at the high school level have had previous difficulties. And some have had professional help long before they reach adolescence. It is important to explore their perceptions of those previous experiences to get an understanding of their outlook on treatment. The details they share will not be very reliable, but themes probably will. The following example highlights this issue:

S: I was in ninth grade and I was taking drafting. So I was carrying a Swiss army knife to sharpen the pencils. I was coming down the stairs at school and this big huge Grade 11 muscle-builder jock who looked like he could have eaten me for lunch was coming up the stairs. Right? And so I just shut up and walked down the stairs. And he bumped into me. I said, what the fuck you doing man? I'm just walking down the stairs and you fuck and come and bump into me. Like, what the fuck's the problem, right? I'm not bugging you, why are you such a dip? He goes, "Want to fuckin' make something of it?" I go, suck my dick!

I'm not going to fucking make you, 'cause you got a friend right there and you look like you could eat me alive. Boom! Up against the wall I went. Right? Mind shuts off and body starts operating. Fuck off! Unexpected reaction. Out comes the knife. And I'm screaming, "Come on, come on, come on!"

I: So you never expected that from yourself?

S: Right. Holy shit! Something's wrong I say to myself! So, I scramble, and I go, "I'm not fucking going to stab you, man. This is bullshit. Even if I did stab you, nothing would happen. You'd still beat the shit out of me." I was too small. So we slapped around a little bit, and poom, up against the wall. So we were swearing at each other and this teacher comes by.

I: You still had the knife out?

S: No, the knife was back in my pocket. And the teacher goes, "What's going on?" I said, "Oh, nothing, me and my friend were just screwing around. Right?" And I was going to let it drop. And he goes, "He pulled a knife on me, man. He pulled a knife on me!"

Note. Tony had quickly generated a creative answer for the teacher, a solution which had the potential to get him and his confronter off the hook. The only problem was that the other student wasn't interested in a mutually satisfying outcome. But Tony's intelligence clearly showed in this example, if only to allow him to scramble out of another problematic situation:

I: In other words, he shafted you!

S: Yeah. And so we went into the principal's office. And here I am, this pathetic looking ninth grader against this big huge fucking godzilla. I said, "Sir, look at this, it's a pocket knife." And he goes, "What do you mean, this is a fucking weapon!" And I go, "You're kidding me! I've got things at home that would make this look like a thing to pick up sardines with." *(Laughs)* And so anyway, I had to go see a shrink or they would throw me out. They wanted actual documented proof to see if I was nuts, to see if I was a danger to their school. So I went. I saw her about eight times. And everything I said was just bullshit. Because I just wanted to stay at that school. Now, me going and spending an hour of my time with some flake because some other flake told me to do it—bite it baby!

I: So you operated a certain way for those eight meetings.

S: Oh yeah. I told her exactly what she wanted to hear. And she sent a report back to the school. "Listen, he just snapped, he was under stress, the guy's not dangerous, don't worry about it." Right? I said, "So the letter's at the school, right? I can go back to school, no problem?" And she goes, "Yeah." And then she realized it. She goes, "You've been fucking me around, haven't you?" I said, "Yup." And she goes, "The only reason you came here was to save your ass?" I nodded. She goes, "Well then, we shouldn't meet any more." And I said, "That's the idea!"

I: And there was another therapist before that, wasn't there?

S: That was sixth grade. My mom suggested it. It was specifically focused on why I was messing up in school. Now we talked about a lot of other things, but it all tied in. After the first meeting, I said, that lady is such a fucking crock of bull. But afterward my mom said let's have pizza tonight. I said, oh, this has got some good kickback! Right? And so I went to the second meeting. And then again the next night, "Do you want Chinese food?" Fuck, this is amazing, all I have to do is put up with an hour of shit and I get whatever I want when I come back! I went for about five months. Actually, you know, after the first two or three meetings it wasn't all that bullshit. And I actually sat down and started to enjoy it. And I started going not so much for the kickback but for the actual meetings.

I: So, there was something you felt was worthwhile? What was the difference between that first lady and the second one?

S: For the second shrink, the school had sent me. I was *forced* to go. I didn't have a choice, my hands were tied, and I just didn't like her. And if I don't like somebody, that's it. You know, I still remember the first lady's name—Mrs. Goodman. And we actually got very close and we talked about a lot of things.

I: What do you think you got out of those meetings? Sounds like something worthwhile happened.

S: Yeah. She held up a mirror, like you're doing. But I was constantly on guard. I didn't want to go too far with her because when you're a young kid you're always suspicious of your parents, right? I was sure she was in contact with my mom. And the minute I left the office, she'd be phoning my mom to tell her what we'd been talking about. I liked her, even though I thought she was telling my mom everything I said. She was still really nice.

I: Now, tell me about our meetings and the connection between you and me? Are there any things that are the same? And what's different from your previous experiences?

S: Okay. A lot of things are different. You don't have any one-way mirrors in your room. Two, there's no little secret office you could stash all the recording stuff in. You laid the tape recorder on the table in front of us and I know when you're taping. You put it right up front. And not only that, I'm here because I want to be. It's true my mom introduced me, but I'm here basically of free will. It will be because I say so.

I: Also the roof won't collapse at home if you decide to stop coming and you won't get kicked out of school if you don't come.

S: Yeah. We're just sitting around, relaxed and all and it also has a direct tie-in to why I screw up, generally. And with the other person, it was a very tense atmosphere. I had to watch what I was saying.

I: So you were on guard.

S: Most of the time.

I: So that's another pattern.

S: Right. I don't like to be told what to do.

I: Yes, but there's another piece.

S: I've missed it.

I: Sounds to me like not only were you being told what to do, but . . .

S: Wait—I think I got it. If I didn't go, there were bad consequences for me.

I: Right. And to put it in your language—they had some power over you.

S: Right. And that's the worst of all.

Pattern of Gamelike Relationships

Patterns are also evident in the *interpersonal games* CD underachievers play. The following example describes a "satisfying" sexual relationship between Tony (17 years) and a 24-year-old separated woman. Note Tony's short-term planning expertise:

S: A year and a half ago there was a lady who moved in on my street who was 24, married, and had a kid. And then about three months later, after they moved, they broke up. And he moved away. She had the kid Monday to Friday, he had him Friday nights to Monday morning. And for his birthday they had bought him a little kitten. And my sister always puts milk out to get the kitten over because she loves kittens. And one night I was stepping out to have a butt and it was about ten and my parents were downstairs watching a movie and I opened the screen door, stepped outside, and poom! I saw this thing go burning into the house and I go, what the fuck is that? And then I put two and two together and I thought, okay the cat. So I thought, I'm going to have my butt before I do anything. So I sat on the porch and I had a butt and went inside afterward, started looking around for the cat. Found him in the furnace room. Grabbed the cat, played with it a bit and said, shit it's twelve o'clock, this lady's probably going to be freaking out. I'd better take the cat back. Everyone else in the family was already asleep. So I said, well, I'll take the cat back and I'll slip back in and my parents won't even know I was gone. She answered the door in her negligee. So I said, your cat was in my house. Do you want him back or do I keep him? And she said, "No, no, no, I'll take him back." And I decided, okay, I'll play. So I was standing at the door and she goes, "So how did he get in?" And I explained. Then she said, "Well it's really late, I'd better be going." I said, okay, fine. So I went back and had a butt, checked on my parents to make sure they were blotto. I went back, she looked out the window, smiled, nodded, and came back downstairs. "I don't have two cats!" she explained. I said innocently: But I'm locked out! While bringing your cat back I locked myself out. *(Tony smiled.)* I'm a sneaky little devil aren't I?

I: Mm hmm.

S: So she said, "Oh, well, why don't you call your parents and let them know." I said, thanks. So I went in and grabbed the phone and dialed my friend's number who I knew was at the cottage.

I: No answer?

S: *(Laughing)* Ring, ring, ring. And she said, "Well, okay, I'll tell you what, why don't you sit here a few minutes and call them back." I said, okay. So she wanders into the kitchen and goes, "Do you want a cup of coffee?" I said, oh yeah. So she put a coffee pot on and she said, "Why don't you try your parents again." I said, okay fine. So I phoned—ring, ring, ring. Guess what? Nobody answers. I wonder why! And so I said, no, still no answer, looks like I'll be sleeping in the garage. That's okay, I got butts, I'll be fine I guess. And she said,

"No, I can't let you do that. You're stuck outside because you brought my cat back. I can't leave you in the garage." So I said, well, what am I going to do, crash here? And she goes, "Well, you can have the couch if you want." I said, okay fine. So I grabbed the couch and she went back upstairs and I crashed. And I made sure I set my alarm watch and made sure I was up at six, because I knew my parents on a Saturday morning would not be up before eight. At six I woke up as usual like a thundering train and I went upstairs and knocked on her door and said, listen, I'm cutting out. I'm sure my parents will be awake by now. They're always up early Saturdays. She said, "Well, if you hold on a second I'll get you a cup of coffee." I said, okay fine. So, she went downstairs and she was in jeans and a cut off. She was making coffee and she goes, "You weren't locked out last night were you?" And I think to myself, okay, now I've really got to be crafty. If I'm setting myself up, I'm really going to get shafted. The shit's going to hit like a high torqued turbine. And if not, it's going to have fringe benefits. So I said, no. And she goes, "And you didn't dial your phone number last night, did you?" And I go, how do you know? And she goes, "I know your phone number because I phoned your mom and asked her for a pound of butter before. So why did you want to stay?" And I go, I don't know, it just looked like you were playing a game and I figured I'd play too. She goes, "Oh, well, how would you like to play the same game later?" I go, when's later? And she goes, "How about next weekend? And I said, okay, when? She says, "Well, I'm always out in the backyard gardening and so let me know." And I said, so how about this coming Friday night? And she said, "Oh, I've got plans." I said, okay and started to turn away. She said, "Well, wait a minute, they're not really that important I can cancel them." And I'm thinking, one point for me! I said, okay, well listen I think I can get out of the house about eight. She said okay. So I went over. She ordered pizza and offered me a beer. So we proceeded to get blotto, she did anyway. It takes me more than twelve by myself to get blotto. I had seven, she had five and she was plastered out of her skull. She goes upstairs and I hear her puke her guts out. I go, oh, God! So she must have forced herself to puke to get it out of her system which I've done many a time to come home sober. So she comes back downstairs and says she's feeling a lot better. She says, "What do you say we jump in the sack?" I said, sounds fine with me. At one o'clock I said, listen, I got to start getting ready to scram. I got dressed, cruised out the door. I said, am I going to see you again?

And she said, "Yeah, sure, next Friday." So this went on for about three months and you know, after a while it was like the age wasn't any difference. And besides, the pizza and beer were good.

Patterns of Betrayal, Anger, and Hurt

CD underachievers also experience predictable *interpersonal difficulties* at home, with peers, and at school. And patterns are evident in these problematic relationships. The major themes include betrayal, anger, hurt, and lessons learned:

S: When I was in seventh grade, my teacher said: "Listen Tony, I know you. You don't have the best work habits, you're lazy, you don't like to do work. All you have to do in this course is your homework and you'll pass." So, I did my homework and I failed! I said, what the fuck is going on? You said I'd pass. He said, "No, I said if you did your homework you'd do okay." I said, well I'm *not* okay, moron. I failed, right? And he says to me, "Well you should have also studied before tests." I said, well thanks for telling me, you fucking goof! And he goes, "Listen don't swear at me." I go, no you listen, you let me down. If you'd told me I had to study a little bit before tests, I would have studied for the odd test. But no—all you said I had to do was my homework. And now I failed and I've got to do the course over again. Thanks a fucking lot, shit head. And I walked out. Surprisingly, I didn't get expelled, suspended, or even a detention for it. *(Smiles)* I was pleased with that.

I: So you felt betrayed.

S: Yeah! He let me down.

Note. Whatever the facts, Tony had portrayed his Grade 7 teacher as a person who betrayed him. A similar theme appeared in Tony's description of an unsatisfying peer relationship:

S: Anyway, Robyn and I spent a great summer together and she'd come down every weekend and go back every weekend and she'd come down Friday night and leave Sunday night. So the day before she was supposed to leave she told me that while she was seeing me in Toronto, she'd also been seeing this guy, Zack. Anyway, I go, yeah, as a boyfriend or a friend? And she goes, "Sometimes a boyfriend, sometimes a friend." And knowing Robyn as I knew her, I knew that boyfriend meant "in the sack." So I was pretty upset. My natural reaction was—fuck you bitch! Went upstairs, cranked up my stereo, dragged out my electric guitar, and sat there violently attacking my guitar. I listened to some really good heavy metal, and then I took her to the train station and said, "bye, bye." And then the next summer, she came back. And so I said, okay, listen, if we're going to spend some time together this summer, we're going to lay down some ground rules. Number one: No screwing around with other people. And then we set down a bunch of little rules, you know, like when she'll be available to take calls at the residence she was staying at. It wound up that out of the whole summer of phoning her twice a week, I actually got through to her about four times. I mean, she was never there! So, I said, okay, it's time to protect myself. I'm not going to sit here and wait if she's going to be fucking around. But she'd come over on the weekend and deny she was involved with anyone else. And again, like a moron, I left myself wide open. Before she left, she handed me the same damn line. "I screwed around when I was there, but it was only because I was lonely and Tony you weren't there with me." That's when I said, fuck you bitch! And so I didn't even see her off. I didn't write her and now I'm waiting to see if she calls again. And if she does, it'll be fuck it bitch! Click! Hang up on her forever.

I: Okay. Sounds like there's an awful lot of anger in you about what happened.

S: I was pissed, completely!

I: You were reaching out, and you're the one who asked her to make some kind of agreement to be there on the other end. And she wasn't. And you find yourself in a position where somebody has not come through. How did you feel about it?

S: Well, now I feel differently, but at the time I was hurt.

I: And what do you do with hurt?

S: Translated it into anger. I was very suspicious. I was pissed off and depressed.

I: And?

S: And, I learned to never leave yourself open.

I: But it sounds like you cared so much about her that you were willing to connect with her the following summer.

S: Yeah. Those who do not study history are doomed to repeat it. Famous quote.

I: Yeah. So there are some things that you learned.

S: I've got a perfect quote for it, just give me a minute. What is it now? Sort of have a good time, be with her, but never get close and never leave yourself open, because then you wind up getting hurt. If there are attachments, then it's gonna hurt.

I: Is this a pattern too?

S: Well, I won't let myself get hurt first anymore.

I: Are you okay with that solution?

S: For now—you bet. When it looks like someone is about to end it with me, I end it first. It's better to have loved and won than loved and lost!

I: What do you mean by winning?

S: Getting in and out fast.

Tony has exposed his vulnerability and provided an area for work in therapy. Patterns of betrayal, anger, and sadness are frequently part of the CD underachiever's experience. For change to occur, these themes will require much exploration.

Functional versus Dysfunctional Patterns

The patterns detected in therapy are not all dysfunctional. In fact, some may involve highly functional responses to very difficult circumstances. As these emerge, they need to be acknowledged as contextually adaptive, even though it is hoped that as change occurs, the frequency of such experiences will diminish. A dramatic example from Tony's thirteenth session follows:

S: I really liked Flora. But she hooked up with this slime guy El Creapo, as street scum as they come. And because I wanted to protect her, I wasn't going to let El Creapo fuck her up. So as much as possible, I was around him when she was. But some guy fucked up a "coke" deal and I got blamed for getting two guys thrown in the can for trafficking. The third guy who managed to get away wasted about three others and started hunting me down. And at that point I said, this is life or death. I went and picked up a Browning high power for about $175—no serial numbers. And I started carrying it. I came face to face with the leader of this gang and he said, "You're the asshole who fucked up our coke deal and got two of our buddies sent to jail. And you're going to burn for it." And I said, I think before you jump I should show you something. I got a wallet here that says you'd better fucking listen. He was up against the wall and the Browning was about a foot and a half from his face. He was looking right down the barrel and I said, you'd better listen. I said, we've a serious problem here. I don't like getting the rap for something I didn't do and I don't like getting killed. And I will kill you—of that I had no doubt. I'd been fucked around before and I'm not going to let another scum like you fuck me around. And if it comes down to it, I'm going to blow you away right here, right now. He goes, "Oh fuck, man! Fuck! Don't kill me, don't kill me!" I go, I think we should talk. I didn't rat on you to the cops because I don't rat on anybody. Ratting gets me in shit and I don't like that situation. The only reason you're still alive right now is the fact that I didn't rat on you. The only reason this gun is pointing in your face is so you'll listen. I don't want to blow you away because that's going to put me in a lot of shit. But if you still think that I ratted on you and you're going to come after me, then I'm going to waste you. He said, "Well then fuck, who the hell ratted on me?" I said, I don't know, but you'd better check that out because I'm going to let you walk now. But you'd better know that I didn't rat. If you come after me again, this won't just be in my hand, it'll be all over your face. He goes, "You're serious aren't you?" I said, yeah, I'm serious. And he said, "If you didn't rat on me, who did?" I said, man I don't know, but my best guess is the guy who told you I did.

I: Sounds like a good move, Tony.

S: And it turned out actually that he was the one. And he's disappeared. I don't know where he is now. So that guy walked and I ditched the Browning and that was the end of that scene.

I: *(Pauses)* I think you handled it in a very savvy way. You protected yourself, you didn't overreact, you got him to think about things he hadn't considered, and you even suggested a solution to his problem.

S: Yeah, but for awhile there it was close.

I: Sure. And it could have gone either way.

S: Absolutely.

Assuming the veracity of the story, Tony had dealt effectively with an explosive encounter, showing intelligence and self-control in his handling of the situation. Often, CD underachievers exhibit a type of savvy or "street smarts" that cannot be captured by formal IQ testing. These high risk patterns should be identified but not confronted because they are functional within a given context. The chance for positive change increases if these cognitive talents can be rechanneled in the fulfillment of different goals.

Stage 3. Change

The Tasks and Limitations of Change

Once the stages of engagement and pattern search have been completed, the arduous task of change begins. For change to occur, the student must be able to identify old patterns, take responsibility for them, and be willing to practice controlling them while developing and solidifying new patterns. The student must be willing to process his or her attempts at change to detect difficulties and identify potential solutions. A strong therapist-client relationship increases the probability of change because it provides an environment for practicing, evaluating, refining, and supporting positive risks.

There are limitations to change for every student with these problems. Internal antichange forces include long-standing impulsivity and immediate gratification tendencies, powerful self-esteem reinforcements from antisocial activities and the obstacles in facing academic skill gaps. In addition, negative transference reactions may also hinder Stage 3 work. External antichange forces may include negative influences of specific family members, peers, and segments of the community. Negative countertransference reactions may also hinder Stage 3 success. The therapist must remain keenly aware of how he or she reacts to positive or negative client change because these reactions reflect the therapist's investment in change.

The Uneven Pace and Direction of Change

For CD underachievers, the course of change rarely occurs quickly and is never linear. Two steps forward, one step back, one step sideways, and time-out from walking are all to be expected. As constructive change occurs, old patterns may reemerge. This reflects the struggle for change both within and around the student. Further, even when change is more lasting, it does not result in a remade human being. Positive change means that self-defeating patterns are diminished in frequency and intensity and that constructive patterns emerge often alongside some of the older problematic patterns.

The following excerpt illustrates Tony's struggle for academic pattern change:

S: Well, you know that I'm now on independent study for the rest of the school term.

I: What does that mean?

S: *(Smiles)* It means that the teachers have tried everything to get me to do my work—and nothing worked.

I: You look pleased with yourself.

S: I am. But there's a kicker here. Independent study means that I don't have to come to class. Actually, it means they don't want me to come to class.

I: That's what you don't have to do.

S: *(Tony interrupts)* I know, I know. What do I have to do? All I have to do is turn in my homework assignments on time and take the tests, and if I pass I'll get my credit.

I: So you're on your own. But you said that there was a kicker.

S: Yeah. I think that they've begun to figure me out after three years. If I miss any assignments, I get docked. For each test I miss, I get docked.

I: Sounds pretty clear to me.

S: And here's the real kicker. If I fail, I'm gone—I can't come back. I'm toast.

I: Toast?

S: Harv get with. Yeah toast, as in burnt!

I: So they've had to put down the "final rule" so to speak.

S: Right. And guess what?

I: You told them to go screw themselves?

S: *(Laughs)* No, no! That's the old me. I have worked my ass off for the last two weeks and I haven't missed any assignments.

I: How come?

S: Because I don't want to get kicked out of school.

I: So with this structure, you may actually get your credits?

S: I'd put money on it.

I: But what happens if you need help?

S: That's what great. Every one of my teachers is willing to meet with me privately if I need help. And I can still hang around the school.

Even though Tony had not initiated the new school structure, he was willing to abide by it. His teachers knew that Tony was not bashful about asking for help. They also knew that to require Tony to attend all classes was unrealistic and would lead to his expulsion. They were willing to employ structures that Tony might be able to use in a beneficial way.

The preceding example illustrates how structural changes may be helpful, but their timing is critical. Had the school offered an independent program before Tony's 16th birthday, Tony would have known that they could not expel him.

The following excerpt illustrates Tony's struggle for relationship change:

S: Yeah, right. Now, there's a girl at school. She swims twice a day, every day except for Sundays. And she can bench press more than I can.

I: So, she's got talent and self-discipline.

S: She can beat the Canadian record holder in her event. She's also incredibly bright.

I: Mm hmm.

S: But what blows my mind about all this is that no matter how well she does, the minute she hits 32, 33 agewise, she's out of swimming. And she won't have reaped enough benefits to live without working, so she'll have to go and find a real job. Now that kind of dedication for something that's not going to set you up for the rest of your life is fucking beyond me. I can't even start to comprehend that. It just doesn't make sense to me! Why the hell anybody would do that is beyond me. And I really blew it when I pointed that out to her. If, and this is like saying if God came down and became my best friend, if, by any chance this girl and I got together, you would see the ultimate in reversal of roles.

I: Meaning?

S: I would not use her, I would not dump her and move on. I would not cheat on her.

I: I wonder why not?

S: *(Sighs)* I don't know. This is what blows my mind. I don't know why I'm so attracted to this girl. If I actually started going out with her, and if she asked me, I would honestly lick-shine the bottom of her shoes if she wanted me to.

I: I've never heard you talk about anybody like that before.

S: I mean, you want to talk shaky. I've got one toe on a hair between two sticks three hundred feet off the ground. I can't understand why! I don't know why! The first time I saw her I thought she was an ugly guy. That was just a brief glance. But then the more I looked at her the more I realized how amazingly good looking she was. And the more I got to know her the more good looking she got. And I don't know what's happened because she's nowhere near my type. This is one person I can't even nail down. And that's what's scary because usually people I can nail down pretty quick. I mean, I should know her inside out by now. And ninety percent of the time I miss things that are so obvious about her that I wind up kicking myself about it. I don't know. I just don't know *(sighs)* what it is, why it is, how it is. *(Pauses)* I said to her, I don't know whether you know or not, but um, I like you. I mean, I couldn't believe I was saying something that honest and blunt. And she goes, "I know." And I said: No, I mean like a lot! Sometimes when we're talking about your swimming and I come off sounding like a big jerk it's really only because I'm desperately trying hard to be supportive and I don't know how. And she said, "Yeah, I know."

I: She had an idea already about what you were saying?

S: Yeah. And she sort of looks at me and goes, "Anything else?" And I go, I guess not. And she goes, "Okay." And she left!

I: Sounds very interesting and different from the way you've talked about other girls. How does somebody who has operated for years by making sure not to let any female in and to use them—how does somebody suddenly change?

S: I don't know. All I know is that I put myself in a pretty risky situation. And for the first time, I don't want to blow this. I want it to work. At least I want to try and make it work. *(Pauses)* And, I mean, the chances of me actually going out with this girl realistically I'd say are worse than of me getting out of high school in the next two months. There's a lot of things standing in my way. I'm not a swimmer, which I thought might have been a bonus. Second, compared to her I'm in as much shape as a Mack truck with no tires and no engine on blocks compared to a Porsche 911, twin turbo. I mean, she's got special shoes for running which have a platform that guarantees you will always stay on the top of your toes. And I can't even walk! *(Laughs)* So we're totally opposite.

I: Sounds like you're not only excited about the possibility of a relationship with her but you're also worried.

S: Yeah, exactly. She's the type of woman who I've never had to deal with and who doesn't respond the way all the other women have responded in the past.

I: Sounds also like you've been thinking a lot about her.

S: Yeah and about me too. Like, I thought of saying, okay, for her next swim meet I'll send her a dozen roses before she swims with just a little card saying, you know, good luck, just showing support. Then I thought about it and I said to myself, no, that's what I do for anybody else. That won't work with her.

I: You mean that you've been trying to analyze how you operate and decide whether to change or not?

S: Exactly. I looked at what would work and I couldn't find anything! I don't know what to do! This is the first time in my life I've been totally lost with a woman!

I: What would you like us to do about this issue?

S: I'd like to figure out how I might ruin it and figure out how to stop myself from doing that.

I: Great!

Changing the Polarity of Perceptions

Motivation for change in relationships derives from many sources. In the preceding example, it stemmed from a romantic interest whose nature was qualitatively different from previous experiences. Just as CD underachievers perceive relationships with adults dichotomously (patsies to be manipulated vs. enemies to be avoided), they often perceive peer relationships in dichotomous ways.

In Stage 3, an important responsibility of Tony's therapist is to provide some counterbalance to the student's portrayal of this new love interest as someone who is not just intriguing but perfect. If, and probably when things don't work out, Tony will quickly discount the value of that relationship and his anger will transform his idyllic portrayal into the old pattern of discounting others.

From a theoretical viewpoint, the expansion of relationship perceptions is no different than getting CD underachievers to explore options to academic roadblocks and to generate, practice, and sustain more realistic solutions. The key problem-solving questions of Stage 3 are:

- What problem am I willing to work on now?
- What are some reasonable solutions to the problem?
- What will probably get in the way when I try to solve it?
- How can I prevent this from happening?
- How will I know when I am beginning to change?
- How can I maintain the changes I make?
- What will I lose as I change, and how will I react and cope with these losses?

Tony's "plan" in the earliest stages of this unfolding heterosexual relationship was to be perfect, assuming that doing so would solidify the relationship. The effort exhausted him and when it didn't produce an immediate "payoff," he got angry:

I: Okay. How do you feel?

S: I feel rejected, and I feel definitely pissed off. Off the bitch!

I: So your style is to show anger, not hurt.

S: Most of the time.

I: By labeling her a bitch, you've changed the way you've always talked about her here.

S: Oh yeah. Well, I have and I haven't. I've got her on two pedestals. I've got her on one big beautiful solid gold one, and then I've got her on another ivory one that says bitch.

I: And the difference between the two is?

S: The difference is, that the one that's in gold is imagination—it'll never become reality! The one that's in ivory is reality.

I: Okay. Can you describe what the elements in that gold pedestal are for you?

S: I saw trust, I saw caring, I saw dedication.

I: Both ways, from her to you and from you to her?

S: *(Hesitates)* One and a half ways, with me being the one and her the half. *(Pauses)* You know, to my dying day she's going to be perfect.

I: Now what adjectives would you use to describe the ivory pedestal?

S: Bitch! And another one that just hit me like a sledgehammer—slut. In other words, just generally everything bad I can think of. To be disposed of, to be stepped on, to be abused.

I: Do you see any connection between those two images?

S: *(Pauses)* I guess one is a total flip side of the other.

I: What you're saying is you have two basic views of women. They are either the gold pedestal in which you are willing to give and give and give . . .

S: *(Interrupts)* And give, and give, and give.

I: Or, they're garbage. And there are no shades or colors in between.

S: Not in my world! I'm either the puppeteer or the puppet.

I: So what you're saying is that you really don't know any other way of operating in a relationship with somebody else where you are neither the puppet nor the puppeteer.

S: *(Pauses for a long moment)* No, I guess that's right. But how can I be something else?

I: Well, how would that something else be different? What would it contain?

S: I guess it would be a companion type thing—more equal, more trusting.

I: And how do people develop trust in each other?

S: By not crossing each other.

I: Okay, but how does that happen?

S: It happens when you decide to take time to build the trust.

I: Okay. So you need *time* for that to develop. And what stops you from taking the time?

S: *(Pauses)* I guess I get angry quickly when things don't work out.

I: Right. That's what you focus on. And once you get angry?

S: I want to get back, I want to get even.

I: Because?

S: Because she rejected me.

I: Has she really rejected you?

S: *(Long pause)* You know, not really. I guess I just wanted her to accept me faster.

I: I guess waiting is hard.

S: *(Sighs)* It sure is.

I: Do you want to try improving your ability to wait?

S: Yeah.

In Stage 3, exploration of anger often leads to a focus on more hidden feelings of hurt, rejection, and helplessness. It is by developing a better understanding of these feelings and their accompanying thoughts that more lasting change is possible. These students have extreme dichotomous perceptions of the universe that are rooted in dichotomous reactions to their experiences—anger and the attempt to retake control of life's circumstances versus sadness and its accompanying sense of helplessness. The following exchange occurred somewhat later in the same session:

S: *(Sighs)* I think it was when I was a little kid. And by little kid I mean early primary school, from Grade two on, mostly from Grade two to Grade five. I was zero on the popularity list at school, if not in the negatives. I was pretty much the wimp and the mama's boy. And I spent most of my time ducking from bullies because I used to get thrashed a lot, especially by this one kid, Stanley. And it was really ridiculous because one day he pushed me too far and I just whaled him one on the side of the head. And he was holding his head and crying and screaming for about five minutes. And instead of pressing on, beating the shit out of him and putting an end to it, I went off into a corner and bawled my eyeballs out. And when he recovered, he came and punched the shit out of me. And I spent ninety-nine percent of my time in school ducking behind the bushes, ducking in the corridors, going as fast as I can to the principal's office with three guys on my ass. And as a result, my social life with the chicks was like, below zero. While everybody else was having a great time with this tease with great knockers in Grade six, I was ducking in hallways. And I tried a couple of times for a couple of the girls in my class and got rejected really badly. In fact, Stanley came over and started knocking me around for even bothering this chick.

I met up with Stanley in an alleyway behind a bar a year and a half ago. He came over and said, "Tony, how about giving me a butt." And I said, no way. I don't owe you a dime and you're not getting dick out of me, you asshole. He took a swing at me and caught me right in the side of the head. And my head went whack! I looked at him and I just saw a wall of red. He says, "What are you going to do now, start crying like you did when you were a little kid?" I just looked at him and said, Stan—I have only one thing to say to you. And I just went, whack! And I just drove him one right in the face. He stumbled back and he was down on his knees on the ground. And instead of walking away, I went over, grabbed him by the hair, pulled him up and drove a knee in his face. And I took out about ten years of being beaten on that day. I left him lying in that alley behind the bar, a pulp I had never seen before in my life. He was just a wreck. His whole face was just a solid wall of blood. And I'm sure I cracked at least three of his ribs. I mean, after I kneed him in the face he couldn't stand. I set him up against the wall and just started pounding the shit out of him. And every time I'd hit him I'd say, who's crying now, you cock sucker! You think you're so tough? How about this? Whack! Whack! Whack!

I: In other words, you started to pay back the years of frustration in all one dose.

S: And in spades. It lasted about ten minutes. It got to the point where I had to walk away because I'd just picked up a lead pipe I had found and I was ready to pummel the shit out of his skull. So I decided it was time to walk because I don't think he was even conscious when I finished. So, I managed to walk from that one. How I got the control to walk I don't know. I think that even though I've been kicked around for ten years I decided it was enough. There was still a little bit of the wimp and the coward and the mama's boy left in me to stop short from really nailing him.

I: Hmmm.

S: I think it was that little edge that held me back. I mean, I've been in some bad brawls since. And I was in one brawl where we both had blades out and I cut him pretty rough right along the arm here and once right across the chest. His shirt was laid wide open across here. And blood was just coming down and he was still coming at me, right? And I thought for sure if I don't kill this guy, he's just going to knife me in the back when I walk away. And I managed to plant the heel of my combat boot right in the center of his face and knock him out. And I just took his blade, went up to the fence, stuck it in the fence and went—whap! Snapped the blade, dropped it and walked. Now, I was pretty much berserk while that fight was going on. I mean, I was fighting for my life. And the fact that I didn't kill the guy with the blade really surprised me after I walked away.

I: Again, you had a chance in both situations because you had the upper hand.

S: Oh yeah. I mean, I took some heavy damage. My gut was laid open and at least one of my ribs was broken. The other was cracked and I mean I was having a hard time seeing and breathing. I was spitting up blood. So I mean, I wasn't in any great shape either but I did have the upper hand. I could very easily have finished him! And that would have been game over. That time I was protecting myself! That time I didn't want to face a murder rap.

I: Sounds to me that you had a terrible time in elementary school.

S: Oh, yah. Today though people would never guess.

I: How did it feel then?

S: I really don't want to talk about it, but I felt like it was never going to end, like it was out of control, like I was trapped.

I: So the teachers in the school . . .

S: *(Interrupts)* Please Harv, be real. They hardly knew what was happening.

I: So how did you feel?

S: I felt scared, I felt alone.

I: Very vulnerable?

S: Of course.

I: So, what you learned about relationships was . . .

S: I started thinking—why not annihilate everyone else, why me? Eat or be eaten. *(Pauses)* Hey, that's sounds like opposites, like the way I operate these days.

I: Mm hmm. And just as you learned things then, you can learn new things now. You are no longer trapped in that helpless situation.

S: Yeah. A great general once said that to win a war you should always have two things—the upper hand and superior fire power. You know, before I pummeled Stanley I was like a dog who had been kicked too much. So I decided that nobody's fucking with me again—I'm going to guarantee it. I used to carry every weapon from a pocket knife to a Walter PFK, including a switchblade, butterfly knife, Chinese Stars, nunchakus, lock blades, or stilettos. There was a period of about three weeks when I was walking around with a Browning high power, semi-automatic pistol in my jacket. And it was basically for survival. Once the situation was over, I ditched it.

I: How old were you when you ditched it?

S: Sixteen.

I: Yeah. Now I know why there are no shades and colors. Sounds like you went from one extreme to the other. What you learned was that life is an extreme.

S: Right!

I: What's sad about this for me is that you've protected yourself in ways in which you ended up getting shafted too.

S: Yeah, but for a time it was well worth it.

I: And also what's sad for me is that you won't get some of the things you really want or need, like friendship, closeness, intimacy. And I guess the question is—can you still protect yourself and open up at the same time?

S: Right, that's a key question.

Tony had just described the transition from being a victim of bullies to becoming tough and invulnerable. But he had been trapped by the polarity of these extremes. Facing this issue in therapy brought with it the chance for alternatives—options which involved many shades and colors rather than just black and white.

Evidence of Change

For the conduct-disordered student, evidence of change can come from changes in behavior in school, at home, and/or in the community. Documented improvement of school marks, fewer incidents of rule violations, and improved relationships with teachers and students are examples of such change. But some of the earliest signs of change come from exploring changes in thinking. The following illustrates a change in Tony's philosophy:

S: I read the *Art of Warfare.*

I: Yeah.

S: It has three rules: (1) If your enemy is smaller than you, crush him; (2) if your enemy's the same size as you, go toe to toe; (3) if your enemy's bigger, regroup and then try to defeat.

I: Okay. What's your point?

S: Well, I realized that those were the rules I used to live by. Somewhere along the way these three simple rules got changed. Now they're (1) if your enemy's smaller, crush him if need be; (2) if he's equal, go toe to toe only if you have to; (3) if your enemy's bigger, run, try and hide, and only if you have no choice, attack.

I: That's interesting but I don't understand. Why would you change when the old system was working for you?

S: I think I found a reason. You know a man who suddenly gets all the money in the world. For the first year or two he has a great time, buying himself Ferraris, pools, anything he wants. After a while he gets bored. There's boredom in perfection and I'd perfected a system. And I realized that if I pushed the system any further, if I increased the stakes, I'm going to get fried.

I: But I thought you were the guy who told me some time in mid-October that there was a high that you got from the chase. Are you getting bored with that kind of high?

S: I'm getting bored with that kind of high. That's my first impression. Second of all, this escapade with the cops and the nunchakus has got me on two years' probation—my name is on the computer for two years. So if I fuck up anyhow, my ass is going to the wall for sure. So I've got to play the ponies very carefully.

I: Oh! Okay. Are you actually telling me that you think it's important to check out the risks involved because it's your ass that could be on the line?

S: Right.

I: So it sounds like you've decided to operate somewhat differently both because of something inside you as well as pressure from outside.

S: Yes. It's true that I'm thinking a bit differently but I have to admit that I'm worried about getting nailed.

In the preceding example, the impetus for change came from both internal and external sources. Any fluctuation in either source could alter the overall momentum of change. A definite sign of change in clients is a willingness to share increasingly *vulnerable aspects* of their lives. Tony provided just such an example in his twentieth therapy session:

S: The only situation that seems to have changed is that time seems to be moving a lot quicker. Like, I've been meeting with my teacher on Monday about math. And it feels like a month or two months, like ages ago since I've seen him. It's just that time is moving so quick.

I: What does that mean to you?

S: Well, when things were moving slow, it was day to day. You knew it was day to day because you could feel it moving slowly. It was very easy to channel and target because things that happened maybe three, four, or five days ago were still right on top of you. But now I feel that time is moving so fast. I think maybe it's not so much that the anger has lessened. Targets are appearing but they're disappearing so quickly again that the whole scenario that would trigger the next one is already so far gone that it's like, not even remembered any more.

I: Has it ever happened before in your life like this?

S: No, nothing's ever seemed to just rip by in fast gear. Like, I went to the cottage with my buddies just this past weekend. And now it's like I don't remember the weekend. It's like it was a million years ago.

I: Were you totally "bombed" on the weekend?

S: No! No! No! That's just it. I had two beers the whole weekend. And it was a good weekend. It's just that we talked a lot about our families.

I: Oh! And what sort of things came up?

S: *(Pensively hesitates)* I thought maybe—well, my dad just had his six-tieth birthday just three days ago. And that seems a long time ago— just two days ago! And I think maybe it's because my dad doesn't look a day over forty even though he's sixty! Sixty years old—that's re-tirement age! He's getting old and he's my dad!

I: So?

S: I think maybe subconsciously seeing my dad turn sixty sort of threw something at me. I said to myself: Holy shit, you're getting old too! So, I mean, maybe that was it. But I don't know for sure.

I: Okay. Why would it bother you more now? He had a birthday a year ago and he was fifty-nine. It didn't hit you then.

S: Yeah. Last year, family functions really didn't mean much; and the year before that too. I was still young enough to say, I'm still a kid and I've forgotten my dad's birthday, so I didn't get him anything. So birthdays, Christmas, it was no real big deal. I think this year what sort of did it was my mom told me a week before that my dad's birthday was coming up. And then the day before, she told me again and I didn't even remember her saying anything about my dad's birthday the week before. I think that's when I started noticing time was moving a little quickly. And then when my dad turned sixty, I think it just sort of hit me how fast time was actually moving. I mean, my dad literally doesn't have that much time left. I mean, he's old! He's getting old and I'm aging just as quickly as he is!

I: But why would it bother you now?

S: *(Sighs)* Maybe because I see my dad mellowing with age and just in the last couple of weeks we've been talking about how I've been mellowing. You know, I'm not quite as obnoxious as I usually have been. So, I don't know. That's the only connection I can make. I began to realize: Hey, I'm almost twenty now!

I: And what does that mean to you?

S: That means that I'm going to have to start taking responsibility for my actions. It means that he's getting closer and closer to the tombstone. It means that he won't be around forever. *(Tears begin to well up in Tony's eyes)*.

I: So you're worried about losing him?

S: *(Sobs)* Yes! And I want to get as much out of it before it goes.

I: Right. Ideally, what would you like to get out of the relationship between you and your dad before he passes away? *(Pauses, noticing the client's facial reaction to the question)*. You know, you look like you never thought about that before. You look thoughtful and also a little afraid.

S: Yeah. Um, *(clears throat, hesitates, and sighs)*. Um . . . Well, the one thing I think I've always wanted is for my dad to feel proud of me.

I: Does that mean that you feel like you really haven't given him something he could be proud of yet?

S: Yeah.

I: And you don't feel terrific about that?

S: *(Head down)* No. Not really.

I: Okay. Why are you struggling with this more now than a year ago, two years ago, three years ago?

S: Well, I think we can sort of tie it in with the math. For the last eighteen years, I've done absolutely dick fucking all, especially in school. I mean I've done lots of things my dad can see as worthwhile. But my school grades have always been in the toilet. And I know it really made my dad happy whenever my grades went up. And I think I see now that I don't have that much left in school and I really honestly don't think that if I can't make him proud of me by the time I get out of school, I don't think I'll be able to, period! And I don't have much time left to do it.

I: So what you're saying is there's something precious you would like to see and you have control over whether it happens.

S: I have all the control over whether it happens.

I: You know, Tony, you sound more serious and mature.

S: You want to know the truth? I'm farther from an answer now than I've ever been before because the old answers don't apply. *(Pauses)* And I think that's one of the things I'm worried about. It's always been easy in the past for me to shrug things off, pass them on, have somebody else carry them. And that's why I've gone through all of my history up to date. I've avoided caring so much so that I wouldn't get stuck in this situation.

I: Sounds though that how you feel about your dad has changed things.

S: That's what's rough.

Tony had begun to face issues of interpersonal responsibility and in the process had exposed his vulnerability and confusion. Often such revelations scare CD underachievers, who judge that this will weaken them. That is why such revelations are often followed by some acting out and/or missing subsequent sessions. A month after the preceding exchange, Tony revealed an even more powerful experience.

S: Yeah, the last time I cared for someone, it ended up scary—the person got killed.

I: Are you serious?

S: Yup. Got hit by a bus. (Tony's eyes began to fill with tears).

I: Take your time.

S: *(Long pause)* A long time ago, there was this girl that I started seeing. We were about 12. It was my first real crush and it developed into an incredible relationship. She knew I loved her, I knew she loved me, and we worked from there. We didn't take advantage of each other— it was just incredible!

I: What was her name?

S: Debra. *(Pauses)* So anyway, Debra and I went everywhere and did everything together. It was just incredible! And her parents didn't know. Her parents were very, very strict. If her parents knew she was seeing somebody, she would have been grounded forever. And then her dad would have hunted me down with a shotgun. I mean, most of the time we would be sneaking out in the middle of the night or at the movies on Saturdays with our friends. But we were really together. This went on for four or five months. Actually, it was weird because the first time we saw each other was at a dance that the school was having and she was a friend of somebody's. I was looking around, feeling bored. I looked and I saw her. She was just turning and I was just turning and our eyes locked. It was as if we both just went and said, ah, there you are. Just fucking incredible! And one day, after several months of being in happy bliss, we were crossing under a highway overpass and a Greyhound bus ran her down.

I: You mean you actually saw the accident?

S: Yeah . . . *(Pauses)* I just . . . *(Pauses)* My whole system just shut right down. *(Long pause)* . . . And after I just stumbled across the street.

I: So you weren't hit?

S: No. She was crossing just in front of me. You know, walking in front of me . . . *(Pauses)* I wandered around for a while . . . I knew she was gone. The bus hit her and ran over her. I knew she was dead. My whole system just shut down.

I: Sounds like you were in shock.

S: Oh fuck! It was like I'd snorted a pound of cocaine. I just went into a cocoon for the rest of the day and then I went home. *(Tony paused as tears streamed down his face.)* Then I shut the memory out. And the only time I ever spoke of her was when I was totally sloshed out of my mind and for some reason I was on a self-pity trip and she's like the ultimate in self-pity trips. And to today, I mean, I still haven't recovered.

I: *(Subdued tone)* I can hear it in your voice as you're describing it.

S: I didn't let myself cry then. And I haven't let myself cry because I know that if I do, I don't know if I'll be able to stop. That was pretty rough.

I: Yeah. And you're still carrying the pain around, although you don't do anything public with it. You don't do much with it yourself, it's just there.

S: Um hum *(Tony's eyes welled up again)*.

I: *(Pauses)* So in a sense, Ann's the first female you've allowed yourself to care for since you lost Debra.

S: It's really rough because, at the time I went to have a cigarette afterward so I would simmer down. And I felt some liquid on my arm, and I thought I was crying so I looked down.

I: And there were no tears?

S: It was blood and I wasn't cut—so it had to be hers. *(Pauses and sighs)*. It was rough.

I: Yeah. *(Pauses)* Are you telling me that from that point on, you have been shut down and that the possibility of feeling again only got touched recently by Ann?

S: *(Thoughtfully)* I hadn't thought there was a connection, simply because that's buried so far away that it doesn't come out. I've only had night terrors once in my life. Night terrors are supposed to be your ultimate fear when your subconscious lets loose. And it was a giant snake. Nothing else. Debra's just buried so far down that nothing can get to it.

I: When did you have that night terror?

S: Oh, three years ago. I thought I was going to die. Actually, I woke up in my closet holding my cross and an air rifle. I had the barrel pointed in my mouth.

I: Oh, God.

S: And I just like sprung awake. I've never been more scared than when I had that night terror. That night terror was . . . I mean nothing will bring Debra back. Nothing will bring that back . . . *(Sighs and cries softly)*.

The externally tough, uncaring manipulator had revealed a frightened, hurt, and angry teenager who had struggled to survive a major loss. He had lived daily as a victim of bullies in elementary school, he had been rejected by peers, both male and female. And he had survived the death of his first girlfriend by shutting off the past and fighting with those in the present. He had rejected meaningful long-term heterosexual relationships as too risky and had learned to take what he could get in the moment. He yearned for what he once had but he had gotten trapped in a mind-set that such aspirations were no longer possible for him.

What did Tony do with what had been uncovered? In the very next session, he returned having worked through additional issues:

S: I've been thinking a lot about what we've talked about and a lot of the pain came back. I mean, it was pretty rough. And then I said, okay, is the pain always going to be there if I don't keep the system shut down? I said, well, two things can happen. One, I can go back to being the more fragile me. And there's a chance, if I look, I might find what I had or close to what I had with Deb. And then I started thinking, well, that's impossible I haven't found it up until now. And then I stopped and looked back and said, no, it's not impossible! The reason I haven't found it isn't because it's not there. It's because I haven't been looking!

I: Yup, I agree.

S: And then I said, well, what do I think my chances are? And I looked around the bar and that was a stupid thing to do.

I: *(Chuckles)* That's a poor place to take a sample?

S: And I realized that. And I said, well, let's take a look at the people who are immediately around me and see who I come up with. And the first person actually that I thought of was Ann. And I said, well, what would happen if we had connected. And I thought about it and that didn't take long. Once I opened myself to the idea that more than likely, if I'd looked, I could have found what I had with Deb. And out of my immediate area I was able to find two other people already. I said, wow this is incredible! My mind said, see, see what you found. You haven't even gone two steps and you've found two. This is great. And I started thinking, why don't I develop? I said, granted, there is a large chance I might get hurt again. I don't think I'll get hurt quite to the same degree as I was the first time because that would be a little difficult. I said, well, is it worth it? And I looked back on the last two years and I said, yeah, I think it is. And I started thinking of people. And then I said, well, maybe what I should do is to go out and see if I still know how to feel, see if I still know how to care or whether it's a waste of my time.

Tony had continued to process the issue and appeared willing to invest some time in testing out new relationships. At least one cognitive danger still remained. Tony continued to perceive relationships in either/or terms. Before he could truly engage at a different level, he would have to face these extremes.

Using the Student-Therapist Relationship for Change

One of the therapist's most powerful tools during the change phase is the *therapeutic relationship,* which can provide a context for dealing with treatment issues. For example, playing games in relationships is a predictable CD underachiever theme that can be addressed this way.

Confronting the client's manipulation of the therapist serves several important purposes, especially *after* the therapy alliance has been established. First, it brings a predictable problem into the treatment relationship. Second, it demonstrates to the student that the therapist is aware of the manipulation within their relationship. This may even strengthen the therapeutic alliance because CD underachievers respect those who can "see through them." Third, it provides an excellent arena within which to observe, explore, and change manipulative patterns. Fourth, if there are no changes in the frequency and intensity of client manipulations within the therapeutic relationship, it is reasonable to assume that the same is true for relationships outside treatment. In other words, it can be a barometer of the extent of change.

Termination

> And then they are supposed to leave. But when is "then"?
>
> Beitman (1987, p. 262)

Issues of Planned Termination

In the literature on psychotherapy with CD underachievers, little emphasis has been placed on treatment termination. How do both therapist and student avoid prolonging treatment while ensuring that they have met enough to maintain change?

For these clients, the possibility of termination exists from the very first session. Many terminate prematurely (often more than once), attend sporadically, or never permit constructive engagement. Others take periodic breaks from treatment, sometimes because of the need to consolidate gains or slow the pace of change.

But for those CD underachievers who have made significant gains, what are the signs that termination is appropriate? Planned termination should be considered when there has been documented change in academic achievement and in interpersonal relationships. But if we wait until both goals are fully met, we might never terminate.

Frequently, therapist and client begin to gradually decrease the frequency of sessions as change occurs. In a sense, changing needs have resulted in mini-terminations. The student will often avail him- or herself of periodic check-ins, especially when new crises emerge. These contacts tend to be of much shorter duration, some lasting only one session. Many expect that the therapist will continue to be "on-call" for them, a lingering sign of their narcissism.

Most CD underachievers who have changed significantly tend to initiate the subject of termination. This may reflect their need to control the relationship, but it may also simply reflect their realistic assessment of a decreasing investment in the therapeutic relationship and increasing investments in other significant relationships and activities.

It is important for the therapist to examine his or her reactions to impending termination. Is the therapist having difficulty saying good-bye, and if so, why? In what ways is the therapist holding on to the student? It is also very important that the therapist allow the client to take most of the credit for change. The greater the sense of client ownership, provided there is reasonable acknowledgment of the therapist's contributions, the greater the chance of sustained improvement.

Impulsive termination is contraindicated. It is important that the issue of termination be processed as any other issue. Saying goodbye, reminiscing, sharing credit, reviewing progress, highlighting lingering patterns, describing future hopes and pointing out potential difficulties all require time.

The following excerpt contains the initial discussion of termination between Tony and his therapist:

S: Oh, let me tell you! And you know what's really neat?

I: No, go ahead.

S: Well, I said, honestly now, would all this have happened if you and I hadn't talked? And granted, fairly regularly, periodically, Deb would come back to mind, and the minute it started to come back to mind, I pondered it for a little bit and then vroom, it got sent off. It's weird because I honestly don't think I would have thought about all these things, felt all these things, done all these things if we hadn't—if I hadn't brought the subject up and if we hadn't started to take a crack at it.

I: Right. But you never would have brought it up unless you felt enough trust in our relationship.

S: Oh yeah, for sure.

I: You've really thought this through step by step, you've been honest enough with yourself and me to face some of the questions you were talking about as you tried to figure this out.

S: I think just bringing it to you was enough. I've made a big leap! *(Pauses)* But, I don't know whether it's done, whether it's in the middle, whether it's still changing. I don't know where it's going from here, and something inside is just saying that now would not be a good time for us to stop seeing each other.

I: Interesting that you've raised the issue of us stopping. It's a fair issue.

S: I've been thinking about it some. You know my grades have improved a lot. My English mark is a 74, Economics—70, Health—80, and Dramatic Arts—85.

I: I know. And those marks are great!

S: Well, ya, but Drama and Health were really a joke. But I really had to work hard in Econ and English.

I: Okay, so you've really brought your school grades up.

S: Ya. I'm even thinking about university now.

I: Okay. Sounds like there are some things we can continue to talk about.

S: Right. But maybe not every week.

I: Sounds fine with me. How would you like to arrange things?

S: Part of me wants to continue but another part wants to try things on my own. Know what I mean?

I: Sure. It makes sense. We've processed a lot of things.

S: Yeah, we sure have. I think I'd like to stop coming regularly. I'd like to set up another appointment in about a month. Just to check in sort of. Okay?

I: Sure, Tony. That'd be fine.

Interpersonal change is more difficult to document than changes in school performance, partly because relationships are more subtle. Documentation sources include reports from the student, observation of changes in the therapeutic relationship, and/or information from friends, parents, teachers, and community authorities. What follows is a brief therapy excerpt from Tony's third-to-last therapy session that highlights the issue of relationship change:

S: Okay. You know I met this girl from Montreal a few months ago, at the beginning of the summer, you know.

I: You mean Gina?

S: Yeah. Well, before the summer ended we talked. We talked a lot about whether we should see other people, you know.

I: You mean like dating other people?

S: Right. And we've talked a lot on the phone since she went back to Montreal. And she said, "Look, I'm not telling you to forget about me. But if you need somebody to take care of you until the term ends, it's okay, I understand." Now, Harv, if you were on the receiving end of that line, what would you have thought?

I: What do I think *you* would have thought, or *I* would have thought?

S: What would *you* have thought.

I: What I would have thought is, that that's consistent with Gina because of the way you described her, *her* needs always came last, that she was generous to a fault, that she would consider others before she would consider herself.

S: Yeah, okay.

I: Now, if I were to try to guess that you thought, you would be suspicious.

S: *(Smiles)* Right. Next question—suspicious of what?

I: Suspicious that she's freeing *herself* up in the same way.

S: Bingo! It's the first thing that ran through my mind. The first thing that ran through my mind. So I said, wait a minute here. Are you trying to say that we should see other people? And her instant reaction was, "No, no, you don't understand. I'm going to stay faithful, but if you need to sleep with somebody while you're there, just don't tell me about it." So, this was like free permission for me to go out and do what the hell I wanted, as long as I came back at the end of the school year. I've had three offers since I've been at university, all of them very attractive. Not nearly as attractive as Gina—nobody is!

I: So it's like, there isn't another female on the face of this earth that is as beautiful as Gina? But that also fits with a tendency of yours to state issues or facts in extreme terms. Like, you hate somebody, or you are absolutely crazy about them.

S: Yeah, that's the way it used to be with me. But, you know, I'm starting to see the shades of grey. Believe it or not, I'm starting to see the shades of grey.

I: Shades of grey? What do you mean?

S: Gina is great, she's good for me, but she's not perfect. And yet, I turned all three offers down. And you want to hear the scary part? I was happy that I did!

I: *(Laughs)* Oh, oh—I think it's time for medication.

S: *(Roars with laughter)* It made me feel really good inside to turn them down! It made me feel really good inside to turn them down and know that I was never going to mention it to Gina and get a possible reward from her for having turned them down.

I: In other words, using it for some future credit?

S: Right. It made me feel like a million bucks to know it was an unselfish act. And that scared the shit out of me. And there's something else.

I: What's that?

S: Coming to university this year, I sort of stopped and looked around. And I guess I just sort of realized my own mortality. I stopped and realized, okay, four years for a BA, so that I can get a job. So I finish school and I start looking for a job. You remember our first couple of sessions? I didn't think I would live to be 30!

I: Sure. You thought you would be either a policeman by the age of 21, or you'd be dead.

S: Yeah. And I'm starting to realize, holy shit, okay, here I am wishing that Gina and I would last forever and have a family and settle down and all that kind of bullshit. And that means I'm going to be like, 25 getting a job, 30 buying a house, 35 having kids! Like, 55 before the kids are basically on their own and can function for themselves! And I guess just coming to university I realized, holy shit! I've really got a long way to go! And I just sort of realized that, whoa, life doesn't end at 30. Like, I'm not going to be dead by 30. Like, I'm actually going to go places and do things.

In the last session, Tony and his therapist reviewed the themes they had worked on during a span of 39 sessions. They also speculated about the future and identified recurring problems:

I: There is one problem for me. The problem is how you translate your intentions into action. I think you would never have thought about slowing yourself down, about taking time to develop a relationship, about giving without automatically figuring out how your giving would result in your receiving, about getting really close, and staying close. Three years ago you would never even have thought about these things.

S: Um hum. You're right.

I: Now, in the future you've got to think about how to continue monitoring yourself, you've got to think about how to keep up your crap detection skills, because they are still part of you.

S: *(Laughs)* Um hum.

I: So, spend some time enjoying your maturity, okay. But be careful. That's all I'm saying. You're so good that you could . . .

S: Screw myself with my old style?

I: That's right. You've done it before. So how do you crap detect on yourself on a continuing basis?

S: Right. You know, when I first started doing this counseling thing, I did it for my mom. And then I shifted to doing it for me. And there's steps that I never, not never, but more than likely I would have taken a lot longer to take, had I not taken them here with you.

I: Yeah, that's fair.

S: And lately with you and me it's been sort of like, we don't get together unless there's been some sort of next step. So, from here I really don't know. I assume the next time we'll get together is if things work out with Gina and if they're going along properly. And if I implement what I say I'm implementing, I guess that would be the next time.

I: Okay. So the reasons for you and me to meet have changed.

S: Right.

Confirmation of subtle changes in Tony's relationships were reported by his mother. He was willing to delay gratification and risk a monogamous, longer-term relationship. However, there was a lingering suspicion on the part of those who knew him that somewhere, somehow, the old patterns would emerge again. These suspicions were well founded. *Characterological remnants* remained. Tony's relationship patterns had changed, but the changes produced modulations, not quantum transformations.

To what extent was Tony typical of Conduct Disorder underachievers? Tony's history (see Chapter 2) accurately reflects childhood-onset CD underachievement. Yet Tony's antisocial behavior was rarely extreme. His individual intellectual assessment placed him in the average range, although it became clear in therapy that he had a keen mind and verbal facility which were not apparent in his IQ score. His parents exhibited some predictable family difficulties both within their marriage and in their discordant child-rearing practices.

During impending termination, decisions about decreasing the frequency of sessions, about deciding whether to set a specific termination date, and about whether to maintain the same level of formality to the end should all be addressed. For these underachievers, losing a meaningful therapy relationship stands in dramatic contrast to the loss of other less positive encounters. But it may also arouse unresolved feelings (especially anger) anchored in earlier unsatisfying or conflicted relationship terminations.

The termination stage provides the therapist with an excellent opportunity to process two losses—the student's and the therapist's. Almost all clinicians who have helped CD underachievers improve their academic performance and modify their interpersonal relationships report a sense of loss at termination. Some also continue to be skeptical about the permanency of the changes they have witnessed. Succeeding within a structured academic environment is one thing. For the student to maintain the gains in the work world will test the strength of the changes.

At a one-year follow-up, Tony had completed his first year at university, having done reasonably well in four courses while failing one. He planned to retake the failed Natural Science course during his second year. He was working part-time to pay for his education, although he reported that he was having difficulty saving money. And he continued to experience highs and lows in relationships with his girlfriends.

And as is typical in treatment of personality disorders in adults, successful treatment with CD underachievers almost invariably involves some dropping back in for "checkups." Often these occur when the individual becomes worried about slipping back into the old patterns or when the "slipping" has already occurred. Generally, reestablishment of rapport and an agenda occur quickly and easily. There is a relationship on which to build.

TERMINATION OF UNSUCCESSFUL THERAPY

How should the therapist deal with termination for those CD underachievers who don't change or who get worse? It is important not to continue ineffective treatment after a reasonable trial period. Prolonging unsuccessful treatment will leave the client with a more negative view of treatment and may preclude any future treatment.

Also, it is imperative not to collude with the student by continuing unproductive treatment. If treatment continues despite little or no progress, parents, teachers, probation officers, and others may conclude that work is being done and progress is just around the corner. It is important that the therapist not permit such a false impression to linger.

SUMMARY

Individual cognitively oriented therapy for CD underachievers includes issues of engagement, pattern search, change, and termination. The examples in this chapter came mainly from one student who was seen for a total of 39 sessions during a period of about four years. This approach should be used, when appropriate, in combination with professional assistance for parents, incorporating school personnel and community representatives.

Chapter 7

Frequently Asked Questions about CD Underachievers

1. *Is it possible for a student to exhibit the personality characteristics of a Conduct Disorder and still be achieving?*

Most certainly. Many individuals successfully manipulate others. Their basic philosophy of life does not differ a great deal from the one Tony presented, but they are usually much less self-destructive and are rewarded for their efforts. Exactly what factors make for an achieving CD and what make for a CD underachiever are not clear, although the suspicion is that the outcome differences are due to a combination of factors, including internal, familial, environmental, and chance variables.

> Conduct Disorder individuals who are achieving are rarely diagnosed, not only because they are unlikely to come to the attention of psychologists and other professionals, but also because professionals rarely consider the possibility that Conduct Disorder permits success. Achieving conduct-disordered individuals are more likely to come to the attention of professionals when the manipulative pattern begins to affect interpersonal relationships. (Mandel & Marcus, 1988, p. 252)

2. *Is there any variation across CD underachievers, or do they all pretty much sound and look the same?*

There is wide variation within the CD underachiever group, including intellectual, familial, environmental, and academic differences. Some CD underachievers have average intellect while others may exhibit superior intelligence. Some come from extremely problematic family backgrounds (e.g., childhood-onset), while others have relatively stable family histories (e.g., adolescent-onset). Some have an impulsive nature, while others are better able to control themselves. Some may be provocative, hostile, and aggressive, while others tend to be less openly confrontive, choosing to manipulate in more discreet ways. Some are more directly tied into a problematic peer group, while others tend to be more isolated socially.

3. *Do CD underachievers change on their own without professional help? If they do change, what critical ingredients produce that change?*

Most CD underachievers tend to persist in their behavior patterns throughout their lives unless some constructive intervention occurs. This need not always include professional mental health assistance. Traumatic events may have an impact, as will significant others who have the strength and skill to successfully resist being manipulated. Some school structures and school personnel are much more suited to help the CD underachiever, and many of these characteristics have been discussed in the preceding chapters. In general, however, the earlier the onset and the more serious and numerous the risk factors, the more difficult it is to change this pattern once it has taken hold.

4. *As they grow into their 20s, 30s, 40s, what happens to those CD underachievers who have not received professional help?*

Many persons with this disorder continue their self-defeating behavior patterns well into their 30s. Mandel and Marcus (1988) have described some of the work and relationship problems that such individuals create. There is a generally held clinical view that such individuals do show signs of change on their own as they reach their middle years. It is possible that by middle age some can't maintain their earlier pace of hustling. Physical changes in these middle years may contribute to decreasing motivation to maintain the pattern or may even precipitate a request for professional help.

> The major issues which usually precipitate such requests revolve around concerns that the individual no longer has the energy required to maintain previous methods of operating, combined with a growing sense of social isolation and aloneness, which is a direct consequence of their past actions. (Mandel & Marcus, 1988, p. 254)

In essence, some conduct-disordered individuals begin to experience "pattern burnout." Nevertheless, they will have caused considerable damage, both to others and to themselves.

   5. *What methods should teachers use to control the acting-out patterns of CD underachievers? Should teachers try to become therapists for CD underachievers?*

Understandably, teachers find it difficult to deal with such students in the classroom (Iddiols, 1985) and tend to enlist external authority, usually in the form of the vice-principal or principal. This may lead to suspensions and/or expulsion from the school, recommendations for psychological assessment and mental health assistance, and so on. Teachers may be "impressed" initially or charmed by CD underachievers but tend to become disenchanted as the behavior patterns emerge.

   Teacher affective reactions can run the full gamut from initial interest to frustration, anger, and resentment at having "failed" or at having been betrayed or used. Some teachers, however, as is the case with some therapists, tend to work well with these students and become a significant positive force in their lives. When this has occurred, the teacher has used (either consciously or not) many of the approaches and methods highlighted in this text.

   Teachers must be very careful not to "treat" the CD underachiever. Each adult in the student's life plays a specific role, as parent, teacher, or school principal. Each role carries with it specific responsibilities, such as taking restrictive or disciplinary action or involving other authority figures. These responsibilities must not be abrogated in the name of therapeutic aims. Some leeway is available within each role, but the therapeutic approach advocated here is not designed for teachers. Nevertheless, some of the general principles can be helpful in dealing with CD underachievers in the classroom.

   6. *How do CD underachievers usually end up in counseling?*

Such students seldom enter counseling voluntarily. Most seek therapy under some form of external pressure from family members, school personnel, or the courts. If the student claims to be seeking counseling on his or her own, one might reasonably suspect that it represents an attempt to circumvent an external pressure. For example, a client may seek help from a guidance counselor knowing that this action will diminish the threat of school expulsion.

  7. *How long does individual counseling with a CD underachiever usually take?*

There is wide variation in the total number of sessions needed to produce meaningful behavior change. The length of treatment depends on many factors, including the severity of the behavior difficulties, the degree of support at home, the nature of academic deficits, the extent to which the school is well organized and effectively run, and the nature of the peer group influence.

As a general rule, the more severe the pathology, the less positive the present environment, and the earlier the onset of difficulties, the greater the length of treatment. Another general rule is that CD underachievers who are overtly sad and vulnerable are more amenable to treatment than those who deny their psychological pain.

Therapy tends to be either very short and unproductive or long term with many interesting ups and downs. For those treatments that end after relatively few sessions, a working therapeutic relationship rarely develops. This may be due to many factors including the inability or unwillingness of either participant to move beyond the initial manipulations.

CD underachievers who remain in treatment for more than a few sessions tend to be in treatment longer than other types of underachievers. Other concurrent forms of treatment (e.g., academic remediation, family therapy) may add to the length of treatment as well.

  8. *Are we any more successful in treating CD underachievers today than we were 20 years ago?*

Many of the earlier treatment reports of CD underachievers implied that such individuals were not suited for "talking" therapies. This clinical wisdom was based on the use of more traditional approaches which tended to be unsuccessful and often reported premature termination. More recent work has pointed to increasing length of treatment as well as increased success, although success rates are generally not as high when compared with other types of underachievers (Mandel & Marcus, 1988).

9. *Does the matching of therapist sex and student sex make any differ-ence in the process or outcome of treatment?*

There does not appear to be any research on this particular topic that di-rectly addresses this issue with CD underachievers. From a clinician's viewpoint, however, it seems better to pair male CD underachievers with male therapists and female CD underachievers with female therapists in individual treatment. Such clients, through their behavior and percep-tions, express strong and often negative attitudes and feelings about mem-bers of the opposite sex. These are more easily handled by same-sex therapists who may not be as personally offended by such attitudes and perceptions. In addition, sexual seductiveness tends to lose its manipu-lative power in same-sex therapist/client combinations.

10. *During the course of treatment, what kinds of inquiries are made of the therapist by parents and/or teachers of CD underachievers?*

Once the student is in treatment, parents often perceive the therapist as a resource and support in their continuing struggles with their child. They may telephone or attempt to enter into conversations with the therapist when they pick up their child. They may ask for advice, especially dur-ing crises precipitated by their child. Most of these discussions should take place with the student present. Any contacts that occur without the student should be reported to the student so that therapeutic trust can be maintained.

It is also important that the therapist not isolate him- or herself from potentially rich sources of information. This is especially true in the case of CD underachievers, who may selectively withhold such external information.

School personnel are also interested in finding out how treatment is progressing and can be valuable sources of information regarding a stu-dent's school behavior. Similar principles should be used as were de-scribed for dealing with parents.

Periodically, school personnel will seek the therapist's advice about how harsh or lenient to be now that treatment has begun. A teacher may believe that the school should "lighten up" and allow the student in treat-ment time to make significant changes. Although this attitude is to be commended the CD underachiever will quickly exploit it. My advice is to ask school personnel to evaluate whether their rules and regulations are fair to all students and whether they have been clearly and fully conveyed. If the answer is in the affirmative, they should maintain structures. No special consideration should be given by the school just because a student is in treatment for the disorder.

11. *What difficulties would novice or experienced therapists have in working with a CD underachievers?*

Most novices tend to allow themselves to be used in much the same way the CD underachiever has used significant others. Novices tend to provide less structure, be less directive and far less confrontive, hoping that their positive attitude and offer of a relationship will trigger changes in the student. These issues should be dealt with early in supervision.

For experienced clinicians, the problems are often quite different. These involve an increasing detachment and unwillingness on the therapist's part to engage with the client. Often this comes from unsuccessful treatment experiences with other CD underachievers. The therapist has adapted to previous failures either by avoiding work with such students or by minimizing the personal investment of time and energy in new CD underachievers.

12. *Does the approach recommended here require any predictable changes in the therapist during the course of treatment?*

Yes. The therapist must be prepared to begin with a structured, active, directive, cognitive-behavioral approach and shift to a more supportive approach as the student changes. In essence, the therapist must be able to perceive the growth in the client, and if it occurs, shift both orientation and attitude.

13. *Is individual or group therapy indicated for CD underachievers?*

Simultaneous or sequential use of both individual and group therapy tends to produce better outcome than either of the approaches used in isolation. Individual sessions can be aimed at a much greater depth, while the group therapy can focus on improving social skills and dealing with peer pressure. There may even be value in remedial academic group work with high-achieving students as tutors.

One consideration is whether to form a homogeneous group consisting only of other CD underachievers or whether to arrange heterogeneous group membership. A mixed grouping is indicated, because it will make it more difficult for the CD underachiever to pair up with deviant peers. In fact, several studies reviewed in Chapter 3 have shown that homogeneous CD underachiever groups are contraindicated in therapy.

Appendix

Instruments and Procedures to Assess Conduct Disorder

The following assessment instruments and structured procedures (e.g., systematic observation or diagnostic interviews) have been used in the study, assessment, and treatment of behavior problem children and adolescents and their families. The list headings indicate the categories of information elicited by the various instruments and procedures.

The Child and Adolescent

Achievement Motivation Profile (AMP) (Friedland et al., 1996).

Adolescent Antisocial Self-Report Behavior Checklist (Kulik, Stein, & Sarbin, 1968).

Adolescent Problem Inventory (Freedman, Rosenthal, Donahoe, Schlundt, & McFall, 1978).

Child Behavior Checklist (Achenbach, 1993; Achenbach & Edelbrock, 1983).

Children's Action Tendency Scale (Deluty, 1979).

Children's Hostility Inventory (self-report and parent report) (Kazdin, Rodgers, Colbus, & Siegel, 1987).

Children's Depression Inventory (Kovacs, 1981).

Daily Parent Report (Chamberlain & Reid, 1987).

Eyberg Child Behavior Inventory (Burns & Patterson, 1990; Eyberg, 1980; Eyberg & Robinson, 1983; Robinson, Eyberg, & Ross, 1980).

Impulsivity Scale (Hirschfield, 1965).

Interview for Aggression (self-report and parent report) (Kazdin & Esveldt-Dawson, 1986).

Minnesota Multiphasic Personality Inventory (Adolescent form) (Butcher, Graham, Williams, & Kaemmer, 1992).

Multiscore Depression Inventory (Berndt, 1986).

The New York Teacher Rating Scale for Disruptive and Antisocial Behavior (Miller et al., 1995).

Parent Daily Report (Chamberlain & Reid, 1987; Patterson & Bank, 1986).

Perceived Competence Scale for Children (Harter, 1982).

Revised Behavior Problem Checklist (Quay & Peterson, 1987).

Self-Control Rating Scale (Kendall & Wilcox, 1979; Kendall & Zupan, 1981).

Self-Report Delinquency Scale (Elliott, Dunford, & Huizinga, 1987).

Self-Report Early Delinquency Scale (Moffit & Silva, 1988d).

Semi-Structured Diagnostic Interview for Underachievers (SSDIU) (Mandel & Mandel, 1995; Mandel & Marcus, 1988; Mandel, Roth, & Berenbaum, 1968).

Standardized Observation Codes (Wahler & Cormier,1970; Wahler, House, & Stambaugh, 1976).

Structured Observation Procedures (Forehand & McMahon, 1981).

The Symptom Checklist (Patterson, Reid, Jones, & Conger, 1975).

Telephone Interview Report on Stealing and Social Aggression (Patterson, Reid, Jones, & Conger, 1975).

The Child's and Adolescent's Cognitive Processing

Attributional Style Assessment (Asarnow & Callahan, 1985).

Interpersonal Awareness (Selman, 1980).

Interpersonal Problem-Solving Strategies Assessment (Asarnow & Callahan, 1985).

Means-Ends Problem-Solving Task (Shure & Spivack, 1972).

Purdue Elementary Problem Solving Inventory (Feldhusen, Houtz, & Ringenbach, 1972).

The Family

Behavioral Parent Interview (Patterson & Bank, 1986).

Conflict Behavior Questionnaire (Prinz, Foster, Kent, & O'Leary, 1979; Robin & Weiss, 1980).

Dyadic Parent-Child Interactional Coding System (Eyberg & Robinson, 1983).

Family Crisis List (Patterson, 1982, 1983).

Family Interaction Coding System (Patterson, Ray, Shaw, & Cobb, 1969; J. B. Reid, 1978).

Family Process Code (Dishion et al., 1984).

Issues Checklist (Robin & Weiss, 1980).

Parents

Dyadic Adjustment Scale (assessing marital relationship) (Spanier, 1976).

O'Leary-Porter Scale (assessing overt marital hostility) (Porter & O'Leary, 1980).

Parent Competency Inventory (Ballenski & Cook, 1983).

Peers

Index of Peer Relations (Hudson, 1992).

Inventory of Parent and Peer Attachment (Armsden & Greenberg, 1987).

Peer and Self-Rating Scale (Glow & Glow, 1980).

Peer Nomination of Aggression (Lefkowitz et al., 1977).

School

Behavioral Coding Systems (for schools) (Harris, Kreil, & Orpet, 1977; Walker & Fabre, 1992).

School Situations Questionnaire (Barkley, 1981).

Sutter-Eyberg Student Behavior Inventory (Funderburk & Eyberg, 1989).

Community

Community Interaction Checklist (Wahler, Leske, & Rogers, 1979).

Inpatient Behavior

Adolescent Antisocial Behavioral Checklist (Curtiss et al., 1983).

References

Achenbach, T. M. (1993). Taxonomy and comorbidity of conduct problems: Evidence from empirically based approaches. *Development and Psychopathology, 5*, 51–64.

Achenbach, T. M., & Edelbrock, C. S. (1983). *Manual for the Child Behavior Checklist and Revised Child Behavior Profile*. Burlington, VT: University of Vermont, Department of Psychiatry.

Agee, V. L. (1979). *Treatment of the violent, incorrigible adolescent*. Lexington, MA: D.C. Heath.

Agnew, R. (1990). The origins of delinquent events: An examination of offender accounts. *Journal of Research in Crime and Delinquency, 27*, 267–294.

Alessi, N. E., McManus, M., Grapentine, W. L., & Brickman, A. (1983). The characterization of depressive disorders in serious juvenile offenders. *Journal of Affective Disorders, 6*, 9–17.

Alexander, J. F. (1973). Defensive and supportive communications in normal and deviant families. *Journal of Consulting and Clinical Psychology, 40*, 223–231.

Alexander, J. F., Barton, C., Schiavo, R. S., & Parsons, B. V. (1976). Systems-behavioral intervention with families of delinquents: Therapist characteristics, family behavior, and outcome. *Journal of Consulting and Clinical Psychology, 44*, 656–664.

Alexander, J. F., Holtzworth-Munroe, A., & Jameson, P. B. (1994). The process and outcome of marital and family therapy research: Review and evaluation. In A. E. Bergin & S. L. Garfield (Eds.), *Handbook of psychotherapy and behavior change* (4th ed.). New York: Wiley.

Alexander, J. F., & Parsons, B. V. (1973). Short-term behavioral intervention with delinquent families: Impact on family process and recidivism. *Journal of Abnormal Psychology, 81*, 219–225.

Alexander, J. F., & Parsons, B. V. (1982). *Functional family therapy*. Monterey, CA: Brooks/Cole.

Allen, J. P., Aber, J. L., & Leadbeater, B. J. (1990). Adolescent problem behaviors: The influence of attachment and autonomy. *Psychiatric Clinics of North America, 13,* 455–467.

Allen, J. P., Leadbeater, B. J., & Aber, J. L. (1994). The development of problem behavior syndromes in at-risk adolescents. *Development and Psychopathology, 6,* 323–342.

Amber, A. -M. (1992). *The effect of children on parents.* Binghamton, NY: Haworth Press.

Amber, A. -M. (1994a). A qualitative study of peer abuse and its effects: Theoretical and empirical implications. *Journal of Marriage and the Family, 56,* 119–130.

Amber, A. -M. (1994b). An international perspective on parenting: Social change and social constructs. *Journal of Marriage and the Family, 56,* 529–543.

American Psychiatric Association. (1987). *Diagnostic and statistical manual of mental disorders* (3rd ed., rev.). Washington, DC: Author.

American Psychiatric Association. (1994). *Diagnostic and statistical manual of mental disorders* (4th ed.). Washington, DC: Author.

Anderson, J. C., Williams, S., McGee, R., & Silva, P. (1987). DSM-III disorders in preadolescent children. *Archives of General Psychiatry, 44,* 69–76.

Anderson, K. E., Lytton, H., & Romney, D. M. (1986). Mother's interactions with normal and conduct-disordered boys: Who affects whom? *Developmental Psychology, 22*(5), 604–609.

Andrew, J. (1977). Delinquency: Intellectual imbalance? *Criminal Justice and Behavior, 4,* 99–104.

Andrews, V. C., Garrison, C. Z., Jackson, K. L., Addy, C. L., & McKeown, R. E. (1993). Mother-adolescent agreement on the symptoms and diagnoses of adolescent depression and conduct disorders. *Journal of the American Academy of Child and Adolescent Psychiatry, 32,* 731–738.

Apter, A., Gothelf, D., Orbach, I., Weizman, R., Ratzoni, G., Har-Even, D., & Tyano, S. (1995). Correlation of suicidal and violent behavior in different diagnostic categories in hospitalized adolescent patients. *Journal of the American Academy of Child and Adolescent Psychiatry, 34,* 912–918.

Arbuthnot, J., & Gordon, D. (1986). Behavioral and cognitive effects of a moral reasoning development intervention for high-risk behavior disordered adolescents. *Journal of Consulting and Clinical Psychology, 54,* 208–216.

Armsden, G. C., & Greenberg, M. T. (1987). The Inventory of Parent and Peer Attachment: Individual differences and the relationship to psychological well-being in adolescence. *Journal of Youth and Adolescence, 16,* 427–454.

Asarnow, J. R., & Callahan, J. W. (1985). Boys with poor adjustment problems: Social cognitive processes. *Journal of Consulting and Clinical Psychology, 53,* 80–87.

Atkeson, B. M., & Forehand, R. (1981). Conduct disorders. In E. J. Mash & L. G. Terdal (Eds.), *Behavioral assessment of childhood disorders.* New York: Guilford Press.

Austin, R. L. (1978). Race, father-absence, and female delinquency. *Criminology, 15,* 487–504.

Ayllon, T., Garber, S., & Pisor, K. (1975). The elimination of discipline problems through a combined school-home motivational system. *Behavior Therapy, 6,* 616–626.

Bachman, J. G., Johnston, L. D., & O'Malley, P. M. (1978). Delinquent behavior linked to educational attainment and post-high school experiences. In L. Otten (Ed.), *Colloquium on the correlates of crime and the determinants of criminal behavior.* Arlington, VA: MITRE Corp.

Baer, R. A., & Nietzel, M. T. (1991). Cognitive and behavioral treatment of impulsivity in children: A meta-analytic review of the outcome literature. *Journal of Clinical Child Psychology, 20,* 400–412.

Ballenski, C. B., & Cook, A. S. (1982). Mother's perceptions of their competence in managing selected parenting tasks. *Family Relations Journal of Applied Family and Child Studies, 31,* 489–494.

Barkley, R. A. (1981). *Hyperactive children: A Handbook for diagnosis and treatment.* New York: Guilford Press.

Barkley, R. A. (1987). *Defiant children: A clinician's manual for parent training.* New York: Guilford Press.

Barley, W. D. (1986). Behavioral and cognitive treatment of criminal and delinquent behavior. In W. H. Reid, D. Dorr, J. I. Walker, & J. W. Bonner (Eds.), *Unmasking the psychopath: Antisocial personality and related syndromes.* New York: Norton.

Bates, J. E., Bayles, K., Bennett, D. S., Ridge, B., & Brown, M. M. (1991). Origins of externalizing behavior problems at eight years of age. In D. Pepler & K. Rubin (Eds.), *The development and treatment of childhood aggression.* Hillsdale, NJ: Erlbaum.

Baum, C. G., & Forehand, R. (1981). Long-term follow-up assessment of parent training by use of multiple outcome measures. *Behavior Therapy, 12,* 643–652.

Bear, G. C., & Richard, H. C. (1981). Moral reasoning and conduct problems in the classroom. *Journal of Educational Psychology, 73,* 644–670.

Beitman, B. D. (1987). *The structure of individual psychotherapy.* New York: Guilford Press.

Belson, W. A. (Ed.). (1975). *Juvenile theft: The causal factors.* London: Harper & Row.

Bennett, T., & Wright, R. (1984). *Burglars on burglary.* Aldershot, England: Gower.

Berkowitz, L. (1989). Frustration-aggression hypothesis: Examination and reformulation. *Psychological Bulletin, 106,* 59–73.

Bernal, M. E., Klinnert, M. D., & Schultz, L. A. (1980). Outcome evaluation of behavioral parent training and client-centered parent counseling for children with conduct problems. *Journal of Applied Behavioral Analysis, 13,* 677–691.

Berndt, D. J. (1986). *The Multiscore Depression Inventory (MDI).* Los Angeles, CA: Western Psychological Services.

Berndt, D. J., & Zinn, D. (1984). Prominent features of depression in affective and conduct disordered inpatients. In D. Offer, K. Howard, & E. Ostrov (Eds.), *Patterns of self-image.* San Francisco: Jossey-Bass.

Berrueta-Clement, J. R., Schweinhart, L. J., Barnett, W. S., Epstein, A. S., & Weikart, D. P. (1984). *Changed lives: The effects of the Perry Preschool Program on youths through age 19* (Monographs of the High/Scope Educational Research Foundation No. 8). Ypsilanti, MI: High/Scope.

Berrueta-Clement, J. R., Schweinhart, L. J., Barnett, W. S., & Weikart, D. P. (1987). The effects of early educational intervention on crime and delinquency in adolescence and early adulthood. In J. D. Burchard & S. N. Burchard (Eds.), *Primary prevention of psychopathology: Vol. 10. Prevention of delinquent behavior.* Newbury Park, CA: Sage.

Biederman, J., Faraone, S., Mick, E., & Lelon, E. (1995). Psychiatric comorbidity among referred juveniles with major depression: Fact or artifact? *Journal of the American Academy of Child and Adolescent Psychiatry, 34,* 579–590.

Biederman, J., Munir, K., & Knee, D. (1987). Conduct and oppositional defiant disorder in clinically referred children with attention-deficit disorder: A controlled family study. *Journal of the American Academy of Child and Adolescent Psychiatry, 26,* 724–732.

Biederman, J., Newcorn, J., & Sprich, S. (1991). Comorbidity of ADHD with conduct, depressive, anxiety, and other disorders. *American Journal of Psychiatry, 148,* 564–577.

Bierman, K. L. (1990). Improving the peer relations of rejected children. In B. B. Lahey & A. E. Kazdin (Eds.), *Advances in clinical child psychology.* New York: Plenum Press.

Bierman, K. L., & Wargo, J. B. (1995). Predicting the longitudinal course associated with aggressive-rejected, aggressive (nonrejected), and rejected (nonaggressive) status. *Development and Psychopathology, 7,* 669–682.

Bird, H. R., Gould, M. S., & Staghezza, B. M. (1993). Patterns of diagnostic co-morbidity in a community sample of children aged 9 through 16 years. *Journal of the American Academy of Child and Adolescent Psychiatry, 32,* 361–368.

Bisnaire, L. M. C., Firestone, P., & Rynard, D. (1990). Factors associated with academic achievement in children following parental separation. *American Journal of Orthopsychiatry, 60,* 67–76.

Blakey, C. H., & Davidson, W. S. (1984). Behavioral approaches to delinquency: A review. *Advances in Child Behavioral Analysis and Therapy, 3,* 241–272.

Block, J., & Gjerde, P. F. (1986). Distinguishing antisocial behavior and undercontrol. In D. Olweus, J. Block, & M. Radke-Yarrow (Eds.), *Development of antisocial and prosocial behavior: Research, theory, and issues.* Orlando, FL: Academic Press.

Blumstein, A., Cohen, J., Roth, J. A., & Visher, C. A. (Eds.). (1986). *Criminal careers and career criminals.* Washington, DC: National Academy of Sciences.

Bornstein, P. H., Schulberg, D., & Bornstein, M. T. (1987). Conduct disorders. In V. B. Van Hasselt & M. Hersen (Eds.), *Handbook of adolescent psychology* (pp. 245–264). New York: Pergamon Press.

Bowlby, J. (1946). *Forty-four juvenile thieves, their characters and homelife.* London: Tindall & Cox.

Bowman, R. P., & Myrick, R. D. (1987). Affects of an elementary school peer facilitator program on children with behavior problems. *School Counselor, 34,* 369–378.

Brandt, D. E., & Zlotnick, S. J. (1988). *The psychology and treatment of the youthful offender.* Springfield, IL: Thomas.

Braukman, C. J., & Fixsen, D. L. (1975). Behavior modification with delinquents. In M. Hersen, R. M. Fisher, & P. M. Miller (Eds.), *Progress in behavior modification* (Vol. 1.). New York: Academic Press.

Breiner, J. L., & Forehand, R. (1981). An assessment of the effects of parent training on clinic-referred children's school behavior. *Behavioral Assessment, 3,* 31–42.

Brennan, P., Mednick, S., & Kandel, E. (1991). Congenital determinants of violent and property offending. In D. J. Pepler & K. H. Rubin (Eds.), *The development and treatment of childhood aggression.* Hillsdale, NJ: Erlbaum.

Brickman, A. S., McManus, M. M., Grapentine, W. L., & Alessi, N. (1984). Neuropsychological assessment of seriously delinquent adolescents. *Journal of the American Academy of Child Psychiatry, 23,* 453–457.

Brier, N. (1995). Predicting antisocial behavior in youngsters displaying poor academic achievement: A review of risk factors. *Developmental and Behavioral Pediatrics, 16,* 271–276.

Brigham, T. A. (1989). *Self-management for adolescents: A skills training program.* New York: Guilford Press.

Brigham, T. A., Hopper, C., Hill, B., de Armas, A., & Newsom, P. (1985). A self-management program for disruptive adolescents in the school: A clinical replication analysis. *Behavior Therapy, 16,* 99–115.

Brody, G. M., & Forehand, R. (1985). The efficacy of parent training with maritally distressed and nondistressed mothers: A multimethod assessment. *Behavior Research and Therapy, 23,* 291–296.

Brophy, J. (1979). Advances in teacher research. *Journal of Classroom Interaction, 15,* 1–7.

Brown, G. M., & Greenspan, S. (1984). Effect of social foresight training on the school adjustment of high-risk youth. *Child Study Journal, 14,* 61–77.

Buckle, A., & Farrington, D. P. (1984). An observational study of shoplifting. *British Journal of Criminology, 24,* 63–73.

Burchard, J. D., & Harig, P. T. (1976). Behavior modification and juvenile delinquency. In H. Leitenberg (Ed.), *Handbook of behavior modification and behavior therapy.* Englewood Cliffs, NJ: Prentice-Hall.

Burns, G. L., & Patterson, D. R. (1990). Conduct problem behaviors in a stratified random sample of children and adolescents: New standardization data on the Eyberg Child Behavior Inventory. *Psychological Assessment, 2,* 391–397.

Butcher, J., Graham, J., Williams, C., & Kaemmer, B. (1992). *The Minnesota Multiphasic Personality Inventory-Adolescent.* Minneapolis, MN: National Computer Systems.

Cadoret, R. J. (1978). Psychopathology in adopted-away offspring of biologic parents with antisocial behavior. *Archives of General Psychiatry, 35,* 176–184.

Cadoret, R. J., Cain, C., & Crowe, R. R. (1983). Evidence for gene-environment interaction in the development of adolescent antisocial behavior. *Behavior Genetics, 13,* 301–310.

Cairns, R. B., & Cairns, B. D. (1986). The developmental-interactional view of social behavior: Four issues in adolescent aggression. In D. Olweus, J. Block, & M. Radke-Yarrow (Eds.), *Development of antisocial and prosocial behavior: Research, theories, and issues.* New York: Academic Press.

Cairns, R. B., & Cairns, B. D. (1992). The sociogenesis of aggressive and antisocial behaviors. In J. McCord (Ed.), *Facts, frameworks, and forecasts: Advances in criminological theory* (Vol. 3). New Brunswick, NJ: Transaction Press.

Cairns, R. B., Cairns, B. D., & Neckerman, H. J. (1989). Early school dropout: Configuration and determinants. *Child Development, 60,* 1437–1452.

Cairns, R. B., Cairns, B. D., Neckerman, H. J., Ferguson, L. L., & Gariepy, J. L. (1989). Growth and aggression: 1. Childhood to adolescence. *Developmental Psychology, 25*(2), 320–330.

Cairns, R. B., Cairns, B. D., Neckerman, H. J., Gest, S. D., & Gariepy, J. L. (1988). Social networks and aggressive behavior: Peer support or peer rejection? *Developmental Psychology, 24,* 815–823.

Camp, B. W., Blom, G. E., Hebert, F., & van Doorninck, W. J. (1977). "Think aloud": A program for developing self-control in young aggressive boys. *Journal of Abnormal Child Psychology, 5,* 167–169.

Campagna, A. F., & Harter, S. (1975). Moral judgement in sociopathic and normal children. *Journal of Personality and Social Psychology, 31,* 199–205.

Campbell, A., & Muncer, S. (1990). Causes of crime: Uncovering a lay model. *Criminal Justice and Behavior, 17,* 410–419.

Campbell, M., Adams, P. B., Small, A. M., Kafantaris, V., Silva, R. R., Shell, J., Perry, R., & Overall, J. E. (1995). Lithium in hospitalized aggressive children with conduct disorder: A double-blind and placebo-controlled study. *Journal of the American Academy of Child and Adolescent Psychiatry, 34,* 445–453.

Campbell, S. B. (1990). *Behavior problems in preschool children: Clinical and developmental issues.* New York: Guilford Press.

Campbell, S. B., & Ewing, L. J. (1990). Follow-up of hard-to-manage preschoolers: Adjustment at age 9 and predictors of continuing symptoms. *Journal of Child Psychology and Psychiatry, 31*(6), 871–889.

Capaldi, D. M., & Patterson, G. R. (1987). An approach to the problem of recruitment and retention rates for longitudinal research. *Behavioral Assessment, 9,* 169–177.

Carr, M., Borkowski, J. G., & Maxwell, S. E. (1991). Motivational components of underachievement. *Developmental Psychology, 27,* 108–118.

Caspi, A., Elder, G. H., & Bem, D. J. (1987). Moving against the world: Life course patterns of explosive children. *Developmental Psychology, 23*(2), 308–313.

Caspi, A., Lynam, D., Moffitt, T. E., & Silva, P. A. (1993). Unraveling girls' delinquency: Biological, dispositional and contextual contributions to adolescent misbehavior. *Developmental Psychology, 29*(1), 19–30.

Chalmers, J., & Townsend, M. (1990). The effects of training in social perspective: Taking on socially maladjusted girls. *Child Development, 61,* 178–190.

Chamberlain, P. (1990). Comparative evaluation of specialized foster care for seriously delinquent youths: A first step. *Community Alternatives: International Journal of Family Care, 2*(2), 21–36.

Chamberlain, P., & Reid, J. B. (1987). Parent observation and report of child symptoms. *Behavioral Assessment, 9,* 97–109.

Chandler, M. J. (1973). Egocentrism and antisocial behavior: The assessment and training of social perspective-taking skills. *Developmental Psychology, 9,* 326–332.

Chess, S., & Thomas, A. (1987). *Origins and evolution of behavior disorders: From infancy to early adult life.* Cambridge, MA: Harvard University Press.

Chiles, J. A., Miller, M. L., & Cox, G. B. (1980). Depression in an adolescent delinquent population. *Archives of General Psychiatry, 37,* 1179–1184.

Chilton, R. J., & Markle, G. E. (1972). Family disruption, delinquent conduct and the effect of subclassification. *American Sociological Review, 37,* 93–99.

Cicchetti, D., & Richters, J. E. (1993). Developmental considerations in the investigation of conduct disorder. *Development and Psychopathology, 5,* 331–344.

Cimler, E., & Beach, L. R. (1981). Factors involved in juveniles' decisions about crime. *Criminal Justice and Behavior, 8,* 275–286.

Cleckley, H. (1964). *The mask of sanity* (4th ed.). St. Louis: Mosby.

Cloniger, C. R., & Guze, S. B. (1970). Psychiatric illness and female criminality: The role of sociopathy and hysteria in the antisocial woman. *American Journal of Psychiatry, 127,* 303–311.

Cloniger, C. R., Reich, T., & Guze, S. B. (1978). Genetic-environmental interactions and antisocial behavior. In R. D. Hare & D. Schalling (Eds.), *Psychopathic behavior: Approaches to research.* New York: Wiley.

Cloward, R. A., & Ohlin, L. E. (1960). *Delinquency and opportunity.* New York: Free Press.

Coie, J. D., & Jacobs, M. R. (1993). The role of social context in the prevention of conduct disorder. *Development and Psychopathology, 5,* 263–275.

Coie, J. D., & Kupersmidt, J. B. (1983). A behavioral analysis of emerging social status in boys' groups. *Child Development, 54,* 1400–1416.

Coie, J. D., Terry, R., Lenox, K., Lochman, J., & Hyman, C. (1995). Childhood peer rejection and aggression as predictors of stable patterns of adolescent disorder. *Development and Psychopathology, 7,* 697–713.

Coleman, J. S., & Hoffer, T. (1987). *Public and private high schools.* New York: Basic Books.

Colorado Juvenile Justice & Delinquency Prevention Council. (1987). *Using school-based programs to improve students' citizenship in Colorado.* Denver, CO: Author.

Comings, D. E. (1995). The role of genetic factors in conduct disorder based on studies of Tourette Syndrome and ADHD probands and their relatives. *Developmental and Behavioral Pediatrics, 16,* 142–157.

Conduct Problems Prevention Research Group. (1992). A developmental and clinical model for the prevention of conduct disorder: The FAST Track Program. *Development and Psychopathology, 4,* 509–528.

Copple, C., Cline, M., & Smith, A. (1987). *Paths to the future: Long-term effects of Head Start in the Philadelphia school district.* Washington, DC: U.S. Department of Health and Human Services.

Cornish, D. B., & Clarke, R. V. (Eds.). (1986). *The reasoning criminal.* New York: Springer-Verlag.

Costello, E. J., & Angold, A. (1993). Toward a developmental epidemiology of the disruptive behavior disorders. *Development and Psychopathology, 5,* 91–101.

Crabtree, L. H. (1982). Hospitalized adolescents who act out: A treatment approach. *Psychiatry, 45,* 147–158.

Craft, M. I. (1965). *Ten studies into psychopathic personality,* Bristol, England: John Wright.

Craig, W., & Pepler, D. (1994). *Naturalistic observation of bullying and victimization in the school yard.* Publication of the LaMarsh Research Centre on Violence and Conflict Resolution, York University, Toronto, Ontario, Canada.

Crick, N. R., & Dodge, K. A. (1994). A review and reformulation of social information processing mechanisms in children's social adjustment. *Psychological Bulletin, 115,* 74–101.

Cromwell, P. F., Loson, J. N., & Avary, D. W. (1991). *Breaking and entering.* Newbury Park, CA: Sage.

Crowe, R. (1974). An adoption study of antisocial personality. *Archives of General Psychiatry, 31,* 785–791.

Cunningham, C. E., Bremner, R., & Boyle, M. (1995). Large group community-based parenting programs for families of pre-schoolers at risk for disruptive behavior disorder: Utilization, cost effectiveness, and outcome. *Journal of Child Psychology and Psychiatry, 36,* 1141–1159.

Curry, G. D., & Spergel, I. A. (1992). Gang involvement and delinquency among Hispanic and African-American adolescent males. *Journal of Research in Crime and Delinquency, 28*(3), 273–291.

Curry, J. F., & Craighead, W. E. (1990). Attributional style in clinically depressed and conduct-disordered adolescents. *Journal of Consulting and Clinical Psychology, 58,* 109–116.

Curtiss, G., Rosenthal, R. H., Marohn, R. C., Ostrov, E., Offer, D., & Trujillo, J. (1983). Measuring delinquent behavior in inpatient treatment settings: Revision and validation of the Adolescent Antisocial Behavior Checklist. *Journal of the American Academy of Child Psychiatry, 22,* 459–466.

Cusson, M. (1983). *Why delinquency?* Toronto, Ontario, Canada: University of Toronto Press.

Dadds, M. R., Sanders, M., Behrens, B. C., & James, J. E. (1987). Marital discord and child behavior problems: A description of interaction during treatment. *Journal of Clinical Child Psychology, 16,* 192–203.

Dadds, M. R., Schwartz, S., & Sanders, M. R. (1987). Marital discord and treatment outcome in behavioral treatment of child conduct disorders. *Journal of Consulting and Clinical Psychology, 55,* 396–403.

Davidson, W. S., Blakely, C. H., Redner, R., Mitchell, C. M., & Emshoff, J. G. (1985). *Diversion of juvenile offenders: An experimental comparison.* East Lansing: Michigan State University, Ecological Psychology Program.

Davidson, W. S., & Redner, R. (1988). The prevention of juvenile delinquency: Diversion from the juvenile justice system. In R. Price, E. Cowen, R. Lorion, & J. Ramos-McKay (Eds.), *Fourteen ounces of prevention.* Washington, DC: American Psychological Association.

Davidson, W. S., & Robinson, M. J. (1975). Community psychology and behavior modification: A community-based program for the prevention of juvenile delinquency. *Journal of Corrective Psychiatry and Behavior Therapy, 21,* 1–12.

Davidson, W. S., & Seidman, E. (1974). Studies of behavior modification and juvenile delinquency: A review, methodological critique, and social perspective. *Psychological Bulletin, 81,* 998–1011.

Davidson, W. S., & Wolfred, T. R. (1977). Evaluation of a community-based behavior modification program for prevention of delinquency: The failure of success. *Community Mental Health Journal, 13,* 296–306.

Daugherty, T. K., & Quay, H. C. (1991). Response preservation and delayed responding in childhood behavior disorders. *Journal of Child Psychiatry and Psychology, 32,* 453–461.

Delameter, A. M., & Lahey, B. B. (1983). Physiological correlates of conduct problems and anxiety in hyperactive and learning-disabled children. *Journal of Abnormal Child Psychology, 11,* 85–100.

Deluty, R. H. (1979). Children's Action Tendency Scale: A self-report measure of aggressiveness and submissiveness in children. *Journal of Consulting and Clinical Psychology, 47,* 1061–1071.

DiLalla, L. F., & Gottesman, I. I. (1989). Heterogeneity of causes for delinquency and criminality: Life-span perspectives. *Development and Psychopathology, 1,* 339–349.

Dishion, T. J. (1990). The peer context of troublesome child and adolescent behavior. In P. Leone (Ed.), *Understanding the troubled and troublesome youth.* Beverly Hills, CA: Sage.

Dishion, T. J., Capaldi, D., Spracken, K. M., & Li, F. (1995). Peer ecology of male adolescent drug use. *Development and Psychopathology, 7,* 803–824.

Dishion, T. J., French, D., & Patterson, G. R. (1995). The development and ecology of antisocial behavior. In D. Cicchetti & D. Cohen (Eds.), *Manual of developmental psychopathology.* New York: Cambridge Press.

Dishion, T. J., Gardner, K., Patterson, G. R., Reid, J., Spyrou, S., & Thibodeaux, S. (1984). *The family process code: A multidimensional system for observing family interactions.* Eugene, OR: Castalia.

Dishion, T. J., Loeber, R., Stouthamer-Loeber, M., & Patterson, G. R. (1984). Skills deficits and male adolescent delinquency. *Journal of Abnormal Child Psychology, 12,* 37–54.

Dishion, T. J., Patterson, G. R., Stoolmiller, M., & Skinner, M. L. (1991). Family, school, and behavioral antecedents to early adolescent involvement with antisocial peers. *Developmental Psychology, 27,* 172–180.

Dodge, K. A. (1980). Social cognition and children's aggressive behavior. *Child Development, 51,* 162–170.

Dodge, K. A. (1985). Attributional bias in aggressive children. *Advances in Cognitive-Behavioral Research and Therapy, 4,* 73–110.

Dodge, K. A. (1990). Nature versus nurture in childhood conduct disorder: It's time to ask a different question. *Developmental Psychology, 26,* 698–701.

Dodge, K. A. (1991). The structure and function of reactive and proactive aggression. In D. Pepler & K. Rubin (Eds.), *The development and treatment of childhood aggression.* Hillsdale, NJ: Erlbaum.

Dodge, K. A. (1993a). The future of research on the treatment of conduct disorder. *Development and Psychopathology, 5,* 311–319.

Dodge, K. A. (1993b). Social-cognitive mechanisms in the development of conduct disorder and depression. *Annual Review of Psychology, 44,* 559–584.

Dodge, K. A., Bates, J., & Pettit, G. S. (1990). Mechanisms in the cycle of violence. *Science, 250,* 1678–1683.

Dodge, K. A., Bates, J., Pettit, G. S., & Valente, E. (1995). Social information-processing patterns partially mediate the effects of early physical abuse on later conduct problems. *Journal of Abnormal Psychology, 104,* 632–643.

Dodge, K. A., Coie, J. D., & Brakke, N. P. (1982). Behavior patterns of socially rejected and neglected preadolescents: The roles of social approach and aggression. *Journal of Abnormal Child Psychology, 10,* 389–410.

Dodge, K. A., & Newman, J. P. (1981). Biased decision-making processes in aggressive boys. *Journal of Abnormal Psychology, 90,* 375–379.

Dodge, K. A., Price, J. M., Bachorowski, J. A., & Newman, J. P. (1990). Hostile attribution bias in severely aggressive adolescents. *Journal of Abnormal Psychology, 99,* 385–392.

Donovan, J. E., & Jessor, R. (1985). Structure of problem behavior in adolescence and young adulthood. *Journal of Consulting and Clinical Psychology, 53*(6), 890–904.

Donovan, J. E., Jessor, R., & Costa, F. M. (1988). Syndrome of problem behavior in adolescence: A replication. *Journal of Consulting and Clinical Psychology, 56,* 762–765.

Doren, D. M. (1987). *Understanding and treating the psychopath.* New York: Wiley.

Dryfoos, J. G. (1990). *Adolescents at risk: Prevalence and prevention.* New York: Oxford University Press.

Dubow, E. F., Huesmann, L. R., & Eron, L. D. (1973). Promoting prosocial behavior in aggressive elementary schoolboys. *Behavior Research and Therapy, 24,* 227–230.

Dumas, J. E. (1989). Treating antisocial behavior in children: Child and family approaches. *Clinical Psychology Review, 9,* 197–222.

Dumas, J. E., & Wahler, R. G. (1983). Predictors of treatment outcome in parent training: Mother insularity and socioeconomic disadvantage. *Behavioral Assessment, 5,* 301–313.

Durlak, J. A., Furhman, T., & Lampman, C. (1991). Effectiveness of cognitive-behavioral therapy for maladapting children: A meta-analysis. *Psychological Bulletin, 110,* 204–214.

Dykman, R. A., & Ackerman, P. T. (1993). Behavioral subtypes of Attention Deficit Disorder. *Exceptional Children, 60,* 132–141.

Earls, F. (1987). Sex differences in psychiatric disorders: Origins and developmental influences. *Psychiatric Developments, 1,* 1–23.

Earls, F., Reich, W., Jung, K. G., & Cloninger, C. R. (1988). Psychopathology in children of alcoholic and antisocial parents. *Alcoholism: Clinical and Experimental Research, 12,* 481–487.

Earls, F., & Reiss, A. J., Jr. (1992). *Annual report of the program on human development and criminal behavior for the John D. and Catherine T. MacArthur Foundation.* Boston: Harvard School of Public Health.

Egan, G. (1976). Confrontation. *Group and Organizational Studies, 1*(2), 223–243. La Jolla, CA: University Associates.

Elliott, D. S., Dunford, F. W., & Huizinga, D. (1987). The identification and prediction of career offenders utilizing self-reported and official data. In J. D. Burchard & S. N. Burchard (Eds.), *Preventing delinquent behavior.* Newbury Park, CA: Sage.

Elliott, D. S., Huizinga, D., & Ageton, S. S. (1985). *Explaining delinquency and drug use.* Newbury Park, CA: Sage.

Elliott, D. S., Huizinga, D., & Menard, S. (1989). *Multiple problem youth: Delinquency, substance abuse, and mental health problems.* New York: Springer-Verlag.

Elliott, D. S., & Voss, H. L. (1974). *Delinquency and dropout.* Lexington, MA: D.C. Heath.

Elliott, F. A. (1978). Neurological aspects of antisocial behavior. In W. Reid (Ed.), *The psychopath.* New York: Brunner/Mazel.

Ellis, P. L. (1982). Empathy: A factor in antisocial behavior. *Journal of Abnormal Child Psychology, 10,* 123–134.

Emery, R. E. (1982). Interparental conflict and the children of discord and divorce. *Psychological Bulletin, 92,* 310–330.

Emery, R. E., & Marholin, D. (1977). An applied behavior analysis of delinquency: The irrelevancy of relevant behavior. *American Psychologist, 32,* 860–873.

Erikson, E. (1963). *Childhood and society.* New York: Norton.

Eron, L. D., & Huesmann, L. R. (1990). The stability of aggressive behavior—Even unto the third generation. In M. Lewis & S. M. Miller (Eds.), *Handbook of developmental psychopathology.* New York: Plenum Press.

Eron, L. D., Huesmann, L. R., & Zelli, A. (1991). The role of parental variables in the learning of aggression. In D. Pepler & K. Rubin (Eds.), *The development and treatment of childhood aggression.* Hillsdale, NJ: Erlbaum.

Esser, G., Schmidt, M. H., & Woerner, W. (1990). Epidemiology and course of psychiatric disorders in school-age children: Results of a longitudinal study. *Journal of Child Psychology and Psychiatry, 31,* 243–263.

Exner, J. E. (1986). *The Rorschach: A comprehensive system* (2nd ed., Vol. 1). New York: Wiley.

Eyberg, S. M. (1980). Eyberg Child Behavior Inventory. *Journal of Clinical Child Psychology, 9,* 29.

Eyberg, S. M., & Robinson, E. A. (1983). Conduct problem behavior: Standardization of a behavioral rating scale with adolescents. *Journal of Clinical Child Psychology, 12,* 347–357.

Eysenck, H. J. (1977). *Crime and personality* (3rd ed.). London: Routledge & Kegan Paul.

Fagot, B. I., Hagan, R., Leinbach, M. D., & Kronsberg, S. (1985). Differential reactions to assertive and communicative acts of toddler boys and girls. *Child Development, 56,* 1499–1505.

Faraone, S. V., Beiderman, J., Keenan, K., & Tsuang, M. T. (1991). Separation of DSM-III attention deficit disorder and conduct disorder: Evidence from a family genetic study of American child psychiatry patients. *Psychological Medicine, 21,* 109–121.

Farnworth, M. (1984). Family structure, family attributes and delinquency in a sample of low-income, minority males and females. *Journal of Youth and Adolescence, 13,* 349–364.

Farrington, D. P. (1978). The family backgrounds of aggressive youths. In L. A. Hersov, M. Berger, & D. Shaffer (Eds.), *Aggression and antisocial behavior in childhood and adolescence.* Oxford, England: Pergamon Press.

Farrington, D. P. (1979). Longitudinal research on crime and delinquency. In N. Morris & M. Tonry (Eds.), *Crime and justice.* Chicago: University of Chicago Press.

Farrington, D. P. (1986). Stepping stones to adult criminal careers. In D. Olweus, J. Block, & M. R. Yarrow (Eds.), *Development of antisocial and prosocial behavior.* New York: Academic Press.

Farrington, D. P. (1988). Studying change within individuals: The case of offending. In M. Rutter (Ed.), *Studies of psychosocial risk: The power of longitudinal data.* Cambridge, England: Cambridge University Press.

Farrington, D. P. (1991a). Antisocial personality from childhood to adulthood. *The Psychologist, 4,* 389–394.

Farrington, D. P. (1991b). Childhood aggression and adult violence: Early precursors and later-life outcomes. In D. Pepler & K. Rubin (Eds.), *The development and treatment of childhood aggression.* Hillsdale, NJ: Erlbaum.

Farrington, D. P. (1992). Explaining the beginning, progress, and ending of antisocial behavior from birth to adulthood. In J. McCord (Ed.), *Facts, frameworks, and forecasts: Advances in criminological theory.* New Brunswick, NJ: Transaction.

Farrington, D. P. (1993). Motivations for conduct disorder and delinquency. *Development and Psychopathology, 5,* 225–241.

Farrington, D. P. (1995). The development of offending and antisocial behavior from childhood: Key findings from the Cambridge Study in Delinquent Development. *Journal of Child Psychology and Psychiatry, 36,* 929–964.

Farrington, D. P., Berkowitz, L., & West, D. J. (1982). Differences between individual and group fights. *British Journal of Social Psychology, 21,* 323–333.

Farrington, D. P., Gallagher, B., Morley, L., St. Ledger, R. J., & West, D. J. (1986). Unemployment, school leaving, and crime. *British Journal of Criminology, 26,* 335–356.

Farrington, D. P., Knapp, W. S., Erickson, B. E., & Knight, B. J. (1980). Words and deeds in the study of stealing. *Journal of Adolescence, 3,* 35–49.

Farrington, D. P., & Knight, B. J. (1980). Four studies of stealing as a risky decision. In P. D. Lipsitt & B. D. Sales (Eds.), *New directions in psycholegal research.* New York: Van Nostrand Reinhold.

Farrington, D. P., Loeber, R., Elliott, D. S., Hawkins, J. D., Kandel, D. B., Klein, M. W., McCord, J., Rowe, D. C., & Tremblay, R. E. (1990). Advancing knowledge about the onset of delinquency and crime. In B. B. Lahey & A. E. Kazdin (Eds.), *Advances in clinical child psychology* (Vol. 13). New York: Plenum Press.

Farrington, D. P., Loeber, R., & Van Kammen, W. B. (1990). Long-term criminal outcomes of hyperactivity-impulsivity-attention deficit and conduct problems in childhood. In L. N. Robins & M. Rutter (Eds.), *Straight and devious pathways from childhood to adulthood.* Cambridge, England: Cambridge University Press.

Farrington, D. P., & West, D. J. (1981). The Cambridge study in delinquent development (United Kingdom). In S. A. Mednick & A. E. Baert (Eds.), *Prospective longitudinal research: An empirical basis for the primary prevention of psychosocial disorders.* New York: Oxford University Press.

Farrington, D. P., & West, D. J. (1990). The Cambridge study in delinquent development: A long-term follow-up of 411 London males. In H. J. Kerner & G. Kaiser (Eds.), *Criminality, personality, behavior, and life history.* Berlin, Germany: Springer-Verlag.

Feindler, E. L. (1987). Clinical issues and recommendations in adolescent anger control training. *Journal of Child and Adolescent Psychotherapy, 4,* 267–274.

Feindler, E. L. (1990). Adolescent anger control: Review and critique. In M. Hersen, R. M. Eisler, & P. M. Miller (Eds.), *Progress in behavior modification* (Vol. 26). Newbury Park, CA: Sage.

Feindler, E. L. (1991). Cognitive strategies in anger control intervention. In P. C. Kendall (Ed.), *Child and adolescent behavior therapy: Cognitive-behavioral procedures.* New York: Guilford Press.

Feindler, E. L., & Ecton, R. B. (1986). *Adolescent anger control: Cognitive-behavioral techniques.* Elmsford, NY: Pergamon Press.

Feindler, E. L., & Guttman, J. (1994). Cognitive-behavioral anger control training. In C. W. LeCroy (Ed.), *Handbook of child and adolescent treatment manuals.* New York: Lexington Books.

Feindler, E. L., Marriott, S. A., & Iwata, M. (1984). Group anger control training for junior high school delinquents. *Cognitive Therapy and Research, 8,* 299–311.

Feldhusen, J., Houtz, J., & Ringenbach, S. (1972). The Purdue Elementary Problem-Solving Inventory. *Psychological Reports, 31,* 891–901.

Feldman, L. (Ed.). (1988). *Partnerships for Youth 2000: A program models manual.* Tulsa, OK: University of Oklahoma, National Resource Center for Youth Services.

Feldman, R. A. (1992). The St. Louis experiment: Effective treatment of antisocial youths in prosocial peer groups. In J. McCord & R. E. Tremblay (Eds.), *Preventing antisocial behavior.* New York: Guilford.

Feldman, R. A., Caplinger, T. E., & Wodarski, J. S. (1983). *The St. Louis conundrum: The effective treatment of antisocial youths.* Englewood Cliffs, NJ: Prentice-Hall.

Felner, R. A., & Adan, A. M. (1988). The school transitional environment project: An ecological intervention and evaluation. In R. H. Price, E. L. Cowen, R. P. Lorion, & J. Ramos-McKay (Eds.), *Fourteen Ounces of Prevention: A casebook for practitioners.* Washington, DC: American Psychological Association.

Ferber, H., Keeley, S. M., & Shemberg, K. M. (1974). Training parents in behavior modification: Outcomes of and problems encountered in a program after Patterson's work. *Behavior Therapy, 5,* 415–419.

Fergusson, D. M., & Horwood, L. J. (1995). Early disruptive behavior, IQ, and later school achievement and delinquent behavior. *Journal of Abnormal Child Psychology, 23,* 183–199.

Fergusson, D. M., Horwood, L. J., & Lloyd, M. (1991). Confirmatory factor models of attention deficit and conduct disorder. *Journal of Child Psychology and Psychiatry, 32,* 257–274.

Fergusson, D. M., Horwood, L. J., & Lynsky, M. T. (1995). The stability of disruptive childhood behaviors. *Journal of Abnormal Child Psychology, 23,* 379–396.

Fleischman, M. J., & Szyluka, S. A. (1985). A community setting replication of a social learning treatment for aggressive children. *Behavior Therapy, 12,* 115–122.

Fleishman, M., Horne, A., & Arthur, J. (1983). *Troubled families: A treatment program.* Champaign, IL: Research Press.

Fo, W. S. O., & O'Donnell, C. R. (1975). The buddy system: Effect of community intervention on delinquent offences. *Behavior Therapy, 6,* 522–524.

Forehand, R., Griest, D., & Wells, K. C. (1979). Parent behavioral training: An analysis of the relationship among multiple outcome measures. *Journal of Abnormal Child Psychology, 7,* 229–242.

Forehand, R., & Long, N. (1988). Outpatient treatment of the acting out child: Procedures, long-term follow-up data, and clinical problems. *Advances in Behavior and Research Therapy, 10,* 129–177.

Forehand, R., & Long, N. (1991). Prevention of aggression and other behavior problems in early adolescent years. In D. Pepler & K. Rubin (Eds.), *The development and treatment of childhood aggression.* Hillsdale, NJ: Erlbaum.

Forehand, R., & McMahon, R. J. (1981). *Helping the non-compliant child: A clinician's guide to parent training.* New York: Guilford Press.

Forehand, R., Middlebrook, J., Rogers, T., & Steffe, M. (1983). Dropping out of parent training. *Behavior Research and Therapy, 21,* 663–668.

Forehand, R., Wells, K. C., & Geist, D. (1980). An examination of the social validity of a parent training program. *Behavior Therapy, 11,* 488–502.

Forehand, R., Wells, K. C., & Sturgis, E. T. (1978). Predictors of child noncompliant behavior in the home. *Journal of Consulting and Clinical Psychology, 46,* 179.

Forer, B. R. (1950). A structured sentence completion test. *Journal of Projective Techniques, 14,* 15–30.

Forgatch, M. S., Patterson, G. R., & Skinner, M. L. (1988). A mediational model for the effects of divorce on antisocial behavior in boys. In E. M. Hetherington & J. D. Aresteh (Eds.), *Impact of divorce, single parenting, and step-parenting on children.* Hillsdale, NJ: Erlbaum.

Forman, S. (1993). *Coping skills interventions for children and adolescents.* San Francisco: Jossey-Bass.

Forness, S. R., Kavale, K. A., & Lopez, M. (1993). Conduct disorders in school: Special education eligibility and comorbidity. *Journal of Emotional and Behavioral Disorders, 1,* 101–108.

Fowles, D. C. (1988). Psychophysiology and psychopathy: A motivational approach. *Psychophysiology, 25,* 373–391.

Fraser, P. (1996). *Statistical versus self-identification methods in defining academic underachievement in high school students.* Unpublished doctoral dissertation, York University, Department of Psychology, Toronto, Ontario, Canada.

Freedman, B. J., Rosenthal, L., Donahoe, C. P., Schlundt, D. G., & McFall, R. M. (1978). A social-behavioral analysis of skill deficits in delinquent and non-delinquent boys. *Journal of Consulting and Clinical Psychology, 46,* 1448–1462.

French, D. C., Conrad, J., & Turner, T. M. (1995). Adjustment of antisocial and nonantisocial rejected adolescents. *Development and Psychopathology, 7,* 857–874.

Frick, P., Kamphaus, R. W., Lahey, B. B., Loeber, R., Christ, M. G., Hart, E., & Tannenbaum, T. E. (1991). Academic underachievement and the disruptive behavior disorders. *Journal of Consulting and Clinical Psychology, 59*, 289–294.

Frick, P., Lahey, B. B., Loeber, R., Christ, M. G., Stouthamer-Loeber, M., & Hanson, K. (1992). Familial risk factors to oppositional defiant disorder and conduct disorder: Parental psychopathology and maternal parenting. *Journal of Consulting and Clinical Psychology, 60*, 49–55.

Friedland, J., Marcus, S. I., & Mandel, H. P. (1996). *The Achievement Motivation Profile (AMP)*. Los Angeles, CA: Western Psychological Services.

Funderburk, B. W., & Eyberg, S. M. (1989). Psychometric characteristics of the Sutter-Eyberg Student Behavior Inventory. *Behavioral Assessment, 11*, 297–313.

Gabel, S., Stadler, J., Bjorn, J., Shindledecker, R., & Bowden, C. L. (1995). Homovanillic acid and monoamine oxidase in sons of substance-abusing fathers: Relationship to conduct disorder. *Journal for Studies on Alcohol, 56*, 135–139.

Gaffney, L. R., & McFall, R. M. (1981). A comparison of social skills in delinquent and nondelinquent adolescent girls using a behavioral role-playing intervention. *Journal of Consulting and Clinical Psychology, 49*, 959–967.

Garbarino, J. (1980). Some thoughts on school size and its effects on adolescent development. *Journal of Youth and Adolescence, 9*, 1.

Gardner, F. E. M. (1987). Positive interactions between mothers and conduct-problem children: Is there training for harmony as well as fighting? *Journal of Abnormal Child Psychology, 15*, 283–293.

Garmezy, M. T., Speltz, M. L., & DeKlyen, M. (1993). The role of attachment in the early development of disruptive behavior problems. *Development and Psychopathology, 5*, 191–213.

Gillmore, M. J., Hawkins, D. J., Catalano, R. F., Day, L. E., Moore, M., & Abbott, R. (1991). The structure of behavioral problems in preadolescents. *Journal of Consulting and Clinical Psychology, 59*, 499–506.

Giordano, P. C., Cernkovich, S. A., & Pugh, M. D. (1986). Friendships and delinquency. *American Journal of Sociology, 91*, 1170–1202.

Glaser, B. A., & Horne, A. M. (1994). A treatment program for children with conduct disorders. In C. W. LeCroy (Ed.), *Handbook of child and adolescent treatment manuals*. New York: Lexington Books.

Glow, R. A., & Glow, P. H. (1980). Peer and self-rating: Children's perception of behavior relevant to hyperkinetic impulse disorder. *Journal of Abnormal Psychology, 8*, 471–490.

Gold, M. (1963). *Status forces in delinquent boys*, Ann Arbor: University of Michigan Press.

Gold, M., & Mann, D. (1984). *Expelled to a friendlier place: A study of effective alternative schools.* Ann Arbor: University of Michigan Press.

Goldstein, H. S. (1984). Parental composition, supervision, and conduct problems in youth 12 to 17 years old. *Journal of the American Academy of Child Psychiatry, 23,* 679–684.

Goodstein, M. (1969). The relationship of personality change to therapeutic system and diagnosis. *Dissertation Abstracts International, 30,* 2419-B.

Gorenstein, E. E., & Newman, J. P. (1980). Disinhibitory psychopathology: A new perspective and model for research. *Psychological Review, 87,* 301–315.

Gottfredson, G. D. (1987). Peer group interventions to reduce the risk of delinquent behavior: A selective review and a new evaluation. *Criminology, 25,* 671–714.

Gottfredson, G. D., Gottfredson, D., & Cook, M. (1983). *The school action effectiveness study: Second interim report.* Baltimore: Johns Hopkins University, Center for Social Organization of Schools.

Gough, H. G. (1948). A sociological theory of psychopathy. *American Journal of Sociology, 53,* 359–366.

Gray, J. A. (1987). Perspectives on anxiety and impulsivity: A commentary. *Journal of Research in Personality, 21,* 493–509.

Greenberg, M. T., & Speltz, M. L. (1988). Attachment and the ontogeny of conduct problems. In J. Belsky & T. Nezworski (Eds.), *Clinical implications of attachment.* Hillsdale, NJ: Erlbaum.

Greenberg, M. T., Speltz, M. L., & DeKlyen, M. (1993). The role of attachment in the early development of disruptive behavior problems. *Development and Psychopathology, 5,* 191–213.

Greenwald, H. (1967, Spring). Treatment of the psychopath. *Voices.*

Gregory, R. J. (1974). The causes of psychopathy: Implications of recent research. *Catalog of Selected Documents in Psychology, 4,* 86.

Griest, D. L., Forehand, R., McMahon, R. J., & Wells, K. C. (1980). An examination of differences between nonclinic and behavior-problem clinic-referred children and their mothers. *Journal of Abnormal Psychology, 3,* 497–500.

Griest, D. L., Forehand, R., Rogers, T., Breiner, J., Furey, W., & Williams, C. A. (1982). Effects of parent enhancement therapy on the treatment outcome and generalization of a parent training program. *Behavior Research and Therapy, 20,* 429–436.

Griest, D. L., Forehand, R., & Wells, K. C. (1981). Follow-up assessment of parent behavioral training: An analysis of who will participate. *Child Study Journal, 11*, 221–229.

Griest, D. L., & Wells, K. C. (1983). Behavioral family therapy with conduct disorders in children. *Behavior Therapy, 14*, 37–53.

Grilo, C. M., Becker, D. F., Walker, M. L., Levy, K. N., Edell, W. S., & McGlashian, T. H. (1995). Psychiatric comorbidity in adolescent inpatients with substance use disorders. *Journal of the American Academy of Child and Adolescent Psychiatry, 34*, 1085–1091.

Grinnell, R. M., & Chambers, C. A. (1979). Broken homes and middle-class delinquency: A comparison. *Criminology, 17*, 395–400.

Gross, A. M., & Brigham, T. A. (1980). Behavior modification and the treatment of juvenile delinquency: A review and proposal for future research. *Corrective and Social Psychiatry and Journal of Behavior Technology, Methods and Therapy, 26*, 98–106.

Gross, A. M., Brigham, T. A., Hopper, R., & Bologna, N. C. (1980). Self-management and social skills training: A study with predelinquent and delinquent youth. *Criminal Justice and Behavior, 7*, 161–184.

Guerra, N. G., & Salby, R. G. (1990). Cognitive mediators of aggression in adolescent offenders: Part 2: Intervention. *Developmental Psychology, 26*, 269–277.

Gutelius, M. F., Kirsch, A. D., MacDonald, S., Brooks, M. R., & McErlean, T. (1977). Controlled study of child health supervision: Behavioral results. *Pediatrics, 60*, 294–304.

Halperin, J. M., Newcorn, J. H., Matier, K., Bedi, G., & Sharma, V. (1995). Impulsivity and the initiation of fights in children with disruptive behavior disorders. *Journal of Child Psychology and Psychiatry, 36*, 1199–1211.

Hare, R. D. (1970). *Psychopathy: Theory and research.* New York: Wiley.

Hare, R. D., & Schalling, D. (Eds.). (1978). *Psychopathic behavior: Approaches to research.* Chichester, England: Wiley.

Harrington, R., Fudge, H., Rutter, M., Pickler, A., & Hill, J. (1991). Adult outcome of childhood and adolescent depression: 2. Links with antisocial disorders. *Journal of the American Academy of Child and Adolescent Psychiatry, 30*, 434–439.

Harris, A., Kreil, D., & Orpet, R. (1977). The modification and validation of the Behavioral Coding System for school settings. *Behavior Therapy and Experimental Psychiatry, 12*, 231–236.

Harter, S. (1982). The Perceived Competence Scale for Children. *Child Development, 53*, 87–97.

Hathaway, S. R., & McKinley, J. C. (1963). *The Minnesota Multiphasic Personality Inventory.* Minneapolis: University of Minnesota Press.

Hawkins, J. D., Catalano, R. F., Jones, G., & Fine, D. (1987). Delinquency prevention through parent training: Results and issues from work in progress. In J. Wilson & G. Loury (Eds.), *Children to citizens: Families, schools, and delinquency prevention.* New York: Springer-Verlag.

Hawkins, J. D., Catalano, R. F., & Miller, J. Y. (1992). Risk and protective factors for alcohol and other drug problems in adolescence and early adulthood: Implications for substance abuse prevention. *Psychological Bulletin, 112,* 64–105.

Hawkins, J. D., Catalano, R. F., & Morrison, D. M. (1989). *Seattle Social Development Project: Cumulative effects of intervention in grades 1–4.* Paper presented at the meeting of the Society for Research in Child Development, Kansas, MO.

Hawkins, J. D., Catalano, R. F., Morrison, D. M., O'Donnell, J. O., Abbott, R. D., & Day, L. E. (1992). The Seattle Social Development Project: Effects of the first four years on protective factors and problem behaviors. In J. McCord & R. E. Tremblay (Eds.), *Preventing antisocial behavior.* New York: Guilford.

Hawkins, J. D., Doueck, H. J., & Lishner, D. M. (1988). Changing teaching practices in mainstream classrooms to improve bonding and behavior of low achievers. *American Educational Research Journal, 25,* 31–50.

Hawkins, J. D., & Lam, T. (1987). Teacher practices, social development, and delinquency. In J. D. Burchard & S. N. Burchard (Eds.), *Primary prevention of psychopathology: Vol. 10. Prevention of delinquent behavior.* Newbury Park, CA: Sage.

Hawkins, J. D., & Lishner, D. M. (1987). School and delinquency. In E. Johnson (Ed.), *Handbook on crime and delinquency prevention.* Westport, CT: Greenwood Press.

Hawkins, J. D., Lishner, D. M., Jenson, J. M., & Catalano, R. F. (1987). Delinquents and drugs: What the evidence suggests about prevention and treatment. In B. S. Brown & A. R. Mills (Eds.), *Youth at risk for substance abuse.* Rockville, MD: National Institute on Drug Abuse.

Hawkins, J. D., VonCleve, E., & Catalano, R. F., Jr. (1991). Reducing early childhood aggression: Results of a primary prevention program. *Journal of the American Academy of Child and Adolescent Psychiatry, 30,* 208–217.

Hawkins, J. D., & Weis, J. G. (1985). The social development model: An integrated approach to delinquency prevention. *Journal of Primary Prevention, 6,* 73–97.

Haynes, J. P., & Bensch, M. (1981). The P > V sign of the WISC-R and recidivism in delinquents. *Journal of Consulting and Clinical Psychology, 49,* 480–481.

Hazler, R. J., Hoover, J. H., & Oliver, R. (1991). Student perceptions of victimization by bullies in school. *Journal of Humanistic Education and Development, 29,* 143–150.

Heath, L., Bresdin, L. B., & Rinaldi, R. C. (1989). Effects of media on violence in children: A review of the literature. *Archives of General Psychiatry, 46,* 376–379.

Henggeler, S. W. (1989). *Delinquency in adolescence.* Newbury Park, CA: Sage.

Henggeler, S. W., & Borduin, C. M. (1990). *Family therapy and beyond: A multisystem approach to treating behavior problems of children and adolescents.* Pacific Grove, CA: Brooks/Cole.

Henn, F. A., Bardwell, R., & Jenkins, R. L. (1980). Juvenile delinquents revisited. *Archives of General Psychiatry, 37,* 1160–1163.

Hennessy, M., Richards, P. J., & Berk, R. A. (1978). Broken homes and middle-class delinquency: A reassessment. *Criminology, 15,* 505–528.

Henry, B., Moffitt, T. E., & Silva, P. A. (1992). Disentangling delinquency and learning disability: Neuropsychological function and social support. *The International Journal of Clinical Neuropsychology, 13,* 1–6.

Hersov, L., Berger, M., & Shaffer, D. (1978). *Aggressive and antisocial behavior in childhood and adolescence.* Oxford, England: Pergamon Press.

Hiew, C. C., & MacDonald, G. (1986). Delinquency prevention through promoting social competence in adolescents. *Canadian Journal of Criminology, 28,* 291–302.

Hinshaw, S. P. (1987). On the distinction between attention deficits/hyperactivity, and conduct problems/aggression in child psychopathology. *Psychological Bulletin, 101,* 443–463.

Hinshaw, S. P. (1992a). Academic underachievement, attention deficits, and aggression: Comorbidity and implications for intervention. *Journal of Consulting and Clinical Psychology, 60,* 893–903.

Hinshaw, S. P. (1992b). Externalizing behavior problems and academic underachievement in childhood and adolescence: Causal relationships and underlying mechanisms. *Psychological Bulletin, 111,* 127–155.

Hinshaw, S. P., Lahey, B. B., & Hart, E. L. (1993). Issues of taxonomy and comorbidity in the development of conduct disorder. *Development and Psychopathology, 5,* 31–49.

Hinshaw, S. P., & Mednick, S. A. (1995). Peer relationships in boys with ADHD with and without comorbid aggression. *Development and Psychopathology, 7,* 627–647.

Hirschfield, P. P. (1965). Response set in impulsive children. *Journal of Genetic Psychology, 107,* 117–126.

Hirschi, T. (1969). *Causes of delinquency.* Berkeley: University of California Press.

Hirschi, T., & Hindelang, M. J. (1977). Intelligence and delinquency: A revisionist review. *American Sociological Review, 42,* 571–587.

Hobbs, T. R., & Holt, M. M. (1976). The effects of token reinforcement on the behavior of delinquents in cottage settings. *Journal of Applied Behavior Analysis, 9,* 189–198.

Holmes, S. J., & Robins, L. N. (1987). The influence of childhood disciplinary experiences on the development of alcoholism and depression. *Journal of Child Psychology and Psychiatry, 28,* 399–415.

Hops, H., Walker, H. M., Fleischman, D. H., Nagoshi, J. T., Omura, R. T., Skinrud, K., & Taylor, J. (1978). CLASS: A standardized in-class program for acting-out children: 2. Field test evaluations. *Journal of Educational Psychology, 70,* 636–644.

Horne, A., & Sayger, T. V. (1990). *Treating conduct and oppositional defiant disorders in children.* New York: Pergamon Press.

Howell, A. J., & Enns, R. A. (1995). A high risk recognition program for adolescents in conflict with the law. *Canadian Psychology, 36,* 149–161.

Hoza, B., Molina, B. S. G., Bukowski, W. M., & Sippola, L. K. (1995). Peer variables as predictors of later childhood adjustment. *Development and Psychopathology, 7,* 787–802.

Hudson, W. W. (1992). *The WALMYR assessment scales scoring manual.* Tempe, AZ: WALMYR.

Huesmann, L., & Malamuth, N. M. (1986). Media violence and antisocial behavior: An overview. *Journal of Social Issues, 42*(3), 1–6.

Huizinga, D., Esbensen, F. -A., & Weiher, A. W. (1991). Are there multiple paths to delinquency? *The Journal of Criminal Law and Criminology, 82,* 83–118.

Humphreys, L., Forehand, R., McMahon, R., & Roberts, M. (1978). Parent behavioral training to modify child noncompliance: Effects on untreated siblings. *Journal of Behavior Therapy and Experimental Psychiatry, 9,* 235–238.

Hurwitz, I., Bibace, R. M., Wolff, P. H., & Rowbotham, B. M. (1972). Neurological function of normal boys, delinquent boys, and boys with learning problems. *Perceptual and Motor Skills, 35,* 387–394.

Iddiols, J. (1985). *The relationship between teacher helping strategies and different personality types of underachieving student.* Unpublished honors thesis, York University, Department of Psychology, Toronto, Ontario, Canada.

Jenkins, J. M., & Smith, M. A. (1990). Factors protecting children living in disharmonious homes: Maternal reports. *Journal of the American Academy of Child and Adolescent Psychiatry, 29,* 60–69.

Jenkins, R. L., & Boyer, A. (1968). Types of delinquent behavior and background factors. *International Journal of Social Psychiatry, 14,* 65–76.

Jensen, G. F. (1972). Parents, peers, and delinquent action: A test of the differential association perspective. *American Journal of Sociology, 78,* 562–575.

Jensen, G. F., Erickson, M. L., & Gibbs, J. P. (1978). Perceived risk of punishment and self-reported delinquency. *Social Forces, 57,* 57–78.

Jessor, R., & Jessor, S. L. (1977). *Problem behavior and psychosocial development: A longitudinal study of youth.* New York: Academic Press.

Johnson, D. L. (1988). Primary prevention of behavior problems in young children: The Houston Parent-Child Development Center. In E. L. Cowen, R. P. Lorion, & J. Ramos-McKay (Eds.), *Fourteen ounces of prevention: A handbook for practitioners.* Washington, DC: American Psychological Association.

Johnson, D. L., & Breckenridge, J. N. (1982). The Houston Parent-Child Development Center and the primary prevention of behavior problems in young children. *American Journal of Community Psychology, 10,* 305–316.

Johnson, D. L., & Walker, T. (1987). The primary prevention of behavior problems in Mexican-American children. *American Journal of Community Psychology, 15,* 375–385.

Johnson, E. O., Arria, A. M., Borges, G., Ialongo, N., & Anthony, J. C. (1995). The growth of conduct problem behaviors from middle childhood to early adolescence: Sex difference and the suspected influence of early alcohol use. *Journal of Studies on Alcohol, 56,* 661–671.

Jones, E., & Gerard, H. (1967). *Foundations of social psychology.* New York: Wiley.

Jones, J. D. (1984). Principles of hospital treatment of the aggressive adolescent. In C. R. Keith (Ed.), *The aggressive adolescent: Clinical perspectives.* New York: Free Press.

Jones, M. B., Offord, D. R., & Abrams, N. (1980). Brothers, sisters, and antisocial behavior. *British Journal of Psychiatry, 136,* 139–145.

Jones, R. T., & Kazdin, A. E. (1981). Childhood behavior problems in the school. In S. M. Turner, K. S. Calhoun, & H. E. Adams (Eds.), *Handbook of clinical behavior therapy.* New York: Wiley.

Jouriles, E. N., Murphy, C. M., & O'Leary, K. D. (1989). Interspousal aggression, marital discord, and child problems. *Journal of Consulting and Clinical Psychology, 57,* 453–455.

Jurkovic, G. J. (1980). The juvenile delinquent as a moral philosopher: A structural-developmental perspective. *Psychological Bulletin, 88,* 709–727.

Jurkovic, G. J., & Prentice, N. M. (1977). Relation of moral and cognitive development to dimensions of juvenile delinquency. *Journal of Abnormal Psychology, 86,* 414–420.

Kahn, E. (1931). *Psychopathic personalities.* New Haven, CT: Yale University Press.

Kandel, E., & Mednick, S. A. (1991). Perinatal complications predict violent offending. *Journal of Consulting and Clinical Psychology, 56,* 224–226.

Kandel, E., Mednick, S. A., Kirkegaard-Sorenson, L., Hutchings, B., Knop, J., Rosenberg, R., & Schulsinger, F. (1988). IQ as a protective factor for subjects at high risk for antisocial behavior. *Journal of Consulting and Clinical Psychology, 56,* 224–226.

Kaplan, H. B. (1980). *Delinquent behavior in defense of self.* New York: Pergamon Press.

Kaplan, P. J., & Arbuthnot, J. (1985). Affective empathy and cognitive role-taking in delinquent and nondelinquent youth. *Adolescence, 20,* 323–333.

Kaplan, W. H. (1988). Conduct disorder. In C. J. Kestenbaum & D. T. Williams (Eds.), *Handbook of clinical assessment of children and adolescents.* New York: New York University Press.

Karniski, W. M., Levine, M. D., Clarke, S., Palfrey, J. S., & Meltzer, L. J. (1982). A study of neurodevelopmental findings in early adolescent delinquency. *Journal of Adolescent Health Care, 3,* 151–159.

Kashani, J. H., Beck, N. C., Hoeper, E. W., Fallahi, C., Corcoran, C. M., McAllister, J. A., Rosenberg, T. K., & Reid, J. C. (1987). Psychiatric disorders in a community sample of adolescents. *American Journal of Psychiatry, 144,* 584–589.

Kashani, J. H., Manning, G., McKnew, D. H., Cytryn, L., Husain, A., & Wooderson, P. (1980). Depression among incarcerated delinquents. *Psychiatry Research, 3,* 185.

Kauffman, J. M. (1977). *Characteristics of children's behavior disorders.* Columbus, OH: Merrill.

Kazdin, A. E. (1985). *Treatment of antisocial behavior in children and adolescents: Alternative interventions and their effectiveness.* Chicago: Dorsey Press.

Kazdin, A. E. (1987a). Treatment of antisocial behavior in children: Current status and future directions. *Psychological Bulletin, 102,* 187–203.

Kazdin, A. E. (1987b). *Conduct disorder of childhood and adolescence.* Newbury Park, CA: Sage.

Kazdin, A. E. (1990). Premature termination from treatment among children referred for antisocial behavior. *Journal of Child Psychology and Psychiatry, 31*, 415–425.

Kazdin, A. E. (1991). Aggressive behavior and conduct disorder. In T. R. Kratochwill & R. J. Morris (Eds.), *The practice of child therapy* (2nd ed.). New York: Pergamon Press.

Kazdin, A. E. (1992). Overt and covert antisocial behavior: Child and family characteristics among psychiatric inpatient children. *Journal of Child and Family Studies, 1*, 3–20.

Kazdin, A. E. (1993). Treatment of conduct disorder: Progress and directions in psychotherapy research. *Development and Psychopathology, 5*, 277–310.

Kazdin, A. E. (1995a). Child, parent, and family dysfunction as predictors of outcome in cognitive-behavioral treatment of antisocial children. *Behavior Research and Therapy, 33*, 271–281.

Kazdin, A. E. (1995b). *Conduct disorder of childhood and adolescence* (2nd ed.). Newbury Park, CA: Sage.

Kazdin, A. E., Bass, D., Siegel, T., & Thomas, C. (1989). Cognitive-behavioral therapy and relationship therapy in the treatment of children referred for antisocial behavior. *Journal of Consulting and Clinical Psychology, 57*, 522–535.

Kazdin, A. E., & Esveldt-Dawson, K. (1986). The interview for antisocial behavior: Psychometric characteristics and concurrent validity with child psychiatric inpatients. *Journal of Psychopathology and Behavioral Assessment, 8*, 289–303.

Kazdin, A. E., Esveldt-Dawson, K., French, N. H., & Unis, A. S. (1987a). Effects of parent management training and problem-solving skills training combined in the treatment of antisocial child behavior. *Journal of the American Academy of Child and Adolescent Psychiatry, 26*, 416–424.

Kazdin, A. E., Esveldt-Dawson, K., French, N. H., & Unis, A. S. (1987b). Problem-solving skills training and relationship therapy in the treatment of antisocial child behavior. *Journal of Consulting and Clinical Psychology, 55*, 76–85.

Kazdin, A. E., & Kolko, D. J. (1986). Parent psychopathology and family functioning among childhood firesetters. *Journal of Abnormal Child Psychology, 23*, 437–457.

Kazdin, A. E., Rodgers, A., Colbus, D., & Siegel, T. (1987). Children's Hostility Inventory: Measurement of aggression and hostility in psychiatric inpatient children. *Journal of Clinical Child Psychology, 16*, 320–328.

Kazdin, A. E., Siegel, T., & Bass, D. (1992). Cognitive problem-solving skills training and parent management training in the treatment of antisocial behavior in children. *Journal of Consulting and Clinical Psychology, 60,* 733–747.

Keith, C. R. (Ed.). (1984). *The aggressive adolescent: Clinical perspectives.* New York: Free Press.

Keller, M. B., Lavori, P. W., Beardslee, W. R., Wunder, J., Schwartz, C. E., Roth, J., & Biederman, J. (1992). The disruptive behavioral disorder in children and adolescents: Comorbidity and clinical course. *Journal of the American Academy of Child and Adolescent Psychiatry, 31,* 204–209.

Kelly, F. J., & Baer, D. J. (1971). Physical challenge as a treatment for delinquency. *Crime and Delinquency, 17,* 437–445.

Kelly, M. L. (1989). *School-home notes: A behavioral intervention for parents and teachers.* New York: Guilford Press.

Kelso, J., & Stewart, M. A. (1986). Factors which predict the persistence of aggressive conduct disorder. *Journal of Child Psychology and Psychiatry, 27,* 77–86.

Kendall, P. C. (1984). Cognitive-behavioral self-control therapy for children. *Journal of Child Psychology and Psychiatry, 25,* 173–179.

Kendall, P. C., & Bartel, N. R. (1990). *Teaching problem solving to students with learning and behavior problems: A manual for teachers.* Merion Station, PA: Workbooks.

Kendall, P. C., & Braswell, L. (1985). *Cognitive-behavioral therapy for impulsive children.* New York: Guilford Press.

Kendall, P. C., & Braswell, L. (1993). *Cognitive-behavioral therapy for impulsive children* (2nd ed.). New York: Guilford Press.

Kendall, P. C., Reber, M., McCleer, S., Epps, J., & Ronan, K. R. (1990). Cognitive-behavioral treatment of conduct disordered children. *Cognitive Therapy and Research, 14,* 279–297.

Kendall, P. C., Ronan, K. R., & Epps, J. (1991). Aggression in children/adolescents: Cognitive-behavioral treatment perspectives. In D. Pepler & K. Rubin (Eds.), *Development and treatment of childhood aggression.* Hillsdale, NJ: Erlbaum.

Kendall, P. C., & Wilcox, L. E. (1979). Self-control in children: Development of a rating scale. *Journal of Consulting and Clinical Psychology, 47,* 1020–1029.

Kendall, P. C., & Zupan, B. A. (1981). Individual versus group application of cognitive-behavioral strategies for developing self-control in children. *Behavior Therapy, 12,* 344–359.

Kent, R. N. (1976). A methodological critique of "Interventions for boys with conduct problems." *Journal of Consulting and Clinical Psychology, 44,* 297–302.

Kent, R. N., & O'Leary, K. D. (1976). A controlled evaluation of behavior modification with conduct problem children. *Journal of Consulting and Clinical Psychology, 44,* 586–596.

Kernberg, P. F., & Chazan, S. E. (1991). *Children with conduct disorders: A psychotherapy manual.* New York: Basic Books.

Kessler, J. W. (1963). My son, the underachiever. *PTA Magazine, 58,* 12–14.

Kimbrough, J. (1985). School-based strategies for delinquency prevention. In P. Greenwood (Ed.), *The juvenile rehabilitation reader.* Santa Monica, CA: Rand Corporation.

King, C. (1976). Countertransference and counter-experience in the treatment of violence prone youth. *American Journal of Orthopsychiatry, 46,* 43–53.

Kirgin, K. A., Braukman, C. J., Atwater, J. D., & Wolf, M. M. (1982). An evaluation of teaching-family (Achievement Place) group homes for juvenile offenders. *Journal of Applied Behavior Analysis, 15,* 1–16.

Klein, M. W. (1969). Gang cohesiveness, delinquency, and a street work program. *Journal of Research in Crime and Delinquency, 6,* 135–136.

Klein, N. C., Alexander, J. F., & Parsons, B. V. (1977). Impact of family systems intervention on recidivism and sibling delinquency: A model of primary prevention and program evaluation. *Journal of Consulting and Clinical Psychology, 45,* 469–474.

Kohlberg, L. (1978). Revisions in the theory and practice of moral development. In W. Damon (Ed.), *New directions in child development: Moral development.* San Francisco: Jossey-Bass.

Kolko, D. J., & Kazdin, A. E. (1986). A conceptualization of firesetting in children and adolescents. *Journal of Abnormal Child Psychology, 14,* 49–61.

Kolko, D. J., Loar, L. L., & Sturnick, D. (1990). Inpatient social-cognitive skills training groups with conduct-disordered and attention-deficit disordered children. *Journal of Child Psychology and Psychiatry, 31,* 737–748.

Kolko, D. J., & Milan, M. A. (1983). Reframing and paradoxical instruction to overcome "resistance" in the treatment of delinquent youths. *Journal of Consulting and Clinical Psychology, 51,* 655–660.

Kovacs, M. (1981). Rating scales to assess depression in school-aged children. *Acta Paedopsychiatrica, 46,* 305–315.

Kovacs, M., Krol, R., & Voti, L. (1994). Early onset psychopathology and the risk of teenage pregnancy among clinically referred girls. *Journal of the American Academy of Child and Adolescent Psychiatry, 33,* 106–113.

Kovacs, M., Paulauskas, S. L., Gastonis, C., & Richards, C. (1988). Depressive disorder in childhood: 2. A longitudinal study of comorbidity with and risk for conduct disorders. *Journal of Affective Disorders, 15,* 205–217.

Kovacs, M., & Pollock, M. (1995). Bipolar disorder and comorbid conduct disorder in childhood and adolescence. *Journal of the American Academy of Child and Adolescent Psychiatry, 34,* 715–723.

Kozloff, M. A. (1979). *A program for families of children with learning disabilities and behavior problems.* New York: Wiley.

Krouse, J. H., & Krouse, H. J. (1981). Toward a multimodal theory of academic underachievement. *Educational Psychologist, 16,* 151–164.

Kruesi, M. J. P., Hibbs, E. D., Zahn, T. P., Keysor, C. S., Hamburger, S. D., Bartko, J. J., & Rapoport, J. L. (1992). A two-year prospective follow-up study of children and adolescents with disruptive behavior disorders. *Archives of General Psychiatry, 47,* 419–426.

Kulik, J. A., Stein, K. B., & Sarbin, T. R. (1968). Dimensions and patterns of adolescent antisocial behavior. *Journal of Consulting and Clinical Psychology, 32,* 375–382.

Kupersmidt, J. B., Burchinal, M., & Patterson, C. J. (1995). Developmental patterns of childhood peer relations as predictors of externalizing behavior problems. *Development and Psychopathology, 7,* 825–843.

Lacasse, M. (in press). *Underachievement: Personality types among gifted adolescents.* Unpublished doctoral dissertation, York University, Department of Psychology, Toronto, Ontario, Canada.

Lahey, B. B., Hartdagen, S. E., Frick, P. J., McBurnett, K., Connor, R., & Hynd, G. W. (1988). Conduct disorder: Parsing the confounded relation to parental divorce and antisocial personality. *Journal of Abnormal Psychology, 97,* 334–337.

Lahey, B. B., Loeber, R., Frick, P. J., Hart, E. L., Applegate, B., Zhang, Q., Green, S. M., & Russo, M. F. (1995). Four-year longitudinal study of conduct disorder in boys: Patterns and predictors of persistence. *Journal of Abnormal Psychology, 104,* 83–93.

Lahey, B. B., Loeber, R., Quay, H. C., Frick, P. J., & Grimm, J. (1992). Oppositional defiant and conduct disorders: Issues to be resolved for DSM-IV. *Journal of the American Academy of Child and Adolescent Psychiatry, 31,* 539–546.

Lahey, B. B., McBurnett, K., Loeber, R., & Hart, E. L. (in press). Psychobiology of conduct disorder. In G. P. Sholeuar (Ed.), *Conduct disorders in children and adolescents: Assessments and interventions.* Washington, DC: American Psychiatric Press.

Lahey, B. B., Piacentini, J. C., McBurnett, K., Stone, P., Hartdagen, S., & Hynd, G. (1988). Psychopathology in the parents of children with conduct disorder and hyperactivity. *Journal of the American Academy of Child and Adolescent Psychiatry, 27,* 163–170.

Lally, R. J., Mangione, P. L., & Honig, A. S. (1988). The Syracuse University Family Development Research Program: Long-range impact on an early intervention with low-income children and their families. In D. Powell (Ed.), *Parent education as early childhood intervention: Emerging directions in theory, research practice.* Norwood, NJ: Ablex.

Landy, S., & Peters, R. D. (1992). Toward an understanding of a developmental paradigm for aggressive conduct disorders during preschool years. In R. D. Peters, R. J. McMahon, & V. L. Quinsey (Eds.), *Aggression and violence throughout the lifespan.* Newbury Park, CA: Sage.

Larzelere, R. E., & Patterson, G. R. (1990). Parental management: Mediator of the effect of socioeconomic status on early delinquency. *Criminology, 28,* 301–323.

Laub, J. H., & Sampson, R. J. (1988). Unraveling families and delinquency: A reanalysis of the Glueks' data. *Criminology, 26,* 355–380.

LeBlanc, M., Cote, G., & Loeber, R. (1991). Temporal paths in delinquency. *Canadian Journal of Criminology, 33,* 23–44.

LeBlanc, M., & Frechette, M. (1989). *Male criminal activity from childhood to adulthood: Multilevel and developmental perspectives.* New York: Springer-Verlag.

LeCroy, C. W. (Ed.). (1994a). *Handbook of child and adolescent treatment manuals.* New York: Lexington Books.

LeCroy, C. W. (1994b). Social skills training. In C. W. LeCroy (Ed.), *Handbook of child and adolescent treatment manuals.* New York: Lexington Books.

Ledingham, J. E., & Schwartzman, A. E. (1984). A 3-year follow-up of aggressive and withdrawn behavior in childhood: Preliminary findings. *Journal of Abnormal Child Psychology, 12,* 157–168.

Lefkowitz, M. M., Eron, L. D., Walder, L. O., & Huesmann, L. R. (1977). *Growing up to be violent: A longitudinal study of the development of aggression.* New York: Pergamon Press.

Leitenberg, H. (1986). Primary prevention in delinquency. In J. Burchard & S. Burchard (Eds.), *Prevention of delinquent behavior.* Newbury Park, CA: Sage.

Leonoff, D. (1993). *Parental, peer, and personality factors in adolescent academic underachievement.* Unpublished doctoral dissertation, York University, Department of Psychology, Toronto, Ontario, Canada.

Lewis, C. E. (1991). Neurochemical mechanisms of chronic antisocial behavior (psychopathy): A literature review. *Journal of Nervous and Mental Disease, 179,* 720–727.

Lewis, D. O., Lovely, R., Yeager, C., & Femina, D. (1989). Toward a theory of the genesis of violence: A follow-up study of delinquents. *Journal of the American Academy of Child and Adolescent Psychiatry, 28*(3), 431–436.

Lewis, D. O., Pincus, J., Lovely, R., Spitzer, E., & Moy, E. (1987). Biopsychosocial characteristics of matched samples of delinquents and nondelinquents. *Journal of the American Academy of Child and Adolescent Psychiatry, 26,* 744–752.

Lewis, D. O., Shanok, S. S., Pincus, J. H., & Glaser, G. H. (1979). Violent juvenile delinquents: Psychiatric, neurological, psychological, and abuse factors. *Journal of the American Academy of Child Psychiatry, 14,* 307–319.

Lewis, D. O., Yeager, C. A., Cobham-Portorreal, C. S., Klein, N., Showalter, C., & Anthony, A. (1991). A follow-up of female delinquents: Maternal contributions to the perpetuation of deviance. *Journal of the American Academy of Child and Adolescent Psychiatry, 30,* 197–201.

Lewis, W., & Balla, D. (1976). *Delinquency and psychopathology.* New York: Grune & Stratton.

Lilienfeld, S. O. (1992). The association between antisocial personality and somatization disorders: A review and integration of theoretical models. *Clinical Psychology Review, 12,* 641–662.

Lion, J. R. (Ed.). (1981). *Personality disorders and management (Revised for DSM-III).* Baltimore: Williams & Wilkins.

Liska, A. E., & Reed, M. D. (1985). Ties to conventional institutions and delinquency: Estimating reciprocal effects. *American Sociological Review, 50,* 547–560.

Little, S. A., & Garber, J. (1995). Aggression, depression, and stressful life events predicting peer rejection in children. *Development and Psychopathology, 7,* 845–856.

Lochman, J. E. (1985). Effects of different treatment lengths in cognitive behavioral interventions with aggressive boys. *Child Psychiatry and Human Development, 16,* 45–56.

Lochman, J. E., Burch, P. R., Curry, J. F., & Lampron, L. B. (1984). Treatment and generalization effects of cognitive-behavioral and goal-setting interventions with aggressive boys. *Journal of Consulting and Clinical Psychology, 52,* 915–916.

Lochman, J. E., & Conduct Problems Prevention Research Group. (1995). Screening for child behavior problems for prevention programs at school entry. *Journal of Consulting and Clinical Psychology, 63,* 549–559.

Lochman, J. E., & Curry, J. F. (1986). Effects of social problem-solving training and self-instruction training with aggressive boys. *Journal of Clinical Child Psychology, 15,* 159–164.

Lochman, J. E., & Lampron, L. B. (1988). Cognitive-behavioral interventions for aggressive boys: 7-month follow-up effects. *Journal of Child and Adolescent Psychotherapy, 2,* 21–25.

Lochman, J. E., Lampron, L. B., Gemmer, T. C., & Harris, S. R. (1987). Anger coping intervention with aggressive children: A guide to implementation in school settings. In P. A. Keller & S. R. Heyman (Eds.), *Innovations in clinical practice, A source book* (Vol. 6). Sarasota, FL: Professional Resource Exchange.

Loeber, R. (1982). The stability of antisocial and delinquent child behavior: A review. *Child Development, 53,* 1431–1446.

Loeber, R. (1989). Natural histories of conduct problems, delinquency, and associated substance use: Evidence for developmental progressions. In B. B. Lahey & A. E. Kazdin (Eds.), *Advances in clinical child psychology* (Vol. 11), New York: Plenum Press.

Loeber, R. (1990). Development and risk factors in juvenile antisocial behavior and delinquency. *Clinical Psychology Review, 10,* 1–41.

Loeber, R. (1992). Natural histories of juvenile conduct problems, substance use, and delinquency: Evidence for developmental progressions. In B. B. Lahey & A. E. Kazdin (Eds.), *Advances in clinical child psychology.* New York: Plenum.

Loeber, R., & Dishion, T. J. (1983). Early predictors of male delinquency: A review. *Psychological Bulletin, 94,* 68–99.

Loeber, R., & Dishion, T. J. (1984). Boys who fight at home and at school: Family conditions influencing cross-setting consistency. *Journal of Consulting and Clinical Psychology, 52,* 759–768.

Loeber, R., Dishion, T. J., & Patterson, G. R. (1984). Multiple gating: A multistage assessment procedure for identifying youths at risk for delinquency. *Journal of Research in Crime and Delinquency, 21,* 7–32.

Loeber, R., Green, S. M., Keenan, K., & Lahey, B. B. (1995). Which boys will fare worse? Early predictors of the onset of conduct disorder in a six-year longitudinal study. *Journal of the American Academy of Child and Adolescent Psychiatry, 34,* 499–509.

Loeber, R., Green, S. M., Lahey, B. B., Christ, M. A., & Frick, P. J. (1992). Developmental sequences in the age of onset of disruptive child behaviors. *Journal of Child and Family Studies, 1,* 21–41.

Loeber, R., Green, S. M., Lahey, B. B., & Stouthamer-Loeber, M. (1989). Optimal informants on childhood disruptive behaviors. *Development and Psychopathology, 1,* 317–337.

Loeber, R., Lahey, B. B., & Thomas, C. (1991). Diagnostic conundrum of oppositional defiant disorder and conduct disorder. *Journal of Abnormal Psychology, 100,* 379–390.

Loeber, R., & Schmalling, K. B. (1985a). The utility of differentiating between mixed and pure forms of antisocial child behavior. *Journal of Abnormal Child Psychology, 13,* 315–336.

Loeber, R., & Schmalling, K. B. (1985b). Empirical evidence for overt and covert patterns of antisocial conduct problems: A meta-analysis. *Journal of Abnormal Child Psychology, 13,* 337–352.

Loeber, R., & Stouthamer-Loeber, M. (1986). Family factors as correlates and predictors of juvenile conduct problems and delinquency. In M. Torrey & N. Morris (Eds.), *Crime and justice* (Vol. 7). Chicago: University of Chicago Press.

Loeber, R., & Stouthamer-Loeber, M. (1987). Prediction. In H. C. Quay (Ed.), *Handbook of juvenile delinquency.* New York: Wiley.

Loeber, R., Stouthamer-Loeber, M., Van Kammen, W. B., & Farrington, D. P. (1989). Development of a new measure of self-reported antisocial behavior in young children: Prevalence and reliability. In W. Klein (Ed.), *Self-report methodology in criminological research.* Boston: Kluwer-Nijhoff.

Loeber, R., Stouthamer-Loeber, M., Van Kammen, W. B., & Farrington, D. P. (1991). Initiation, escalation and desistance in juvenile offending and their correlates. *Journal of Criminal Law and Criminology, 82,* 36–82.

Loeber, R., Tremblay, R., Gagnon, C., & Charlebois, P. (1989). Continuity and desistance in early fighting in school. *Development and Psychopathology, 1,* 39–50.

Loeber, R., Weissman, W., & Reid, J. B. (1983). Family interactions of assaultive adolescents, stealers, and non-delinquents. *Journal of Abnormal Child Psychology, 11,* 1–14.

Loeber, R., Wung, P., Kennan, K., Giroux, B., Stouthamer-Loeber, M., Van Kammen, W. B., & Maughan, B. (1993). Developmental pathways in disruptive child behavior. *Development and Psychopathology, 5,* 103–133.

Lynsky, M. T., & Fergusson, D. M. (1995). Childhood conduct problems, attention deficit behaviors, and adolescent alcohol, tobacco, and illicit drug use. *Journal of Abnormal Child Psychology, 23,* 281–302.

Lytton, H. (1990). Child and parent effects in boys' conduct disorder: A reinterpretation. *Developmental Psychology, 26*(5), 683–697.

Maccoby, E. E. (1986). Social groupings in childhood: Their relationship to prosocial and antisocial behavior in boys and girls. In D. Olweus, J. Block, & M. Radke-Yarrow (Eds.), *Development of antisocial and prosocial behavior.* Orlando, FL: Academic Press.

Maenchen, A. (1970). The handling of overt aggression in child analysis. *Psychoanalytic Study of the Child, 39,* 393–406.

Magnusson, D. (1987). Adult delinquency in the light of conduct and physiology at an early age: A longitudinal study. In D. Magnusson & A. Ohman (Eds.), *Psychopathology: An interactional perspective.* Orlando: Academic Press.

Mahy, A. (1994). Validation of the Achievement Motivation Profile (AMP) in a Canadian high school sample. Unpublished masters thesis, York University, Department of Psychology, Toronto, Ontario, Canada.

Mandel, H. P. (1981). *Short-term psychotherapy and brief treatment techniques: An annotated bibliography (1920–1980).* New York: Plenum.

Mandel, H. P., Friedland, J., & Marcus, S. I. (1996). *The Achievement Motivation Profile (AMP): Administration, scoring, and interpretation manual.* Los Angeles: Western Psychological Services.

Mandel, H. P., Friedland, J., Marcus, S. I., & Mandel, D. E. (1996). *The Achievement Motivation Profile (AMP): Computerized interpretative report.* Los Angeles: Western Psychological Services.

Mandel, H. P., & Mandel, D. E. (Eds.). (1995). *Along the path: Case histories of differentially diagnosed underachievers* (2nd ed.). Toronto, Ontario, Canada: York University, Institute on Achievement and Motivation.

Mandel, H. P., & Marcus, S. I. (1988). *The psychology of underachievement: Differential diagnosis and differential treatment.* New York: Wiley.

Mandel, H. P., Marcus, S. I., & Dean, L. (1995). *Could do better: Why children underachieve and what to do about it.* New York: Wiley.

Mandel, H. F., Marcus, S. I., & Mandel, D. E. (1992). *Helping the non-achievement syndrome student* (Rev. ed.). Toronto, Ontario, Canada: York University, Institute on Achievement and Motivation.

Mandel, H. P., Roth, R. M., & Berenbaum, H. L. (1968). The relationship between personality change and achievement change as a function of psychodiagnosis. *Journal of Counseling Psychology, 15,* 500–505.

Mandel, H. P., Weizmann, F., Millan, B., Greenhow, J., & Spiers, D. (1975). Reaching emotionally disturbed children: Judo principles in remedial education. *American Journal of Orthopsychiatry, 45,* 867–874.

Marlatt, G. A., & Gordon, J. (1985). *Relapse prevention.* New York: Guilford Press.

Marohn, R., Dalle-Molle, D., McCarter, E., & Linn, D. (1980). *Juvenile delinquents: Psychodynamic assessment and hospital treatment.* New York: Brunner/Mazel.

Marriage, K., Fine, S., Moretti, M., & Haley, G. (1986). Relationship between depression and conduct disorder in children and adolescents. *Journal of the American Academy of Child Psychiatry, 25,* 687–691.

Martin, H. (1987). *Conduct disorders of childhood and adolescence: A social learning perspective.* New York: Wiley.

Matsueda, R. L., & Heimer, K. (1987). Race, family structure, and delinquency: A test of differential association and social control theories. *American Sociological Review, 52,* 826–840.

Matthews, W., & Reid, W. (1981). A wilderness experience treatment program for offenders. In W. Reid (Ed.), *The treatment of antisocial syndromes.* New York: Van Nostrand Reinhold.

Matthys, W., Walterbos, W., Van Engeland, H., & Koops, W. (1995). Conduct disordered boys' perceptions of their liked peers. *Cognitive Therapy and Research, 19,* 357–372.

Maughan, B., Gray, G., & Rutter, M. (1985). Reading retardation and antisocial behavior: A follow-up into employment. *Journal of Child Psychology and Psychiatry, 26,* 741–758.

McArdle, P., O'Brien, G., & Kolvin, I. (1995). Hyperactivity: Prevalence and relationship with conduct disorder. *Journal of Child Psychology and Psychiatry, 36,* 279–303.

McBurnett, K., Lahey, B. B., Frick, P. J., Risch, C., Loeber, R., Hart, E. L., Christ, M. A., & Hanson, K. S. (1991). Anxiety, inhibition, and conduct disorder in children: 2. Relation to salivary cortisol. *Journal of the American Academy of Child and Adolescent Psychiatry, 31,* 192–196.

McCall, R. B., Evahn, C., & Kratzer, L. (1992). *High school underachievers: What do they achieve as adults?* Newbury Park, CA: Sage.

McConaughy, S. H., & Skiba, R. J. (1993). Comorbidity of externalizing and internalizing problems. *School Psychology Review, 22,* 421–436.

McCord, J. (1979). Some child-rearing antecedents of criminal behavior in adult men. *Journal of Personality and Social Psychology, 37,* 1477–1486.

McCord, J. (1986). Instigation and insulation: How families affect antisocial aggression. In D. Olweus, J. Block, & M. Radke-Yarrow (Eds.), *Development of antisocial and prosocial behavior.* Orlando, FL: Academic Press.

McCord, J. (1991). Family relationships, juvenile delinquency, and adult criminality. *Criminology, 29,* 397–417.

McCord, J. (1993). Conduct disorder and antisocial behavior: Some thoughts about processes. *Development and Psychopathology, 5,* 321–329.

McCord, J., & Tremblay, R. (Eds.). (1992). *Preventing antisocial behavior.* New York: Guilford Press.

McCord, W., & McCord, J. (1964). *The psychopath: An essay on the criminal mind.* New York: Van Nostrand Reinhold.

McAuley, R. (1982). Training parents to modify conduct problems in their children. *Journal of Child Psychology and Psychiatry and Allied Disciplines, 23,* 335–342.

McGee, R., Feehan, M., Williams, S., & Anderson, J. (1992). DSM-III disorders from age 11–15 years. *Journal of the American Academy of Child and Adolescent Psychiatry, 31,* 50–59.

McGee, R., Feehan, M., Williams, S., Partridge, F., Silva, P. A., & Kelly, J. (1990). DSM-III disorders in a large sample of adolescents. *Journal of the American Academy of Child and Adolescent Psychiatry, 31,* 50–59.

McGee, R., Share, D. L., Moffitt, T. E., Williams, S., & Silva, P. A. (1988). Reading disability, behavior problems, and juvenile delinquency. In D. H. Saklofske & S. B. G. Eysenck (Eds.), *Individual differences in children and adolescents: International perspectives.* London: Hodder & Stoughton.

McGee, R., Williams, S., Share, D. L., Anderson, J., & Silva, P. A. (1986). The relationship between specific reading retardation, reading backwardness, and behavioral problems in a large sample of Dunedin boys. *Journal of Child Psychology and Psychiatry, 27,* 597–610.

McGee, R., Williams, S., & Silva, P. A. (1984). Behavioral and developmental characteristics of aggressive, hyperactive, and aggressive-hyperactive boys. *Journal of the American Academy of Child Psychiatry, 23,* 270–279.

McKeough, A., Yates, T., & Marini, A. (1994). Intentional reasoning: A developmental study of behaviorally aggressive and normal boys. *Development and Psychopathology, 6,* 285–304.

McMahon, R. J. (1987). Some current issues in the behavioral assessment of conduct disordered children and their families. *Behavioral Assessment, 9,* 235–252.

McMahon, R. J., & Forehand, R. (1988). Conduct disorders. In E. J. Mash & L. G. Terdal (Eds.), *Behavioral assessment of childhood disorders* (2nd ed.). New York: Guilford Press.

McMahon, R. J., Forehand, R., & Griest, D. L. (1981). Effects of knowledge of social learning principles on enhancing outcome and generalization in a parent training program. *Journal of Consulting and Clinical Psychology, 49,* 526–532.

McMahon, R. J., & Wells, K. C. (1989). Conduct disorders. In R. A. Barkley & E. J. Mash (Eds.), *Childhood disorders* (pp. 73–132). New York: Guilford Press.

McManus, M., Alessi, N. E., Grapentine, W. L., & Brickman, A. (1984). Psychiatric disturbances in serious delinquents. *Journal of the American Academy of Child Psychiatry, 23,* 602–615.

Mednick, S. A., Gabrielli, W. F., & Hutchings, B. (1984). Genetic influences in criminal convictions: Evidence from an adoption cohort. *Science, 224,* 891–894.

Meeks, J. (1980). Conduct disorders. In A. Freedman, H. Kaplan, & B. Sadock (Eds.), *Comprehensive textbook of psychiatry.* Baltimore: Williams & Wilkins.

Meichenbaum, D. H., & Goodman, J. (1971). Training impulsive children to talk to themselves: A means of developing self-control. *Journal of Abnormal Psychology, 77,* 115–126.

Meltzer, L. J., Levine, M. D., Karniski, W., Palfreg, J. S., & Clarke, S. (1984). Analysis of the learning style of adolescent delinquents. *Journal of Learning Disabilities, 17,* 600–608.

Michelson, L. (1986). Cognitive-behavioral strategies in the prevention and treatment of antisocial disorders in children and adolescents. In J. Burchard & S. Burchard (Eds.), *Prevention of delinquent behavior.* Newbury Park, CA: Sage.

Michelson, L., Sugai, D. P., Wood, R. P., & Kazdin, A. E. (1983). *Social skills assessment and training with children.* New York: Plenum Press.

Milich, R., & Landau, S. (1989). The role of social status variables in differentiating subgroups of hyperactive children. In L. M. Bloomingdale & J. M. Swanson (Eds.), *Attention deficit disorder* (Vol. 4). Oxford, England: Pergamon Press.

Miller, G. E., & Prinz, R. J. (1990). Enhancement of social learning family interventions for childhood conduct disorder. *Psychological Bulletin, 108*(2), 291–307.

Miller, L. S., Klein, R. G., Piacentini, J., Abikoff, H., Shah, M. R., Samoilov, A., & Guardino, M. (1995). The New York Teacher Rating Scale for Disruptive and Antisocial Behavior. *Journal of the American Academy of Child and Adolescent Psychiatry, 34,* 359–370.

Miller, W. B. (1958). Lower class culture as a generating milieu of gang delinquency. *Journal of Social Issues, 14,* 5–19.

Miller, W. B. (1962). The impact of a "total community" delinquency control project. *Social Problems, 10,* 168–191.

Mischel, W., Shoda, Y., & Rodriguez, M. C. (1989). Delay of gratification in children. *Science, 244,* 933–938.

Moffitt, T. E. (1990a). Juvenile delinquency and attention-deficit disorder: Developmental trajectories from age 3 to 15. *Child Development, 61,* 893–910.

Moffitt, T. E. (1990b). The neuropsychology of delinquency: A critical review of theory and research. In N. Morris & M. Tonry (Eds.), *Crime and Justice* (Vol. 12). Chicago: University of Chicago Press.

Moffitt, T. E. (1993). The neuropsychology of conduct disorder. *Development and Psychopathology, 5,* 135–151.

Moffitt, T. E. (1993). "Life-course-persistent" and "adolescent-limits" antisocial behavior: A developmental taxonomy. *Psychological Review, 100*(4), 674–701.

Moffitt, T. E., Caspi, A., Dickson, N., Silva, P., & Stanton, W. (1996). Child-onset versus adolescent-onset antisocial conduct problems in males: Natural history from ages 3 to 18 years. *Development and psychopathology, 8,* 399–424.

Moffitt, T. E., Gabrielli, W. F., Mednick, S. A., & Schulsinger, F. (1981). Socioeconomic status, IQ, and delinquency. *Journal of Abnormal Psychology, 90,* 152–156.

Moffitt, T. E., & Henry, B. (1989). Neuropsychobiological assessment of executive function in self-reported delinquents. *Development and Psychopathology, 1,* 105–118.

Moffitt, T. E., & Silva, P. A. (1988a). IQ and delinquency: A direct test of the differential detection hypothesis. *Journal of Abnormal Psychology, 97,* 330–333.

Moffitt, T. E., & Silva, P. A. (1988b). Neuropsychological deficit and self-reported delinquency in an unselected birth cohort. *Journal of the American Academy of Child and Adolescent Psychiatry, 27,* 233–240.

Moffitt, T. E., & Silva, P. A. (1988c). Self-reported delinquency, neuropsychological deficit, and history of attention deficit disorder. *Journal of Abnormal Child Psychology, 16,* 553–569.

Moffitt, T. E., & Silva, P. A. (1988d). Self-reported delinquency: Results from an instrument for New Zealand. *Australian and New Zealand Journal of Criminology, 21,* 227–240.

Moore, D. R., Chamberlain, P., & Mukai, L. H. (1979). Children at risk for delinquency: A follow-up comparison of aggressive children and children who steal. *Journal of Abnormal Child Psychology, 7,* 345–355.

Morris, H. H., Escoll, P. J., & Wexler, R. (1956). Aggressive behavior disorders of childhood: A follow-up study. *American Journal of Psychiatry, 112,* 991–997.

Moskowitz, D. S., & Schwartzman, A. E. (1989). Life paths of aggressive and withdrawn children. In N. Cantor & D. Buss (Eds.), *Emerging trends in personality.* New York: Springer-Verlag.

Moss, G. R., & Rick, G. R. (1981). Overview: Application of operant technology to behavioral disorders of adolescents. *American Journal of Psychiatry, 138,* 1161–1169.

Mrazek, P. J., & Haggerty, R. J. (Eds.). (1994). *Reducing risks for mental disorders: Frontiers of preventive intervention research.* Washington, DC: National Academy Press.

Mullins, E., Quigley, K., & Glanville, B. (1994). A controlled evaluation of the impact of a parent training programme on child behaviour and mothers' general well-being. *Counselling Psychology Quarterly, 7,* 167–179.

Murray, H. A. (1971). *Thematic Apperception Test Manual.* Cambridge, MA: Harvard University Press.

Naglieri, J. A. (1985). *The Matrix Analogies Test.* New York: The Psychological Corporation.

Nasby, W., Hayden, B., & DePaulo, B. M. (1980). Attributional bias among aggressive boys to interpret unambiguous social stimulus as displays of hostility. *Journal of Abnormal Psychology, 89,* 459–468.

Newman, J. P. (1987). Reaction to punishment in extroverts and psychopaths: Implications for the impulsive behavior of disinhibited individuals. *Journal of Research in Personality, 21,* 464–480.

Newman, J. P., & Kosson, D. S. (1986). Passive avoidance learning in psychopathic and nonpsychopathic offenders. *Journal of Abnormal Psychology, 95,* 257–263.

Newman, J. P., Patterson, C. M., & Kosson, D. S. (1987). Response perseveration in psychopaths. *Journal of Abnormal Psychology, 96,* 145–148.

Noam, G. G., Paget, K., Valiant, G., Borst, S., & Bartok, J. (1994). Conduct and affective disorders in developmental perspective: A systematic study of adolescent psychopathology. *Development and Psychopathology, 6,* 519–532.

Noy, S. (1969). Comparison of three types of psychotherapies in promoting growth in behavior disorders. *Dissertation Abstracts International, 29,* 3919-B.

Nucci, L. P., & Herman, S. (1982). Behavioral disordered children's conception of moral, conventional, and personal issues. *Journal of Abnormal Child Psychology, 10,* 411–426.

Nye, F. I. (1958). *Family relationships and delinquent behavior.* New York: Wiley.

O'Donnell, C., Manos, M., & Chesney-Lind, M. (1987). Diversion and neighborhood delinquency programs in open settings. In E. Morris & C. Braukmann (Eds.), *Behavioral approaches to crime and delinquency.* New York: Plenum Press.

O'Donnell, D. J. (1985). Conduct disorders. In J. M. Weiner (Ed.), *Diagnosis and psychopharmacology of childhood and adolescent disorders.* New York: Wiley.

O'Donnell, J., Hawkins, J. D., Catalano, R. F., Abbott, R. D., & Day, L. E. (1995). Preventing school failure, drug use, and delinquency among low-income children: Long-term intervention in elementary schools. *American Journal of Orthopsychiatry, 65,* 87–100.

Offord, D. R. (1982). Family backgrounds of male and female delinquents. In J. Gunn & D. P. Farrington (Eds.), *Abnormal offenders, delinquency, and the criminal justice system.* Chichester, England: Wiley.

Offord, D. R., & Boyle, M. H. (1989). Ontario Child Health Study: Correlates of disorder. *Journal of the American Academy of Child and Adolescent Psychiatry.*

Offord, D. R., Boyle, M. H., & Racine, Y. A. (1991). The epidemiology of antisocial behavior in childhood and adolescence. In D. Pepler & K. Rubin (Eds.), *The development and treatment of childhood aggression.* Hillsdale, NJ: Erlbaum.

Offord, D. R., Boyle, M. H., Szatmari, P., Rae-Grant, N. I., Links, P. S., Cadman, D. T., Byles, J. A., Crawford, J. W., Blum, H. M., Byrne, C., Thomas, H., & Woodward, C. A. (1987). Ontario Child Health Study: 2. Six month prevalence of disorder and rates of service utilization. *Archives of General Psychiatry, 44,* 832–836.

Offord, D. R., Sullivan, K., Allen, N., & Abrams, N. (1979). Delinquency and hyperactivity. *Journal of Nervous and Mental Disease, 167,* 734–741.

Olds, D. L. (1988). The Prenatal-Early Infancy Project. In E. L. Cowen, R. P. Lorion, & J. Ramos-McKay (Eds.), *Fourteen ounces of prevention: A handbook for practitioners.* Washington, DC: American Psychological Association.

Olds, D. L., Henderson, C. R., & Tatelbaum, R. (1986). Preventing child abuse and neglect: A randomized trial of nurse home visitation. *Pediatrics, 78,* 65–78.

Ollendick, T. H., & Hersen, M. (1979). Social skills training for juvenile delinquents. *Behavior Research and Therapy, 17,* 547–555.

Olson, S. L. (1992). Development of conduct problems and peer rejection in preschool children: A social systems analysis. *Journal of Abnormal Child Psychology, 20,* 327–350.

Olweus, D. (1979). Stability of aggressive reaction patterns in males: A review. *Psychological Bulletin, 86,* 852–857.

Olweus, D. (1980). Familial and temperamental determinants of aggressive behavior in adolescent boys: A causal analysis. *Developmental Psychology, 16,* 644–660.

Olweus, D. (1981). Continuity in aggressive and withdrawn, inhibited behavior patterns. *Psychiatry and Social Science, 1,* 141–149.

Olweus, D. (1991). Bully/victim problems among school children: Basic facts and effects of a school-based intervention program. In D. Pepler & K. Rubin (Eds.), *The development and treatment of childhood aggression,* Hillsdale, NJ: Erlbaum.

Olweus, D., Block, J., & Radke-Yarrow, M. (Eds.). (1986). *Development of antisocial and prosocial behavior.* Orlando, FL: Academic Press.

O'Neal, P., & Robins, L. N. (1958). The relation of childhood behavior problems to adult psychiatric states: A thirty-year follow-up study of 150 subjects. *American Journal of Psychiatry, 114,* 961–969.

Packman, J. (1986). *Who needs care.* Oxford, England: Blackwell Scientific.

Padawer, W. J., Bupan, B. A., & Kendall, P. C. (1980). *Developing self-control in children: A manual of cognitive-behavioral strategies.* Minneapolis: University of Minnesota Press.

Parke, R. D., & Slaby, R. G. (1983). The development of aggression. In E. M. Hetherington (Ed.), P. H. Mussen (Series Ed.), *Handbook of child psychology: Vol. 4. Socialization, personality, and social development.* New York: Wiley.

Parrott, C. A., & Strongman, K. I. (1984). Loss of control and delinquency. *Adolescence, 19,* 459–471.

Parsons, B. V., & Alexander, J. F. (1973). Short-term family intervention: A therapy outcome study. *Journal of Consulting and Clinical Psychology, 41,* 195–201.

Patterson, G. R. (1974). Interventions for boys with conduct problems: Multiple settings, treatments, and criteria. *Journal of Consulting and Clinical Psychology, 42,* 471–481.

Patterson, G. R. (1976). The aggressive child. In E. J. Mash, L. A. Hamerlynck, & L. C. Handy (Eds.), *Behavior modification and families.* New York: Brunner/Mazel.

Patterson, G. R. (1979). Treatment for children with conduct problems: A review of outcomes studies. In S. Feshback & A. Fraczak (Eds.), *Aggression and behavior change: Biological and social processes.* New York: Praeger.

Patterson, G. R. (1982). *Coercive family process.* Eugene, OR: Castalia.

Patterson, G. R. (1983). Stress: A change agent for family process. In N. Garmezy & M. Rutter (Eds.), *Stress, coping, and development in children,* New York: McGraw-Hill.

Patterson, G. R. (1986a). The contribution of siblings to training for fighting: A microsocial analysis. In D. Olweus, J. Block, & M. Radke-Yarrow (Eds.), *Development of antisocial and prosocial behavior: Research, theories, and issues.* Orlando, FL: Academic Press.

Patterson, G. R. (1986b). Performance models for antisocial boys. *American Psychologist, 41,* 432–444.

Patterson, G. R., & Bank, L. (1986). Bootstrapping your way in the nomological thicket. *Behavioral Assessment, 8,* 49–73.

Patterson, G. R., Capaldi, D., & Bank, L. (1991). An early starter model for predicting delinquency. In D. Pepler & K. Rubin (Eds.), *The development and treatment of childhood aggression.* Hillsdale, NJ: Erlbaum.

Patterson, G. R., DeBarshye, B. D., & Ramsey, E. (1989). A developmental perspective on antisocial behavior. *American Psychologist, 44,* 329–335.

Patterson, G. R., & Dishion, T. J. (1985). Contribution of families and peers to delinquency. *Criminology, 23,* 63–79.

Patterson, G. R., Dishion, T. J., & Chamberlain, P. (1993). Outcomes and methodological issues relating to treatment of antisocial children. In T. R. Giles (Ed.), *Handbook of effective psychotherapy* (pp. 43–88). New York: Plenum Press.

Patterson, G. R., Ray, R. S., Shaw, D. A., & Cobb, J. A. (1969). *Manual for coding of family interactions* (Rev. ed.). New York: Microfiche Publications.

Patterson, G. R., Reid, J. B., & Dishion, T. J. (1992). *Antisocial boys.* Eugene, OR: Castalia.

Patterson, G. R., Reid, J. B., Jones, R. R., & Conger, R. E. (1975). *A social learning approach to family intervention: Families with aggressive children* (Vol. 1). Eugene, OR: Castalia.

Patterson, G. R., & Stouthamer-Loeber, M. (1984). The correlation of family management practices and delinquency. *Child Development, 55,* 1299–1307.

Peed, S., Roberts, M., & Forehand, R. (1977). Evaluation of the effectiveness of a standardized parent training program in altering the interaction of mothers and their non-compliant children. *Behavior Modification, 1,* 323–350.

Pennington, B. F., & Bennetto, L. (1993). Main effects or transactions in the neuropsychology of conduct disorder? Commentary on "the neuropsychology of conduct disorder." *Development and Psychopathology, 5,* 153–164.

Penzerro, R., & Lein, L. (1995). Burning their bridges: Disordered attachment and foster care discharge. *Child Welfare, 74,* 351–366.

Pepler, D. (1995). *A developmental profile of risks for aggressive girls.* Unpublished manuscript, York University, LaMarsh Research Centre for Violence and Conflict Resolution, Toronto, Ontario, Canada.

Pepler, D., & Craig, W. (1993). School-based social skills training with aggressive children: Necessary, but not sufficient. *Exceptionality Education Canada, 3,* 177–194.

Pepler, D., & Craig, W. (1994). *A peek behind the fence: Naturalistic observations of aggressive children with remote audio-visual recording.* Toronto, Ontario, Canada: York University, LaMarsh Research Centre on Violence and Conflict Resolution.

Pepler, D., Craig, W., & Roberts, W. (1995). Social skills training and aggression in the peer group. In J. McCord (Ed.), *Coercion and punishment in long-term perspectives* (pp. 213–228). New York: Cambridge University Press.

Pepler, D., Craig, W., Ziegler, S., & Charach, A. (1993). A school-based anti-bullying intervention: Preliminary evaluation. In D. Tattum (Ed.), *Understanding and managing bullying.* Oxford, England: Heinemann Books.

Pepler, D., Craig, W., Ziegler, S., & Charach, A. (in press). An evaluation of an anti-bullying intervention in Toronto schools. *Canadian Journal of Mental Health.*

Pepler, D., King, G., & Byrd, W. (1991). A social-cognitively based social skills training program for aggressive children. In D. Pepler & K. Rubin (Eds.), *The development and treatment of childhood aggression.* Hillsdale, NJ: Erlbaum.

Pepler, D., & Rubin, K. (Eds.). (1991). *The development and treatment of childhood aggression.* Hillsdale, NJ: Erlbaum.

Pepler, D., & Slaby, R. (1994). *Theoretical and developmental perspectives on youth and violence.* Toronto, Ontario, Canada: York University, LaMarsh Research Centre on Violence and Conflict Resolution.

Persons, R. W., & Peplinsky, H. B. (1966). Convergence in psychotherapy with delinquent boys. *Journal of Counseling Psychology, 13,* 329–334.

Pettit, G. S., & Bates, J. E. (1989). Family interaction patterns and children's behavior problems from infancy to four years. *Developmental Psychology, 25*(3), 413–420.

Pfeffer, C. R., Plutchik, R., & Mizruchi, M. S. (1983). Suicidal and assaultive behavior in children: Classification, measurement and interrelations. *American Journal of Psychiatry, 140,* 154–157.

Pianta, R. C., & Caldwell, C. B. (1990). Stability of externalizing symptoms from kindergarten to first grade and factors related to instability. *Developmental Psychology, 2,* 247–258.

Pliska, S. R., Rogeness, G. A., & Medrano, M. A. (1988). DBH, MHPG, and MAO in children with depressive, anxiety, and conduct disorders: Relationship to diagnosis and symptoms. *Psychiatry Research, 24,* 35–44.

Plomin, R., Nitz, K., & Rowe, D. C. (1990). Behavioral genetics and aggressive behavior in childhood. In M. Lewis & S. M. Miller (Eds.), *Handbook of developmental psychopathology.* New York: Plenum Press.

Pontius, A. A. (1972). Neurological aspects of some types of delinquency, especially among juveniles. *Adolescence, 7,* 289–308.

Porter, B., & O'Leary, K. D. (1980). Marital discord and childhood behavior problems. *Journal of Abnormal Child Psychology, 8,* 287–295.

Potts, L. J., Barley, W. D., Jones, K. A., & Woodhall, P. K. (1986). Comprehensive inpatient treatment of a severely antisocial adolescent. In W. H. Reid, D. Dorr, J. I. Walker, & J. W. Bonner (Eds.), *Unmasking the psychopath: Antisocial personality and related syndromes.* New York: Norton.

Price, J. M., & Dodge, K. A. (1989). Proactive and reactive aggression in childhood: Relations to peer status and social context dimensions. *Journal of Abnormal Child Psychology, 17,* 455–471.

Price, R. H., Cowen, E., Lorion, R., & Ramos-McKay, J. (1988). *Fourteen ounces of prevention: A casebook for practitioners.* Washington, DC: American Psychological Association.

Price, R. H., Cowen, E., Lorion, R., & Ramos-McKay, J. (1989). The search for effective prevention programs: What have we learned along the way. *American Journal of Orthopsychiatry, 59,* 107–120.

Prinz, R. J., Foster, S., Kent, R. N., & O'Leary, K. D. (1979). Multivariate assessment of conflict in distressed and nondistressed mother-adolescent dyads. *Journal of Applied Behavioral Analysis, 12,* 691–700.

Prochaska, J. O., DiClemente, C. C., & Norcross, J. C. (1992). In search of how people change. *American Psychologist, 47,* 1102–1114.

Provence, S., & Naylor, A. (1983). *Working with disadvantaged parents and children: Scientific issues and practice.* New Haven, CT: Yale University Press.

Puig-Antich, J. (1982). Major depression and conduct disorder in prepuberty. *Journal of the American Academy of Child Psychiatry, 17,* 695–707.

Pullis, M. (1991). Practical considerations of excluding conduct disordered students: An empirical analysis. *Behavior Disorders, 17,* 9–22.

Quay, H. C. (1986). Conduct disorders. In H. C. Quay & J. S. Werry (Eds.), *Psychopathological disorders of childhood* (3rd ed.). New York: Wiley.

Quay, H. C. (Ed.). (1987). *Handbook of juvenile delinquency.* New York: Wiley.

Quay, H. C. (1993). The psychobiology of undersocialized aggressive conduct disorder: A theoretical perspective. *Development and Psychopathology, 5,* 165–180.

Quay, H. C., & Peterson, D. R. (1987). *Manual for the Revised Behavior Checklist.* (Available from H. C. Quay, 2525 Gulf of Mexico Drive, Apt. 5C, Longboat Key, FL 34228.)

Raine, A. (1988). Evoked potentials and antisocial behavior. In T. Moffitt & S. A. Mednick (Eds.), *Biological contributions to crime causation.* Dordrecht, Netherlands: Martinus Nijhoff.

Raine, A., & Jones, F. (1987). Attention, autonomic arousal, and personality in behaviorally disordered children. *Journal of Abnormal Child Psychology, 15,* 583–599.

Raine, A., Venables, P. H., & Williams, M. A. (1990). Autonomic orienting responses in 15-year old male subjects and criminal behavior at age 24. *American Journal of Psychiatry, 147,* 933–937.

Ramsey, E., Bank, L., Patterson, G. R., & Walker, H. M. (in press). From home to school to juvenile court: A social interaction model of the path to delinquency. *Journal of Experimental Child Psychology.*

Reckless, W. C., & Dinitz, S. (1972). *The prevention of juvenile delinquency: An experiment.* Columbus: Ohio State University Press.

Reeves, J. C., Werry, J. S., Elkind, G. S., & Zametkin, A. (1987). Attention deficit, conduct, oppositional, and anxiety disorder in children: 2. Clinical characteristics. *Journal of the American Academy of Child and Adolescent Psychiatry, 26,* 144–155.

Reich, W., Earls, F., Frankel, O., & Shayka, J. J. (1993). Psychopathology in children of alcoholics. *Journal of the American Academy of Child and Adolescent Psychiatry, 32,* 995–1002.

Reich, W., Earls, F., & Powell, J. (1988). A comparison of the home and social environments of children of alcoholic and non-alcoholic parents. *British Journal of Addiction, 83,* 831–839.

Reid, F., & Wineman, D. (1951). *Children who hate.* New York: Free Press.

Reid, J. B. (Ed.). (1978). *A social learning approach to family intervention: Vol. 2. Observation in home settings.* Eugene, OR: Castalia.

Reid, J. B. (1991). Involving parents in the prevention of conduct disorder: Rationale, problems, and tactics. *Community Psychology, 24*(2), 28–30.

Reid, J. B. (1993). Prevention of conduct disorder before and after school entry: Relating interventions to developmental findings. *Development and Psychopathology, 5,* 243–262.

Reid, J. B., Baldwin, D. V., Patterson, G. R., & Dishion, T. J. (1988). Observations in the assessment of childhood disorders. In M. Rutter, A. H. Tuma, & I. S. Lann (Eds.), *Assessment and diagnosis in child psychopathology.* New York: Guilford Press.

Reid, W. H. (Ed.). (1978). *The psychopath: A comprehensive study of antisocial disorders and behaviors.* New York: Brunner/Mazel.

Reid, W. H. (1985). The antisocial personality: A review. *Hospital and Community Psychiatry, 36,* 831–837.

Reid, W. H., Dorr, D., Walker, J. I., & Bonner, J. W. (Eds.). (1986). *Unmasking the psychopath: Antisocial personality and related syndromes.* New York: Norton.

Reiss, A. J., & Rhodes, A. L. (1961). The distribution of juvenile delinquency in the social class structure. *American Sociological Review, 26,* 720–732.

Rhodes, A. L., & Reiss, A. J. (1969). Apathy, truancy, and delinquency as adaptations to school failure. *Social Forces, 48,* 12–22.

Richman, N., Stevenson, J., & Graham, P. J. (1982). *Pre-school to school: A behavioral study.* London: Academic Press.

Richters, J. E., & Cicchetti, D. (1993a). Editorial: Toward a developmental perspective on conduct disorder. *Development and Psychopathology, 5,* 1–4.

Richters, J. E., & Cicchetti, D. (1993b). Mark Twain meets DSM-III-R: Conduct disorder, development, and the concept of harmful dysfunction. *Development and Psychopathology, 5,* 5–29.

Richters, J. E., & Martinez, P. E. (1993). Violent communities, family choices, and children's chances: An algorithm for improving the odds. *Development and Psychopathology, 5,* 609–627.

Riddle, M., & Roberts, A. H. (1977). Delinquency, delay of gratification, recidivism, and the Porteus Maze tests. *Psychological Bulletin, 84,* 417–425.

Roberts, M. W., McMahon, R. J., Forehand, R., & Humphrey, L. (1978). The effect of parental instruction-giving on child compliance. *Behavior Therapy, 9,* 793–798.

Robin, A. K., & Weiss, J. (1980). Criterion-related validity of behavioral and self-report measures of problem solving communication skills in distressed and nondistressed parent-adolescent dyads. *Behavioral Assessment, 4,* 339–352.

Robin, A. L., Bedway, M., & Gilroy, M. (1994). Problem-solving communications training. In C. W. LeCroy (Ed.), *Handbook of child and adolescent treatment manuals.* New York: Lexington Books.

Robins, L. N. (1966). *Deviant children grown up: A sociological and psychiatric study of sociopathic personality.* Baltimore: Williams & Wilkins.

Robins, L. N. (1970). The adult development of the antisocial child. *Seminars in Psychiatry, 6,* 420–434.

Robins, L. N. (1974). Antisocial behavior disturbances of childhood: Prevalence, prognosis, and prospects. In E. J. Anthony & C. Koupernick (Eds.), *The child in his family: Children at psychiatric risk.* New York: Wiley.

Robins, L. N. (1978). Sturdy childhood predictors of adult antisocial behavior: Replications from longitudinal studies. *Psychological Medicine, 8,* 611–622.

Robins, L. N. (1981). Epidemiological approaches to natural history research: Antisocial disorders in children. *Journal of the American Academy of Child Psychiatry, 20,* 566–680.

Robins, L. N. (1986). The consequences of conduct disorder in girls. In D. Olweus, J. Block, & M. Radke-Yarrow (Eds.), *Development of antisocial and prosocial behavior.* Orlando, FL: Academic Press.

Robins, L. N. (1991). Conduct disorder. *Journal of Child Psychology and Psychiatry, 32,* 193–212.

Robins, L. N., & Hills, S. Y. (1966). Assessing the contribution of family structure, class, and peer groups to juvenile delinquency. *Journal of Criminal Law, Criminology, and Police Science, 57,* 325–334.

Robins, L. N., & McEnvoy, L. (1990). Conduct problems as predictors of substance abuse. In L. N. Robins & M. Rutter (Eds.), *Straight and devious pathways from childhood to adulthood.* Cambridge, England: Cambridge University Press.

Robins, L. N., & Price, R. K. (1991). Adult disorder predicted by childhood conduct problems: Results from the NIMH Epidemiologic Catchment Area Project. *Psychiatry, 54,* 113–132.

Robins, L. N., & Ratcliffe, K. S. (1979). Risk factors in the continuation of childhood antisocial behavior into adulthood. *International Journal of Mental Health, 7*(3–4), 6–116.

Robinson, E. A. (1985). Coercion theory revisited: Toward a new theoretical perspective on the etiology of conduct disorders. *Clinical Psychology Review, 5,* 577–626.

Robinson, E. A., Eyberg, S. M., & Ross, A. W. (1980). The standardization of an inventory of child conduct problem behavior. *Journal of Clinical Child Psychology, 48,* 117–118.

Rogeness, G. A., Hernandez, J. M., Macedo, C. A., & Mitchell, E. C. (1982). Biochemical differences in children with conduct disorder socialized and undersocialized. *American Journal of Psychiatry, 139,* 307–311.

Rogers, T. R., Forehand, R., & Geist, D. L. (1981). The conduct disordered child: An analysis of family problems. *Clinical Psychology Review, 1,* 139–147.

Romig, D. A., Cleland, C., & Romig, J. (1989). *Juvenile delinquency: Visionary approaches.* Columbus, OH: Merrill.

Rose, S. L., Rose, S. A., & Feldman, J. R. (1989). Stability of behavior problems in very young children. *Development and Psychopathology, 1,* 5–19.

Rosellini, R., & Lashley, R. L. (1992). Opponent-process theory: Implications for criminality. In J. McCord (Ed.), *Facts, frameworks, and forecasts: Advances in criminological theory.* New Brunswick, NJ: Prentice-Hall.

Rossman, P. G., & Knesper, D. J. (1976). The early phase of hospital treatment for disruptive adolescents: The integration of behavioral and dynamic techniques. *Journal of the American Academy of Child Psychiatry, 15,* 693–708.

Rotenberg, M. (1978). Psychopathy and differential insensitivity. In R. D. Hare & D. Schalling (Eds.), *Psychopathic behavior.* New York: Wiley.

Roth, R. M. (1970). *Underachieving students and guidance.* Boston: Houghton Mifflin.

Roth, R. M., Berenbaum, H. L., & Hershenson, D. (1967). *The developmental theory of psychotherapy: A systematic eclecticism.* Unpublished manuscript, Illinois Institute of Technology, Department of Psychology, Chicago.

Routh, C. P., Hill, J. W., Steele, H., Elliott, C. E., & Dewey, M. E. (1995). Maternal attachment status, psychosocial stressors and problem behaviour: Follow-up after parent training courses for conduct disorder. *Journal of Child Psychology and Psychiatry, 36,* 1179–1198.

Rubin, K. H., Chen, X., McDougall, P., Bowker, A., & McKinnon, J. (1995). The Waterloo Longitudinal Project: Predicting internalizing and externalizing problems in adolescence. *Development and Psychopathology, 7,* 751–764.

Russo, M. F., Lahey, B. B., Christ, M. A. G., Frick, P. J., McBurnett, K., Walker, J. L., Loeber, R., Stouthamer-Loeber, M., & Green, S. (1991). Preliminary development of a Sensation Seeking Scale for Children. *Personality and Individual Differences, 12,* 399–405.

Russo, M. F., Stokes, G. S., Lahey, B. B., Christ, M. A. G., McBurnett, K., Loeber, R., Stouthamer-Loeber, M., & Green, S. M. (1993). A Sensation Seeking Scale for Children: Further refinement and psychometric development. *Journal of Psychopathology and Behavioral Assessment, 15,* 69–86.

Rutter, M. (1960). *Changing youth in a changing society.* Cambridge, MA: Harvard University Press.

Rutter, M. (1978). Early sources of security and competence. In J. S. Bruner & A. Garten (Eds.), *Human growth and development.* London: Oxford University Press.

Rutter, M. (1979). Protective factors in children's responses to stress and disadvantage. In M. W. Kent & J. E. Rolf (Eds.), *Primary prevention in psychopathology: Vol. 3. Social competence in children.* Hanover, NH: University of New England.

Rutter, M. (1982). Epidemiological-longitudinal approaches to the study of development. In W. A. Collins (Ed.), *Minnesota Symposia on Child Psychology: Vol. 15. The concept of development.* Hillsdale, NJ: Erlbaum.

Rutter, M. (1991). Psychosocial resilience and protective factors. In J. Rolf & A. S. Masten (Eds.), *Risk and protective factors in the development of psychopathology.* New York: Cambridge University Press.

Rutter, M., Bolton, P., Harrington, R., LeCouteur, A., MacDonald, H., & Simonoff, E. (1990). Genetic factors in child psychiatric disorders: 1. A review of research strategies. 2. Empirical findings. *Journal of Child Psychology and Psychiatry, 31,* 3–37, 39–83.

Rutter, M., & Giller, H. (1984). *Juvenile delinquency: Trends and perspectives.* New York: Guilford Press.

Rutter, M., Maughan, B., Mortimore, P., & Ouston, J. (1979). *Fifteen thousand hours: Secondary schools and their effects on children.* Cambridge, MA: Harvard University Press.

Rutter, M., & Quinton, D. (1984). Long-term follow-up of women institutionalized in childhood: Factors promoting good functioning in adult life. *British Journal of Developmental Psychology, 18,* 225–234.

Rutter, M., Tizard, B., & Whitmore, K. (1970). *Education, health, and behavior.* London: Longman.

Safer, D. J. (1984). Subgrouping conduct disordered adolescents by early risk factors. *American Journal of Orthopsychiatry, 54,* 603–611.

Samuels, S. K., & Sikorsky, S. (1990). *Clinical evaluations of school-aged children.* Sarasota, FL: Professional Exchange Press.

Sanders, M., & James, J. E. (1983). The modification of parent behavior: A review of generalization and maintenance. *Behavior Modification, 7,* 3–27.

Sarason, I. G., & Ganzer, V. J. (1973). Modeling and group discussion in the rehabilitation of juvenile delinquents. *Journal of Counseling Psychology, 20,* 442–449.

Savitsky, J. C., & Czyzewski, D. (1978). The reaction of adolescent offenders and nonoffenders to nonverbal emotional displays. *Journal of Abnormal Child Psychology, 6,* 89–96.

Sayger, T. V., Horne, A. M., Walker, J. M., & Passmore, J. L. (1988). Social learning family therapy with aggressive children: Treatment outcome and maintenance. *Journal of Family Psychology, 1*(3), 261–285.

Scerbo, A., Raine, A., O'Brien, M., Chan, C. J., Rhea, C., & Smiley, N. (1990). Reward dominance and passive avoidance learning in adolescent psychopaths. *Journal of Abnormal Child Psychology, 18,* 451–464.

Schachar, R., & Logan, G. D. (1990). Impulsivity and inhibitory control in normal development and childhood psychopathology. *Developmental Psychology, 26,* 710–720.

Schachar, R., & Tannock, R. (1995). Test of four hypotheses for the comorbidity of attention deficit hyperactivity disorder and conduct disorder. *Journal of the American Academy of Child and Adolescent Psychiatry, 34,* 639–648.

Schmideberg, M. (1978). The treatment of the juvenile "psychopath." *International Journal of Offender Therapy and Comparative Criminology, 22,* 21–28.

Schonfeld, I. S., Shaffer, D., O'Connor, P., & Portnoy, S. (1988). Conduct disorder and cognitive functioning: Testing three causal hypotheses. *Child Development, 59,* 993–1007.

Schorr, L. B. (1988). *Within our reach: Breaking the cycle of disadvantage.* New York: Anchor Press.

Schulsinger, F. (1972). Psychopathy: Heredity and environment. *International Journal of Mental Health, 1,* 190–206.

Schuster, R. (1976). Trust: Its implication in the etiology and treatment of psychopathic youths. *International Journal of Offender Therapy and Comparative Criminology, 20,* 198–233.

Schwartzbein, D. (1992). *A comparison of family variables of nonproblematic achieving high school students and their parents and non-clinical underachieving high school students and their parents.* Unpublished doctoral dissertation, York University, Department of Psychology, Toronto, Ontario, Canada.

Schweinhart, L. J. (1987). Can preschool programs help prevent delinquency? In J. Q. Wilson & G. C. Loury (Eds.), *From children to citizens: Vol. 3. Families, schools, and delinquency prevention.* New York: Springer-Verlag.

Schweinhart, L. J., & Weikart, D. P. (1988). The High/Scope Perry preschool program. In R. H. Price, E. L. Cowen, R. P. Lorion, & J. Ramos-McKay (Eds.), *Fourteen ounces of prevention: A casebook for practitioners.* Washington, DC: American Psychological Association.

Selman, R. D. (1986). A therapeutic milieu for treating the antisocial substance-abusing adolescent. In W. H. Reid, D. Dorr, J. I. Walker, & J. W. Bonner (Eds.), *Unmasking the psychopath: Antisocial personality and related syndromes.* New York: Norton.

Selman, R. L. (1980). *The growth of interpersonal understanding: Developmental and clinical analyses.* New York: Academic Press.

Shamblin, W. J. (1986). Inpatient treatment of antisocial youth. In W. H. Reid, D. Dorr, J. I. Walker, & J. W. Bonner (Eds.), *Unmasking the psychopath: Antisocial personality and related syndromes.* New York: Norton.

Shanok, S. S., & Lewis, D. O. (1981). Medical histories of female delinquents: Clinical and epidemiological findings. *Archives of General Psychiatry, 38,* 211–213.

Shapiro, S. K., Quay, H. C., Hogan, A. E., & Schwartz, K. P. (1988). Response preservation and delayed responding in undersocialized aggressive conduct. *Journal of Abnormal Psychology, 97,* 371–373.

Shaw, M. C., & McCuen, J. T. (1960). The onset of academic underachievement in bright children. *The Journal of Educational Psychology, 51,* 103–108.

Shinn, M. R., Ramsey, E., Walker, H. M., Steiber, H., & O'Neill, R. E. (1987). Antisocial behavior in school settings: Initial differences in an at-risk and normal population. *Journal of Special Education, 21*(2), 69–84.

Shirk, S. R. (Ed.). (1988). *Cognitive development and child psychotherapy.* New York: Plenum Press.

Short, J. F., & Strodbeck, F. L. (1965). *Group process and gang delinquency.* Chicago: University of Chicago Press.

Short, R. J., & Shapiro, S. K. (1993). Conduct disorders: A framework for understanding and intervention in schools and communities. *School Psychology Review, 22,* 362–375.

Shraga, S. (1986). Therapeutic implications of games with juvenile delinquents. In C. Schaefer (Ed.), *Game play: Therapeutic uses of childhood games.* New York: Wiley.

Shure, M. B., & Spivack, G. (1972). Means-ends thinking, adjustment and social class among elementary school children. *Journal of Consulting and Clinical Psychology, 38,* 348–353.

Shure, M. B., & Spivack, G. (1982). Interpersonal problem-solving in young children: A cognitive approach to prevention. *American Journal of Community Psychology, 10,* 341–356.

Simcha-Fagan, O., & Schwartz, J. E. (1986). Neighborhood and delinquency: An assessment of contextual effects. *Criminology, 24,* 667–699.

Skoff, B. F., & Libon, J. (1987). Impaired executive functions in a sample of male juvenile delinquents. *Journal of Clinical and Experimental Neuropsychology, 9,* 60.

Slaby, R. G., & Guerra, N. G. (1988). Cognitive mediators of aggression in adolescent offenders: Part 1. Assessment. *Developmental Psychology, 24,* 580–588.

Slavin, R. E. (1979). *Using student team learning.* Baltimore: Johns Hopkins University, Center for Social Organization of Schools.

Slavin, R. E., Karweit, R. E., & Madden, N. L. (1989). *Effective programs for children at risk.* Boston: Allyn & Bacon.

Smith, R. J. (1978). *The psychopath in society.* New York: Academic Press.

Snyder, J. (1991). Discipline as a mediator of the impact of maternal stress and mood on child conduct problems. *Development and Psychopathology, 3,* 263–276.

Snyder, J., Edwards, P., McGraw, K., Kilgore, K., & Holton, A. (1994). Escalation and reinforcement in mother-child conflict: Social processes associated with the development of physical aggression. *Development and Psychopathology, 6,* 305–321.

Snyder, J., & Patterson, G. R. (1987). Family interactions and delinquent behavior. In H. Quay (Ed.), *Handbook of juvenile delinquency.* New York: Wiley.

Snyder, J., & White, M. J. (1979). The use of cognitive self-instruction in the treatment of behaviorally disturbed adolescents. *Behavior Therapy, 10,* 227–235.

Solursh, S. (1989). *The distribution of personality types in a differentially diagnosed learning disabled high school sample.* Unpublished honours thesis, York University, Department of Psychology, Toronto, Ontario, Canada.

Spaccarelli, S., Cotler, S., & Penman, D. (1992). Problem-solving skills training as a supplement to behavioral parent training. *Cognitive Therapy and Research, 16,* 1–18.

Spanier, G. B. (1976). Measuring dyadic adjustment: New scales for assessing the quality of marriage and similar dyads. *Journal of Marriage and Family, 38,* 15–28.

Spitzer, R. L., Davies, M., & Barkley, R. A. (1990). The DSM-III-R field trials of disruptive behavior disorders. *Journal of the American Academy of Child and Adolescent Psychiatry, 29,* 690–697.

Sroufe, L. A., Egeland, B., & Kreutzer, T. (1990). The fate of early experience following developmental change: Longitudinal approaches to individual adaptation in childhood. *Child Development, 61,* 1363–1373.

Stanger, C., McConaughy, S. H., & Achenbach, T. M. (1992). Three year course of behavioral/emotional problems in a national sample of 4- to 16-year olds: 2. Predictors of syndromes. *Journal of Child and Adolescent Psychiatry, 31,* 941–950.

Steinberg, L., Dornbusch, S. M., & Brown, B. B. (1992). Ethnic differences in adolescent achievement. *American Psychologist, 47,* 723–729.

Steinberg, M. D., & Dodge, K. A. (1983). Attributional bias in aggressive adolescent boys and girls. *Journal of Social and Clinical Psychology, 1,* 312–321.

Stevenson, H. W., & Stigler, J. W. (1992). *The learning gap: Why our schools are failing and what we can learn from Japanese and Chinese education.* New York: Summit Books.

Stewart, J. T., Myers, W. C., Burket, R. C., & Lyles, W. B. (1990). A review of the pharmacotherapy of aggression in children and adolescents. *Journal of the American Academy of Child and Adolescent Psychiatry, 29,* 269–277.

Stouthamer-Loeber, M. (1986). Lying as a problem behavior in children: A review. *Clinical Psychology Review, 6,* 267–289.

Strain, P. S., Steele, P., Ellis, T., & Timm, M. A. (1982). Long-term effects of oppositional child treatment with mothers as therapists and therapist trainers. *Journal of Applied Behavioral Analysis, 15,* 163–169.

Strasburger, L. H. (1986). The treatment of antisocial syndromes: The therapist's feelings. In W. H. Reid, D. Dorr, J. I. Walker, & J. W. Bonner (Eds.), *Unmasking the psychopath: Antisocial personality and related syndromes.* New York: Norton.

Strasburger, V. C. (1995). *Adolescents and the media: Medical and psychological impact.* Thousand Oaks, CA: Sage.

Strayhorn, J. M. (1994). Psychological competence-based therapy for young children and their parents. In C. W. LeCroy (Ed.), *Handbook of child and adolescent treatment manuals.* New York: Lexington Books.

Stuart, R. B. (1971). Behavioral contracting with the families of delinquents. *Journal of Behavior Therapy and Experimental Psychiatry, 2,* 1–11.

Stuart, R. B., Jayratne, S., & Tripodi, T. (1976). Changing adolescent deviant behavior through reprogramming the behavior of parents and teachers: An experimental evaluation. *Canadian Journal of Behavioral Science, 8,* 132–144.

Stuart, R. B., & Lott, L. B. (1973). Behavioral contracting with adolescents: A cautionary note. *Journal of Behavior Therapy and Experimental Psychiatry, 3,* 161–169.

Stumphauzer, J. (1973). *Behavior therapy with delinquents.* Springfield, IL: Thomas.

Stumphauzer, J. (1976). Modifying delinquent behavior: Beginnings and current practices. *Adolescence, 11,* 13–28.

Sturge, C. (1982). Reading retardation and antisocial behavior. *Journal of Child Psychology and Psychiatry, 23,* 21–31.

Suedfeld, P., & Landon, F. B. (1978). Approaches to treatment. In R. D. Hare & D. Schalling (Eds.), *Psychopathic behavior: Approaches to research.* Chichester, England: Wiley.

Susman, E. J. (1993). Psychological, contextual, and psychobiological interactions: A developmental perspective on conduct disorder. *Development and Psychopathology, 5,* 181–189.

Swaim, R. C., Oetting, E. R., Edwards, R. W., & Beauvais, F. (1989). Links from emotional distress to adolescent drug use: A path model. *Journal of Consulting and Clinical Psychology, 57,* 227–231.

Symkal, A., & Thorne, F. C. (1951). Etiological studies of psychopathic personality. *Journal of Clinical Psychology, 7,* 299–316.

Szatmari, P., Boyle, M., & Offord, D. (1989). ADHD and conduct disorder: Degree of diagnostic overlap and differences among correlates. *Journal of the American Academy of Child and Adolescent Psychiatry, 28,* 865–872.

Szatmari, P., Reitsma-Street, M., & Offord, D. (1986). Pregnancy and birth complications in antisocial adolescents and their siblings. *Canadian Journal of Psychiatry, 31,* 513–516.

Tamayo, A., & Raymond, F. (1977). Self-concepts of psychopaths. *Journal of Psychology, 97,* 71–77.

Taras, S. (1993). Depressive symptoms in a differentially diagnosed non-clinic underachieving high school sample. *Dissertation Abstracts International, 54*(8), 4410.

Tarter, R. E., Hegedus, A. M., Alterman, A. L., & Katz-Garris, L. (1983). Cognitive capacities of juvenile violent, nonviolent, and sexual offenders. *Journal of Nervous and Mental Disease, 171,* 564–567.

Taylor, A. R. (1990). Behavioral subtypes of low-achieving children: Differences in school social adjustment. *Journal of Applied Developmental Psychology, 11,* 487–498.

Tennant, C., Bebbington, P., & Hurry, J. (1981). The short-term outcome of neurotic disorders in the community: The relation of remission to clinical factors to "neutralizing" life events. *British Journal of Psychiatry, 139,* 213–220.

Thelen, M. H., Fry, R. A., Dollinger, S. J., & Paul, S. C. (1976). Use of videotaped models to improve the interpersonal adjustment of delinquents. *Journal of Consulting and Clinical Psychology, 44,* 492.

Thomas, A., Chess, S., & Birch, H. G. (1968). *Temperament and behavior disorders in children.* New York: New York University Press.

Tollefson, N., Hsia, S., & Townsend, J. (1991). Teachers' perceptions of students' excuses for academic difficulties. *Psychology in the Schools, 28,* 146–155.

Tremblay, R. E. (1992). The prediction of delinquent behavior from childhood behavior: Personality theory revisited. In J. McCord (Ed.), *Facts, frameworks, and forecasts.* New Brunswick, NJ: Transactions.

Tremblay, R. E., LeBlanc, M., & Schwartzman, A. E. (1988). The predictive power of first-grade peer and teacher ratings of behavior: Sex differences in antisocial behavior and personality at adolescence. *Journal of Abnormal Child Psychiatry, 16,* 571–583.

Tremblay, R. E., Masse, B., Perron, D., Leblanc, M., Schwartzman, E., & Ledingham, J. E. (1992). Early disruptive behavior, poor school achievement, delinquent behavior, and delinquent personality: Longitudinal analysis. *Journal of Consulting and Clinical Psychology, 60,* 64–72.

Tremblay, R. E., Masse, B., Vitaro, F., & Dobkin, P. L. (1995). The impact of friends' deviant behavior on early onset of delinquency: Longitudinal data from 6 to 13 years of age. *Development and Psychopathology, 7,* 649–667.

Tremblay, R. E., Vitaro, F., Bertrand, L., Leblanc, M., Beauchesne, H., Boileau, H., & David, L. (1992). Parent and child training to prevent early onset of delinquency: The Montreal longitudinal-experimental study. In J. McCord & R. E. Tremblay (Eds.), *Preventing antisocial behavior.* New York: Guilford Press.

Ulrici, D. K. (1983). The effects of behavioral and family interventions on juvenile recidivism. *Family Therapy, 10,* 25–36.

Vaillant, G. E. (1975). Sociopathy as a human process: A viewpoint. *Archives of General Psychiatry, 32,* 178–183.

Van Kammen, W. B., Loeber, R., & Stouthamer-Loeber, M. (1991). Substance use, antisocial, and delinquent behavior in young boys. *Youth and Adolescence, 20,* 445–451.

Virkunnen, M., deJong, J., Bartko, J., Goodwin, F., & Linnoila, M. (1989). Relationship of psychobiological variables to recidivism in violent offenders and impulsive fire setters. *Archives of General Psychiatry, 46,* 604–606.

Wadsworth, M. (1982). *Roots of delinquency: Infancy, adolescence, and crime.* Oxford, England: Martin Robinson.

Wahler, R. G. (1980). The insular mother: Her problems in parent-child treatment. *Journal of Applied Behavior Analysis, 13,* 207–219.

Wahler, R. G., & Cormier, W. H. (1970). The ecological interview: A first step in out-patient child behavior therapy. *Journal of Behavior Therapy and Experimental Psychiatry, 1,* 279–289.

Wahler, R. G., & Dumas, J. E. (1987). Stimulus class determinants of mother-child coercive interchanges in multidistressed families: Assessment and intervention. In J. D. Burchard & S. N. Burchard (Eds.), *Prevention of delinquent behavior.* Newbury Park, CA: Sage.

Wahler, R. G., House, A. E., & Stambaugh, E. E. (1976). *Ecological assessment of child problem behavior: A clinical package for home, school, and institutional settings.* New York: Pergamon Press.

Wahler, R. G., Leske, G., & Rogers, E. S. (1979). The insular family: A deviance support system for oppositional children. In L. A. Hamerlynck (Ed.), *Behavioral systems for the developmentally disabled: 1. School and family environments.* New York: Brunner/Mazel.

Wakefield, V. C. (1992). Disorder as harmful dysfunction: A conceptual critique of DSM-III-R's definition of mental disorder. *Psychological Review, 99,* 232–247.

Walker, H. M., & Fabre, T. R. (1987). Assessment of behavior disorders in the school setting: Issues, problems, and strategies revisited. In N. G. Haring (Ed.), *Assessing and managing behavior disabilities.* Seattle, WA: University of Washington Press.

Walker, H. M., & Fabre, T. R. (1992). Antisocial behavior in young school aged children: Behavioral and ecological characteristics, screening and assessment procedures, and school accommodation and intervention strategies. In G. Adams (Ed.), *Behavior disorders: Theories and characteristics.* Englewood Cliffs, NJ: Prentice-Hall.

Walker, H. M., Hops, H., & Greenwood, C. R. (1981). RECESS: Research and developments of a behavior management package for remediating social aggression in the school setting. In P. S. Strain (Ed.), *The utilization of classroom peers as behavior change agents.* New York: Plenum Press.

Walker, H. M., Retana, G. F., & Gersten, R. (1988). Replication of the CLASS program in Costa Rica. *Behavior Modification, 12,* 133–154.

Walker, H. M., Shinn, M. R., O'Neill, R. E., & Ramsey, E. (1987). A longitudinal assessment of the development of antisocial behavior in boys. *Remedial and Special Education, 8,* 7–16, 27.

Walker, J. L., Lahey, B. B., Hynd, G. W., & Frame, C. L. (1987). Comparison of antisocial behavior in children with conduct disorder with or without co-existing hyperactivity. *Journal of Consulting and Clinical Psychology, 55,* 910–913.

Walker, J. L., Lahey, B. B., Russo, M. F., Christ, M., McBurnett, K., Loeber, R., Stouthamer-Loeber, M., & Green, S. M. (1991). Anxiety, inhibition, and conduct disorder in children: Relations to social impairment. *Journal of the American Academy of Child and Adolescent Psychiatry, 30,* 187–191.

Wall, J. S., Hawkins, J. D., Lishner, D., & Fraser, M. (1981). *Juvenile delinquency prevention: A compendium of 36 program models.* Washington, DC: U.S. Department of Justice, National Institute for Juvenile Justice and Delinquency Prevention.

Walsh, A., Petee, T. A., & Beyer, J. A. (1987). Intellectual imbalance and delinquency: Comparing high verbal and high performance IQ delinquents. *Criminal Justice and Behavior, 14*(3), 370–379.

Waters, E., Hay, D. F., & Richters, J. (1986). Infant-parent attachment and the origins of prosocial and antisocial behavior. In D. Olweus, J. Block, & M. Radke-Yarrow (Eds.), *The development of antisocial and prosocial behavior: Research, theories, and issues.* New York: Academic Press.

Waters, E., Posada, G., Cromwell, J., & Keng-Ling, L. (1993). Is attachment theory ready to contribute to our understanding of disruptive behavior problems? *Development and Psychopathology, 5,* 215–224.

Weathers, L., & Liberman, R. P. (1975). Contingency contracting with families of delinquent adolescents. *Behavior Therapy, 6,* 356–366.

Webster-Stratton, C. (1984). Randomized trial of two parent-training programs for families with conduct-disordered children. *Journal of Consulting and Clinical Psychology, 52,* 666–678.

Webster-Stratton, C. (1985). Predictors of treatment outcome in parent training for conduct disordered children. *Behavior Therapy, 16,* 223–243.

Webster-Stratton, C. (1989). Systematic comparison of consumer satisfaction of three cost-effective parent training programs for conduct problem children. *Behavior Therapy, 20*(1), 103–116.

Webster-Stratton, C. (1990). The relationship of marital support, conflict, and divorce to parent perceptions, behaviors, and child conduct problems. *Journal of Marriage and the Family, 51,* 417–430.

Webster-Stratton, C. (1993). Strategies for helping early school-aged children with oppositional defiant and conduct disorders: The importance of home-school partnerships. *School Psychology Review, 22,* 437–457.

Webster-Stratton, C., Kolpacoff, M., & Hollingsworth, T. (1988). Self-administered videotape therapy for families with conduct problem children. *Journal of Consulting and Clinical Psychology, 56*(4), 558–566.

Wehby, J. H., Dodge, K. A., Valente, E., & Conduct Disorders Prevention Research Group. (1993). School behavior of first grade children identified as at-risk for development of conduct problems. *Behavioral Disorders, 19,* 67–78.

Weikart, D. P., & Schweinhart, L. J. (1987). The High/Scope Cognitively Oriented Curriculum in early education. In J. L. Roopnarine & J. E. Johnson (Eds.), *Approaches to early childhood education.* Columbus, OH: Merrill.

Weikart, D. P., & Schweinhart, L. J. (1992). High/Scope preschool program outcomes. In J. McCord & R. E. Tremblay (Eds.), *Preventing antisocial behavior.* New York: Guilford.

Weinberger, D. A., & Gomes, M. E. (1995). Changes in daily mood and self-restraint among undercontrolled preadolescents: A time-series analysis of "acting out." *Journal of the American Academy of Child and Adolescent Psychiatry, 34,* 1473–1482.

Wells, K. C., & Egan, J. (1988). Social learning and systems family therapy for childhood oppositional disorder: Comparative treatment outcome. *Comprehensive Psychiatry, 29,* 138–146.

Wells, K. C., & Forehand, R. (1981). Child behavior problems in the home. In S. M. Turner, K. Calhoun, & H. E. Adams (Eds.), *Handbook of clinical behavior therapy.* New York: Wiley.

Wells, K. C., Griest, D. L., & Forehand, R. (1980). The use of a self-control package to enhance temporal generality of a parent training program. *Behavior Research and Therapy, 18,* 347–353.

Wells, P., & Farragher, B. (1993). In-patient treatment of 165 adolescents with emotional and conduct disorders: A study of outcome. *British Journal of Psychiatry, 162,* 345–352.

Werner, E. E., & Smith, R. S. (1982). *Vulnerable, but invincible: A longitudinal study of resilient children and youth.* New York: McGraw-Hill.

Werthamer-Larsson, L., Kellam, S. G., & Wheeler, L. (1991). Effect of first grade classroom environment on shy behavior, aggressive behavior, and concentration problems. *American Journal of Community Psychology, 19,* 585–602.

West, D. (1982). *Delinquency: Its roots, careers, and prospects.* London: Heinemann Educational Books.

West, D., & Farrington, D. P. (1973). *Who becomes delinquent?* London: Heinemann Educational Books.

West, D., & Farrington, D. P. (1977). *The delinquent way of life.* London: Heinemann Educational Books.

West, M. O., & Prinz, R. J. (1987). Parental alcoholism and childhood psychopathology. *Psychological Bulletin, 102,* 203–218.

Westman, J. C., & Bennett, T. M. (1985). Learning impotence and the Peter Pan fantasy. *Child Psychiatry and Human Development, 15,* 153–166.

White, J., Moffitt, T. E., Caspi, A. S., Needles, D. J., & Stouthamer-Loeber, M. (1994). Measuring impulsivity and examining its relationship to delinquency. *Journal of Abnormal Psychology, 103*(2), 192–205.

White, J., Moffitt, T. E., Earls, F., Robins, L. N., & Silva, P. A. (1990). How early can we tell? Preschool predictors of boys' conduct disorder and delinquency. *Criminology, 28,* 507–533.

White, J., Moffitt, T. E., & Silva, P. A. (1989). A prospective replication of the protective effects of IQ in subjects at high risk for juvenile delinquency. *Journal of Clinical and Consulting Psychology, 57,* 719–724.

Whitmore, J. (1980). *Giftedness, conflict, and underachievement.* Boston: Allyn & Bacon.

Widom, C. S. (1989). Does violence beget violence? A critical examination of the literature. *Psychological Bulletin, 106,* 3–28.

Williams, E., & Radin, N. (1993). Paternal involvement, maternal employment, and adolescents' academic achievement: An 11-year follow-up study. *American Journal of Orthopsychiatry, 63,* 306–312.

Williams, S., Anderson, J., McGee, R., & Silva, P. A. (1990). Risk factors for behavioral and emotional disorder in preadolescent children. *Journal of the American Academy of Child and Adolescent Psychiatry, 29,* 413–419.

Willock, B. (1986). Narcissistic vulnerability in the hyper-aggressive child: The disregarded (unloved, uncared for) self. *Psychoanalytic Psychology, 3,* 59–80.

Willock, B. (1987). The devalued (unloved, repugnant) self: A second facet of narcissistic vulnerability in the aggressive, conduct-disordered child. *Psychoanalytic Psychology, 4,* 219–240.

Wilson, J. Q. (1987). Strategic opportunities for delinquency prevention. In J. Q. Wilson & G. C. Loury (Eds.), *From children to citizens: Vol. 3. Families, schools, and delinquency prevention.* New York: Springer-Verlag.

Wilson, J. Q., & Herrnstein, R. J. (1985). *Crime and human nature.* New York: Simon & Schuster.

Winnicott, C., Shepherd, R., & Davis, M. (Eds.). (1984). *Deprivation and delinquency*. London: Tavistock.

Wolff, P. H., Waber, D., Bauermeister, M., Cohen, C., & Ferber, R. (1982). The neuropsychological status of adolescent delinquent boys. *Journal of Child Psychology and Psychiatry, 23,* 267–279.

Wolfgang, M. E., Thornberry, T. P., & Figlio, R. M. (1987). *From boy to man, from delinquency to crime*. Chicago: University of Chicago Press.

Yeudall, L. T. (1980). A neuropsychological perspective of persistent juvenile delinquency and criminal behavior. *Annals of the New York Academy of Science, 347,* 349–355.

Yoshikawa, H. (1994). Prevention as cumulative protection: Effects of early family support and education on chronic delinquency and its risks. *Psychological Bulletin, 115,* 28–54.

Young, S. E., Mikulich, S. K., Goodwin, M. B., Hardy, J., Martin, C. L., Zoccolillo, M. S., & Crowley, T. J. (1995). Treated delinquent boys' substance use: Onset, pattern, relationship to conduct and mood disorders. *Drug and Alcohol Dependence, 37,* 149–162.

Zahn-Waxler, C. (1993). Warriors and worriers: Gender and psychopathology. *Development and Psychopathology, 5,* 79–89.

Zahn-Waxler, C., Iannotti, R. J., Cumming, E. M., & Denham, S. (1990). Antecedents of problem behaviors in children of depressed mothers. *Development and Psychopathology, 2,* 271–291.

Zigler, E., & Berman, W. (1983). Discerning the future of early childhood intervention. *American Psychologist, 38,* 894–906.

Zigler, E., Taussig, C., & Black, K. (1992). Early childhood intervention: A promising preventative for juvenile delinquency. *American Psychologist, 47*(8), 997–1006.

Zoccolillo, M. (1992). Co-occurrence of conduct disorder and its adult outcomes with depressive and anxiety disorders: A review. *Journal of the American Academy of Child and Adolescent Psychiatry, 31,* 547–556.

Zoccolillo, M. (1993). Gender and the development of conduct disorder. *Development and Psychopathology, 5,* 65–78.

Zoccolillo, M., Pickles, A., Quinton, D., & Rutter, M. (1992). The outcome of childhood conduct disorder: Implications for defining adult personality disorder. *Psychological Medicine, 22,* 971–986.

Zoccolillo, M., & Rogers, K. (1991). Characteristics and outcome of hospitalized adolescent girls with conduct disorder. *Journal of the American Academy of Child and Adolescent Psychiatry, 30,* 973–981.

Author Index

Subject Index